MEN
of
LEARNING
in
EUROPE

at the End of the Middle Ages

The publisher acknowledges with gratitude
the considerable financial assistance received from

THE FRENCH MINISTRY OF CULTURE

for support of the costs of translation.
Without their support this edition would not have been possible.

MEN
of
LEARNING
in
EUROPE

at the End of the Middle Ages

JACQUES VERGER

Translated by
Lisa Neal and Steven Rendall

UNIVERSITY OF NOTRE DAME PRESS
Notre Dame, Indiana

2000 English Language Edition published in the U.S.A. by
University of Notre Dame Press
Notre Dame, IN 46556
All Rights Reserved

Translated by Lisa Neal and Steven Rendall from the French *Les gens de savoir dans
l'Europe de la fin du Moyen Age* by Jacques Verger, published by Presses
Universitaires de France.

© Presses Universitaires de France, 1997

Library of Congress Cataloging-in-Publication Data

Verger, Jacques.
   [Gens de savoir dans l'Europe de la fin du Moyen Age. English]
   Men of learning in Europe at the end of the Middle Ages / Jacques Verger ;
translated by Lisa Neal and Steven Rendall.
     p.   cm.
   Includes bibliographical references and index.
   ISBN 0-268-03451-6
   1. Europe—Intellectual life.   2. Learning and scholarship—History—
Medieval, 500–1500.   3. Education, Medieval—Europe.
   CB353.V4713   2000
   001.2—dc21   00-026031

Contents

———•◦•———

Part III: Social Realities and Self-Image

Introduction

————•=•·•————

The title of this book calls for some clarification, which will also serve to outline its content and limits.

The chronological and geographical framework should not present any major difficulty. Here, "end of the Middle Ages," refers essentially to the fourteenth and fifteenth centuries. I chose this period because it was the one in which the social group I wished to study first emerged, or at least clearly manifested itself, and because there was enough documentary evidence to make the study possible. The sixteenth century was chosen as a temporal limit (except for the concluding chapter) simply because it was necessary to establish an end date, despite clear continuities on either side of it. On the other hand, I have taken the liberty of occasionally returning to the thirteenth and even the twelfth centuries, because the phenomena I am analyzing at the end of the Middle Ages first emerged then, at least in countries that were already experiencing the great movements of social, religious, political and cultural rejuvenation often called "the twelfth-century Renaissance."

As for the geographic framework of this book, I would have liked to cover the whole of western Europe—in other words, all of Latin Christendom—because the history of this entire area seems to have a number of salient common traits, despite the emergence of the early national states. Unfortunately, the uneven development of research, my own historical and linguistic limitations, and the varying degrees in which European countries evolved socially, politically, and culturally prevented me from achieving my initial goal. Thus I want to apologize for having frequently emphasized French examples which are more familiar to me. However, I have continually placed the French case within a larger context, trying to show what brought it closer to or distanced it from neighboring countries, whether the latter were already on their way toward national monarchy (England and the Iberian kingdoms) or had instead developed a number of city-states and independent principalities

(Italy and Germany). More distant countries (Scotland, Hungary, Bohemia, Poland, and the Scandinavian countries) will be discussed only peripherally in the following pages. Despite these imperfections, the goal of this book remains to describe comparatively a phenomenon observable throughout Europe (with multiple local variants, of course, and with different rates of development depending on the country).

What may be problematic in my title is the expression "men of learning" (*gens de savoir*). Without adhering *a priori* to a rigid definition, I must nonetheless explain from the outset what I mean by this term and why I contend that men of learning constituted a specific social group worthy of study. The expression *gens de savoir* was not used in the Middle Ages. The medieval terms—*vir litteratus* (in Castilian *letrado*), *clericus, magister, philosophus*—only partially cover the group I call men of learning, and for this reason I have opted not to use them. In this context the modern word "intellectual" (*intellectuel*) is anachronistic— a quality Jacques Le Goff acknowledges in the title of his classic and still stimulating work—and not really suitable to designate the group under study here. Only the German expression *die Gelehrten* corresponds more or less to "men of learning."

Other terms could have been chosen—"academic degree recipients" or, to stay closer to medieval language, "graduates" (*graduati*), those holding the university degrees of baccalaureate, master's, or doctorate— but these terms would have been too restrictive, even though the people they designate are in fact part of the larger group that interests me here. Moreover, possession of a formal education is one of the most pertinent criteria in defining men of learning. Nevertheless, among men of learning as I understand the term there were many former students who received no academic degree and others who studied at institutions that did not confer degrees.

"People of the book," an expression historians sometimes use, would be more appropriate than "graduates." The ability not only to read and write but also to use books to maintain certain kinds of competency and to shape social or political practices is in fact one of the most important characteristics of the men I have set out to study in this book. However, this term suggests that these men had an absolute monopoly on books, which was not at all the case, and it gives written activities priority over oral activities that must not be neglected.

The expression "men of learning" ultimately seemed the best choice because, despite its relative lack of precision, it is the most neutral and least presupposes the results of my historical inquiry. As it is used here, the term comprises two elements: first, the mastery of a certain kind and level of knowledge; second, the claim—accepted by contemporaries—to have a practical competency grounded in this acquired knowledge. The existence of individuals fulfilling this double criterion was not entirely new at the end of the Middle Ages, but as I will show, only at this moment in history did the number and influence of men of learning grow so large that they can be considered a specific group able to affect the religious, social, and political evolution of Western civilization.

With a few notable exceptions, in the early Middle Ages the man of learning was simply a *vir litteratus*, in other words, someone who knew how to read and write more or less correct Latin. Moreover, at this time the group of the *litterati* and that of the clerics and monks were nearly identical, laymen being perceived, almost by definition, as uneducated (even though there had always been, at least in the aristocracy, a few secular *litterati*, and there were many ignorant clerics and monks).

Since the twelfth and thirteenth centuries, however, this simplistic opposition has lost its meaning. Not only did the number of secular *litterati* grow considerably, but the simultaneous progress of various areas of knowledge and of institutions of learning caused, at least for the élite, an overall rise in the level of knowledge, making it henceforth impossible to consider as men of learning those who possessed only a minimal level of education—in other words, the ability to read and write. I will therefore deal neither with the problem of literacy in the Middle Ages nor with social groups whose members may have achieved this minimal level but pursued their learning no further (for example, the lower clergy and simple monks).

By the end of the Middle Ages it became possible, for anyone who put forth the requisite effort and had adequate intelligence and financial means, to acquire what was considered at that time advanced knowledge. In the first part of this book, I will try to determine the recognized constituents of learned culture, that is, the kinds of knowledge that normally characterized a man of learning (chapter I). I will then attempt to determine the types of schools (chapter II) and books (chapter III) that enabled these men of learning to become educated and to master the knowledge that was the essential aspect of their social definition.

Stopping at this point, however, would have meant approaching my subject solely from the perspective of a kind of sociology of knowledge, asking once again: "What was an intellectual in the Middle Ages?" Therefore I have found it useful to complement this approach with another, which is pursued in the second and third parts of this book, where I inquire into the competencies men of learning were thought to possess and the role reserved for them in a society that was becoming increasingly diverse and complex.

Men of learning displayed competencies based on the mastery of theoretical and abstract knowledge that allowed them to perform various functions in society. Chapter IV will determine what these functions were, while the levels at which they were exercised will be examined in chapters V and VI. Subsequent chapters move from the exercise of competencies to the sociological reality: Were men of learning distributed among the traditional categories (clergy, aristocracy, bourgeoisie), fulfilling in each a given function? Or did they instead arrive at an awareness of themselves as a group—and at a degree of social and political recognition—sufficient to allow them to transcend the existing social structures (if so, by what means?) and at least to adumbrate an autonomous category (but not, naturally, a monolithic one, because of inevitable internal hierarchies and national or regional particularities)? These questions will be addressed in the final chapters of the book, taking into account objective aspects of social differentiation such as wealth, family structures, and networks of alliances, etc. (chapter VII) as well as the representations by means of which contemporaries tried to grasp this social change, the specificity of these representations being one of the most pertinent criteria of the self-awareness of a group in its formative stages (chapter VIII). A brief conclusion (chapter IX) will emphasize the fact that this phenomenon continued well beyond the conventional date of 1500 and that, in this domain as in so many others, the opposition between the Middle Ages and the Renaissance, though not meaningless, should nonetheless not obscure important continuities.

One last remark—a kind of excuse really—should be addressed to the reader. Because of the limits of my own scholarly competence, I discuss here only Christian men of learning, chiefly orthodox, but also heterodox insofar as possible. I am well aware that there were in western Europe at this time religious minorities containing their own men of learning: The Muslim communities in Spain, Sicily, and southern Italy went into a rapid decline in the thirteenth century, which no doubt brought about, even before their complete disappearance, a gradual dismemberment of their social structures and a reduction in their intellectual activities, which had been so brilliant in the preceding era.

In contrast, the numerous Jewish communities in almost all the countries of medieval Europe maintained a very active intellectual life until the end of the Middle Ages. One can argue that their level of education and knowledge was often more developed than that of the Christian populations. But a discussion of Jewish men of learning in this period would have required a historical and linguistic proficiency that I lack. That is my chief excuse for not undertaking such a discussion; I would not excuse the omission by pointing to the isolation of Jews within the communities in which they lived, an isolation which, though exacerbated in the fourteenth and fifteenth centuries by increasing anti-Semitism on the part of Christians, did not put an end to all contacts between Jews and Christians. Several important recent studies have demonstrated the continuation of such contacts; for instance, a study on Gersonides (1288–1344), a Jewish philosopher who had extensive contacts with the clerics and ecclesiastics of his time, and another on the role of Jewish doctors, consulted by people of all faiths who sometimes audited courses at Christian universities.[1]

PART I

The Foundation of a Culture

M y title, "men of learning," points to the fact that the men I am studying can be distinguished from the rest of society both by their possession of a particular kind of learning and by their conception of culture itself. It is therefore essential from the beginning to try to grasp the parameters and the status of their culture.

I will discuss several questions in the first three chapters of this study: On the mastery of what kinds of knowledge, to the exclusion of others, was these men's culture based? Under what conditions was it acquired? Was it a precious heritage that teachers transmitted orally from one generation to another, or was it instead new turf conquered by minds stimulated by societal expectations? Was memory the sole repository of this knowledge or did books preserve, disseminate, and possibly enrich it as well?

CHAPTER I

Areas of Knowledge

A̲s I said in the introduction, we are concerned here with individuals who had in common a more or less complete mastery of a number of intellectual disciplines that could be considered as constituting the learned culture of their time. This culture cannot be defined simply. In the last centuries of the Middle Ages, it varied from place to place and from one time to another. Nonetheless, learned culture in the principal countries of western Europe maintained a relative unity that was gradually to fade in the modern era. We can therefore enumerate at least its most salient characteristics, provided we keep in mind national particularities and developments.

1. The Bases: Latin and Aristotle

One of the fundamental aspects of learned culture in the Middle Ages is the essential role played by Latin. It can be contended that medieval civilization was bilingual, marked by the cohabitation throughout Europe of Latin and one or several vernacular languages. But what, exactly, is this medieval "bilingualism," this "diglossia"? Since the early Middle Ages, no one "spoke" Latin; it was no longer anyone's mother tongue, nor was it the dominant language of any significant group. Everywhere, new vernacular languages were being established at the same time that they were breaking into vigorous dialects. In areas formerly under Roman rule, different Latin-based languages were spoken: Italian, Catalan, Castilian, Portuguese, Langue d'Oc and Langue d'Oïl. Elsewhere, Anglo-Saxon or Germanic languages triumphed; in Central Europe they melded with Slavic and Hungarian languages; whereas toward the Atlantic coast, Celtic languages were already somewhat marginalized.

At the end of the Middle Ages, these vernacular languages already had a long history and were very widespread. They were spoken by the high aristocracy as well as by the people; many members of the noble and royal classes spoke only a vernacular language as opposed to Latin. The cultural role of vernacular languages was equally well established. Even if some languages (Basque and Breton) were still essentially oral, most gave rise to abundant and diverse written texts. Vernacular languages were not only practical modes of communication, but literary as well. In most European countries masterpieces in various genres—epic, courtly, or satirical poetry, novels, drama, history, etc.—had already been or were soon to be written in vernacular languages. In fact, these languages of "daily use" had also become, more or less early depending on the country, the main languages of management, administration, and even of government. They were used to keep accounts, to write statutes and regulations, to decree laws or render judgments, to speak before an assembly or plead before a court.

In spite of all this, the status and dignity of vernacular languages remained contested. Grammarians acted as if the vernacular didn't exist, until at least the fifteenth century, and it was not taught autonomously.[1] There was, of course, a price to pay for the lack of a theoretical dimension in vernacular languages that may have protected them from an excess of purity and scholarliness. These languages were lexically poor (at least in some registers), morphologically and syntactically irregular, and orthographically unstable.

The contrary was true of Latin. After the Carolingian Renaissance of the eighth and ninth centuries, its prestige continued. This was the era, in fact, when the vernacular languages (at least the romance languages) definitively separated from Latin. The latter, renewed by writing and scholarly activities to a point of relative purity, was then locked into a privileged position as erudite and elitist. Latin's position was all the more privileged because it had no competitor, since other languages of antiquity—Greek and Hebrew in particular—had been almost entirely forgotten in Christian western Europe and were known to only a very few individuals.

Medieval Latin was first of all a sacred language, the language of Scripture, of liturgy, of worship and the sacraments—in other words the language of priests and monks. In the religious domain, the vernacular was practically limited to oral sermons addressed to the laity. The composition or translation in vernacular language of religious works, and of the Bible first among them, was not actually prohibited or unknown, but it was undertaken only occasionally and met with suspicion on the part of the Church, especially if the authors were themselves laymen.

Latin was moreover the language of antiquity and its heritage. Whether it was a matter of Latin texts in the original or Greek texts translated into Latin in antiquity or in the Middle Ages (directly or by way of Arab intermediaries), almost all of those available in Europe at the end of the Middle Ages—texts on grammar, philosophy, science (the natural sciences, mathematics, astronomy, cosmology, etc.), law, medicine, and ancient history, not to mention the writings of the Church Fathers—were still in Latin. The legacy that was transmitted was admittedly incomplete—whole segments of ancient culture had been forgotten by western Europe, in particular everything from Greek literature that had not been translated into Latin. Until the end of the Middle Ages, very few original works were written in the vernacular in the disciplines of scholarly culture. People relied essentially on translations that were belated, few in number, and often mediocre in quality. These translations were not intended for use by men of learning, but instead by a lay public rather difficult to define, quite limited in scope, and comprising individuals from the high aristocracy and the court.

In France, the first translations from ancient Latin works were made in the thirteenth century, but it was not until the middle of the fourteenth century, at the explicit requests of King John II the Good (1350–1364) and especially of Charles V (1364–1380), that a more systematic process was launched on a far grander scale. Consequently, classics like Cicero or Livy were translated into French, along with medieval encyclopedias (Bartholomaeus Anglicus, Thomas de Cantimpré), Saint Augustine's *City of God*, and John of Salisbury's *Policraticus*. The most significant translations were those of Aristotle (*Ethics, Politics, Economics, De caelo*) by Nicolas Oresme, made between 1369 and 1377.

These texts, though they belonged to the learned culture of the time, were not commonly taught in the schools. This was particularly true of Aristotle's texts that represented only very limited aspect of his work, which was not often read in the university but was likely to be of direct concern to men in power. In this latter case, the translations were at least carefully executed, despite many flaws that show to what extent a man of learning such as Oresme, a doctor of theology and formerly professor at the College of Navarre, had difficulty transposing into the vernacular knowledge that he was perfectly familiar with in Latin. Furthermore, Oresme accompanied his translation with long original glosses in the vernacular; in this way, he paved the way for the first political treatises in French, such as the *Songe du vergier*, written at almost the same time by a specialist in Church law, Evrard de Trémaugon.

Other areas of learned culture remained almost exclusively the prerogative of Latin. Modern works written to complement the ancient heritage were in Latin and even newer disciplines specific to medieval culture, such as canon law or scholastic theology, remained entirely Latin.

The language of Scripture and of learned culture, Latin was also naturally the language of teaching. To study meant first of all to study "letters" (*litterae*), in other words, Latin. A person who had studied was thus called a *litteratus*, which meant basically that he knew Latin.

But this issue is complex, and not entirely clear. Was it possible to teach only in Latin, even to young children who didn't know the language? In the fourteenth and fifteenth centuries there were many individuals who had a much better mastery of the vernacular, even in reading and writing, than of Latin. Are we to imagine that these people had earlier learned to read and write exclusively in Latin? How can we explain the fact that they could write in the vernacular while not knowing, or having forgotten, Latin? Though nothing proves the existence of schools teaching in the vernacular, it seems difficult not to imagine that at least part of elementary education was conducted in vernacular languages. Our limited knowledge of this education, however, does not allow us to substantiate this hypothesis.

On the other hand, we do know without a doubt that at the most advanced levels of education Latin remained the universal language in western Europe. This means that anyone who attended school with some regularity not only learned Latin as such but was compelled to use it to study other disciplines taught at the school. As we have seen, Latin was the language of all scholarly disciplines. These were essentially textual disciplines. They were based on "authorities" going back to pagan or Christian antiquity that were written in Latin. Thus it was not possible to gain access to these authorities, commentaries on which were the basic form of teaching in the Middle Ages, if the student did not know Latin. The commentary itself was given in Latin, either orally or in the form of a written "apparatus" or "readings" that were henceforth raised to the level of secondary authorities and considered sources of knowledge in their own right. The tools—tables, concordances, dictionaries—that facilitated the mastery of texts and commentaries were also written in Latin.

In short, it was hardly possible in the Middle Ages to belong to the group of men of learning without being a Latinist. Are we to suppose then that men of learning were the only ones at the end of the Middle Ages who knew Latin? Certainly not. In fact, as I have said, anyone who had learned to read, and a fortiori to write, had received some modicum of Latin. Such a person may not have been able to remember much, but this was not the case for one very specific category, that of the clerics and ecclesiastics, whose liturgical responsibilities required them to use Latin almost daily. We explained in the introduction why we are not including this type of individual in the group of men of learning. It should be borne in mind, however, that most of these people had at least a rudimentary knowledge of Latin that would have enabled them to celebrate mass, administer the sacraments, and preside at the service. Bishops of the time complained much less than their predecessors about the crass ignorance and scandalous barbarity of low-level clergy; the latter may have been hardly able to write or speak Latin but they more or less understood the meaning of the Scriptures, the service, the sacramental rituals and the common prescriptions of canon law repeated in the episcopal legislation.

Returning now to our men of learning, what was the nature of their knowledge of Latin? Here we must remember that though medieval Latin could be considered a living language (and as such exhibiting local particularities and developments), it was nonetheless always a learned language and therefore *artificial* insofar as it was not anyone's mother tongue.

The level of mastery in Latin thus varied considerably from one person to another. University professors were supposedly able to write and even to read it with ease (since they were not allowed to deliver a lecture they had written down in advance). This Latin was scholarly; it was quite technical—almost a jargon—and had a stereotypical vocabulary and elementary syntax that was not used with concern for literary elegance. University students were undoubtedly less comfortable with Latin, despite the rule to speak only Latin in public and inside the colleges. Their Latin must have often resembled the pretentious and ridiculous pidgin spoken by Rabelais' student from the Limousin.

These same differences in the level of Latin are found in administrative practices. Some chancelleries, in particular the pontifical chancellery, employed Latinists of high caliber, meticulous rhetoricians capable of composing in long rhythmical periods the majestic preambles of official documents. In contrast, many statutes, common charters, administrative inquiries, fiscal documents, and judicial decrees, to say nothing of ordinary accounts and notarized acts, even when they were written in Latin, were in a language infinitely less lofty in tone, in "a vulgar Latin accessible to laymen" (*latinum grossum, pro laicis amicum*), as one reads in a 1440 manual for use by councilors in the Paris Parlement entitled *Style de la Chambre des Enquêtes*.[2] This was a Latin very close to the vernacular language, French, both in terms of its sentence structure and its vocabulary; the Latin endings served only to conceal the fact that Latin was a kind of mask worn by thoughts conceived in the vernacular language. Many decrees were recopied on official forms that were used in most chancelleries and by court clerks and notaries, and naturally this only accentuated their stereotypical nature and their linguistic poverty.

However, we should not conclude too rapidly that Latin degenerated at the end of the Middle Ages. The choice in administrative documents of a fairly elementary Latin corresponds to a desire to be understood by the greatest number of readers, even by the most mediocre Latinists (*pro laicis amicum*), without giving up the prestige (and the convenience) of Latin. However, other writers of official documents (or perhaps the same writers in other situations) were perfectly capable of reading Latin treatises or writing in a purer Latin. From the middle of the fourteenth century, humanism, which originated in Tuscany and was then disseminated through all of Italy and beyond the Alps—most notably in Avignon during the papacy of Benedict XIII and in the Paris of Charles VI—found its most fervent partisans in court clerks and chancellery secretaries. These writers, professionals of public writing, were far more likely than academics to seek in Cicero's letters and speeches models to give to their own writings the elegance and persuasiveness that had characterized the best orators of antiquity. A letter from Coluccio Salutati (1331–1406), the great humanist chancellor of the Republic of Florence, then at war with Milan, was more fearsome, people said, than a squadron of cavalry.[3]

Of course, the success of humanism must not hide the slow and inevitable encroachment of the vernacular languages on many domains, literary, political, administrative, and judicial. These languages were easier and more intelligible, and they benefited from the widespread emergence of nationalistic feelings that were then beginning to consider them a component of national and ethnic identity. The vernacular languages' supposed ability to express the spirit of the nation stood in opposition to the Christian, scholarly universalism of Latin.

At times with reticence, at times with relief—since the humanist concern for purity had begun to ridicule the crude or incorrect Latin that many medieval *litterati* were themselves unable to surpass—men of learning themselves started to use the vernacular more and more. Some of them turned into veritable propagandists for the vernacular, following the example of Dante's *De vulgari eloquentia* (1305) by writing the first treatises defending and illustrating their national languages. Thus Nicolas Oresme, in the preface to his translations of Aristotle, recognizes their weaknesses—which he sees as resulting from the fact that the subject had never "been treated and practiced in such a language"—while proudly contending that "to translate such books into French and to render the arts and sciences in French is a most beneficial labor; for it is a noble language of men of great minds and good judgment. And as Cicero says in his book *Academica*, people find weighty matters of great import agreeable and pleasing in the language of their own country."[4]

In everyday practice, men of learning and educated people increasingly used the vernacular. In the fourteenth and fifteenth centuries, Latin appears less frequently in the royal or municipal archives. After 1380–1400, there are few authors, with the exception of those in strictly academic or university disciplines, who have left a work exclusively in Latin. Take, for example, the group considered the "first French humanists": Whereas Nicolas de Clamanges (v. 1362–1437) wrote only in Latin and the works of Laurent de Premierfait (?–1418) consisted solely of French translations of Cicero and Boccaccio, Jean de Montreuil (1354–1418) provided two versions—one Latin and the other French—of his principal treatises of political propaganda (in particular his *Treatise Against the English*), as had Evrard de Trémaugon (*Le songe du vergier*) and Jean Gerson (1363–1429), whose work in Latin, which was connected with the university, hardly equaled in scope his French writings, court sermons and spiritual treatises addressed to "simple folk."

We cannot, however, conclude that the progress made by vernacular languages at the end of the Middle Ages caused a complete decline in the use of Latin among the educated. An argument could be made that the rise of the vernacular reinforced a medieval "diglossia" which, no longer corresponding to simple social dichotomies (learned/common; cleric/lay; *litteratus/illitteratus*),[5] was transposed to the very heart of scholarly disciplines and practices, both written and oral, in the domains of politics, administration and law. The choice of language for individuals progressively proficient in the double register of the vernacular and Latin (to say nothing of the newly emerging renewal of interest in Greek, especially among Italians), henceforth revealed subtle strategies: the concern for political efficacy and linguistic confirmation of national feelings continued to be opposed by an attachment to the Christian and cultural universalism, of which Latin was the guarantor, as well as by need for identity among people whose studies and tastes led them to form themselves into professional castes. To the degree that it lost its cultural legitimacy, Latin, still very staunchly supported by the Church and the schools, gained in value as a sign of social recognition and a constituent element of the established order. Latin remained the language of memory.

The initial constitution of the group of men of learning in the Middle Ages was not limited to the learning of Latin; it was complemented, for whoever went beyond the most elementary level, by an introduction to "philosophy." Until the fifteenth century, this expression designated the content of the basic courses—to use the terms from Antiquity, the seven "liberal arts," divided into the *trivium* (grammar, rhetoric, dialectics) and the *quadrivium* (arithmetic, music, geometry, astronomy). In reality, this traditional classification fell out of use as early as the thirteenth century. Clearly, instruction in Latin corresponded more or less to grammar, possibly combined with rhetoric, when the study of the classics became important. But what fit less easily into the traditional schema was the introduction to dialectics, or rather logic, normally supplemented by a few notions borrowed from disciplines in the *quadrivium* (essentially, a bit of arithmetic and elementary cosmology) and especially by lessons from natural and moral philosophy that were not part of the original curriculum in the arts.

As for the scientific disciplines, ancient authors were read less than small, simple manuals composed in the Middle Ages, for instance, in astronomy, Johannes de Sacrobosco's *De sphaera*, which dates from the first years of the thirteenth century. All the rest, or practically all, was based on Aristotle. His treatises on logic called the *Organon* had long been known and studied in the West; the first part, the *Logica vetus,* was translated at the end of the fifth century by Boethius, and the subsequent treatises (*Logica nova*), were translated in the first half of the twelfth century and taught in Parisian schools as early as 1150. At the end of the Middle Ages, the entire work was available and in general use. To Aristotle's texts were added several more recent manuals, the most widely distributed being the *Summulae logicales* by Peter of Spain (ca. 1210–1277; later Pope John XXI).

For western Europeans at the end of the Middle Ages, Aristotle was more than a master of dialectics. From the thirteenth century on, practically the entire corpus of his philosophical works was available in Latin translation: *Physics, On Metaphysics,* short treatises on natural science (known as *Parva naturalia), De anima* (On the Soul), *De caelo* (On the Heavens), *Meteorologica, Ethics, Politics.* Initially forbidden (1210–1215), the teaching of Aristotle's philosophy was progressively tolerated and then finally officially accepted by the University of Paris (statute of the Faculty of Arts in 1255). Aristotle was taught in most of the faculties of arts founded subsequently, even though it appears that in a number of southern universities (Bologna, Montpellier, Toulouse) grammar and rhetoric remained the principal subjects, with philosophy occupying a less important place.[6] It is not clear whether Aristotle's works were regularly studied in less illustrious schools. Nonetheless, we can conclude that anyone who had received an education of at least a certain level in the Middle Ages—whether in a university or a preparatory school—had been introduced to Aristotle's logic and at least to the most well-known aspects of his philosophy. This broad diffusion of Aristotle's works clearly contrasts with the almost complete ignorance of Plato. The *Timaeus,* the chief work of Plato that had been translated into Latin, was hardly studied in western Europe after the twelfth century.

That does not mean that all medieval intellectuals subscribed to Aristotelianism as a coherent philosophical system. There were of course Aristotelians and even "thoroughgoing Aristotelians." The faculty of arts in Paris from 1260–1270 and the faculty of arts in Padua in the fourteenth and fifteenth centuries were the principle seats of this trend, more often referred to at the time as "Averroist," whose proponents met with hostility on the part of their theologian peers and with the Church's condemnation. Thoroughgoing or heterodox Aristotelianism, understood in light of Averroës' commentaries (1126–1198)—themselves translated from Arabic into Latin around 1220—led to doctrines not very compatible with Christian revelation. The most obvious stumbling blocks concerned the eternity of the world and the unity of the active intellect (in other words, the negation of the soul's existence as a spiritual, individual and immortal substance). In addition, there was the Aristotelian belief in astral determinism and a purely human definition of happiness and virtue, which were identified with philosophical contemplation that takes pleasure in its own knowledge. Despite the caution, whether affected or sincere, of these "Averroïsts," the requirements of Christian metaphysics and morality were far from satisfied and we can well thus understand, without necessarily approving, why the Church was suspicious of such teachings.

The Aristotelianism of educated people in the Middle Ages was quite a different matter. It had to do with a kind of *koïné*, ways of speaking and reasoning, with definitions and concepts, with diverse bodies of knowledge—explicit or implicit—instilled in school and accepted by all as a given. For Aristotelianism was above all a kind of logic, the art of syllogism conceived as a demonstrative technique par excellence. The educated individual in the Middle Ages displayed a natural tendency to couch—correctly or incorrectly—his thoughts and those of his interlocutors in terms of a syllogism. Let us give one example: In France at the time of the Estates General of 1357, Bishop Robert le Coq used an arsenal of syllogisms against his opponents, the royal officials whom he was accusing:

> The said bishop made the following argument: It is well-known that the King had been badly advised and counseled; those named below [the officials] badly advised him; *Ergo*, etc. [i.e. these officials should be relieved of their duties].
>
> Response [of the officials]: The major premise is false, or at least is not manifest, but obscure, and remains to be demonstrated; while the minor premise is even falser, more obscure and more lacking in factual basis.[7]

In addition to dialectics, conceived as the art of rigorous and irrefutable reasoning, Aristotelianism was also a rhetoric, an art of the probable and the plausible founded on a study of "commonplaces" (in Greek, *topoï*) to which one could reduce concrete situations in order to convince a listener. The principles of this technique were taught in the eight books of the *Topics*.

From their study of Aristotle, medieval educated people derived not only techniques of exposition and reasoning but also explanatory schemas and habits of classification that could be applied to all sorts of phenomena. The principle of non-contradiction, the study of "causes" (material, formal, efficient, and final), the distinction between matter and form, substance and accident, potentiality and actuality, and the identification of genera and species were all rational means of defining an object and understanding change. The result was a coherent perception of the world that may be foreign to us now but that men of that time, equipped with these instruments of analysis, related to with little difficulty.

This common perception of the physical universe had as its basis the theory of the four elements and a geocentric cosmogony that placed the immobile earth at the center of concentric celestial spheres. Aristotle also provided, especially in his *De anima*, a physiology and a psychology that explained the fundamental characteristics of living things, flora and fauna as well as human beings. While the movement of the planets and their influence on the sublunar world justified the existence of astrology and provided a scientific justification for the inexhaustible success of predictions and horoscopes, the play of elements and humors determined the constitution of each individual (sanguine, bilious, phlegmatic or melancholic). In addition, the definition of various functions of the soul—from the most primitive vegetative function, common to all living beings, to the intellectual and rational function peculiar to humans—led to an understanding of the continuity and the hierarchies of the biological universe, and also of the somehow organic link between soul and body.

The Aristotelian intellectual edifice was crowned by its moral and political philosophy, whose major texts (*The Ethics* and *Politics*) were taught in schools and universities starting in the second half of the thirteenth century before Oresme translated them into French in the 1370s. Without understanding all the details, which were at times incompatible with Christian revelation, educated people at the end of the Middle Ages remembered at least the definition of virtue as the practice of moderation and measure, and especially numerous political concepts, which were sometimes associated with those of Roman law and came to constitute a kind of commonly accepted vulgate that could be put to different, if not opposing, uses.[8] With this Aristotelian political vulgate can be connected notions widespread at the end of the Middle Ages, such as the distinctions between natural, divine and human law, the original, organic character of the political community (man as "social animal"), the typology of governmental forms (monarchy, aristocracy, democracy) and their possible degeneration, and finally the notion of the "common good" as a goal of political action.

Taken together, this does not constitute a coherent doctrine. In the fourteenth and fifteenth centuries Aristotelianism as such became the target of increasingly acerbic criticism on the part of many philosophers, humanists, jurists, and theologians. Some questioned, in the name of rhetoric and literature, the tyranny of the syllogism; others appealed to the principle of divine freedom to challenge a highly deterministic, if not materialistic, interpretation, and to give priority to a more atomistic or even empirical view of man and nature. However, our goal here is simply to underscore the continuing influence of the Aristotelian schemas and concepts instilled in the formative years, an influence that retained its power precisely because people were often not conscious of it. In the words of Alexandre Koyré, these Aristotelian schemas and concepts achieved a "union of a teleological metaphysics with the experience of common sense"[9] that long continued to seem so self-evident that it allowed them to provide the basis for the fundamentally qualitative rationalism that best defines the intellectual attitude of all those who received a certain level of education in the Middle Ages. Men of learning and the men of letters at the end of the Middle Ages were not necessarily Aristotelians, but they lived in a world largely still perceived in terms of the definitions and categories of Aristotle.

2. Legitimate Disciplines and Marginal Disciplines

The education of medieval men of learning was clearly not limited to these basic elements; rather, the latter were integrated into an overall framework whose contours theoreticians have attempted to determine in terms of systematic classifications of various kinds of knowledge. These classifications, modeled on those of the ancients or the Arabs, were particularly popular among the authors of the twelfth and thirteenth centuries.[10] They were of varying degrees of complexity, but they all came down to an overall schema comprising, on one hand, the preparatory disciplines (*scientiae primitivae*)—arising out of the by then outdated seven liberal arts—and on the other, sacred knowledge, that is, the study of the text of revelation (*sacra pagina*), the sole capstone of a Christian education that could be envisioned after St. Augustine's *De doctrina christiana*. This way of perceiving education—expressed by Hugh of Saint-Victor in his *Didascalicon* (around 1130)—fully justified the primordial role accorded to Latin and to Aristotle, but it relegated a great many disciplines to a marginal position.

The disdain for some disciplines displayed by the proponents of "liberal" and religious education is easy to comprehend, as is its origin, at once ancient and Christian. The "mechanical arts"—considered too technical and linked to manual labor and direct, sullying and even servile contact with tangible matter—were rejected as well as the "profane" or "lucrative" disciplines, which were motivated (at least in the opinion of the Church) by purely worldly ambitions and the desire for profit.

The absence of other disciplines is more difficult to explain. Was it because it was feared they satisfied a kind of "vain curiosity," a gratuitous fondness for intellectualizing and mind-games that disregarded the Christian goals of all study? "One should learn only in order to be enlightened or to be useful to others; learning for the sake of learning is only shameful curiosity," Saint Bernard wrote in his thirty-sixth sermon on the Song of Songs.[11] In addition to these conscious motivations we must take into consideration the equally weighty influence of Scholastic traditions and the corporative reflexes on the part of specialists in various disciplines which, like guilds, were not inclined to make room for potential competitors.

In any case, some domains rapidly escaped from the subordinate position to which theoreticians wanted to limit them, while other domains long suffered from this kind of rejection, which often persisted long after the Middle Ages. It will be worthwhile, though somewhat anachronistic, to compile a list of these rejections and exclusions, which indirectly mark the limits of medieval education, before we discuss the positive aspects of this education.

As we have said, everything having to do with the vernacular, regardless of discipline, was in some sense excluded. Still more generally, no part of what today we call the humanities (*belles lettres*), including Latin humanities, had a place in the schools, at least after the Renaissance of the twelfth century and the "battle of the seven arts" ultimately won by dialectics at the expense of poetry and eloquence. Though medieval students were given a few classical texts in order to illustrate grammar lessons or to introduce students to rhetorical devices, no one tried to instill in them a true literary culture. In contrast, the humanists of the fifteenth and sixteenth centuries were steeped in Greek and Latin texts and drew from them not only stylistic but also aesthetic and moral lessons. This was a marked change from the preceding era; even medieval students would certainly have been able to quote a few *sententiae* of Cicero or a few lines from Virgil or Horace that they had learned from academic collections of *auctores,* but they undoubtedly experienced neither love for the beauty of classical language nor disinterested curiosity about ancient civilizations. As for vernacular languages, we have already noted that medieval men of learning were, at least from around the mid-thirteenth century, able to use them both in writing and speech and in various registers. But this was the result of personal efforts or else of formal instruction that had purely professional goals. Generally speaking, they do not seem to have possessed a true literary culture as we understand the term today.

Did they have a historical culture? This is a rather complex question that requires a negative but qualified reply.[12] The twelfth century was without a doubt the great era of medieval historiography. Monasteries like Saint Denis in France or Saint Alban's in England, together with the princely courts, were the principal seats of historical scholarship; most authors were monks or clerics. History was not taught in the schools but benefited from the increased interest in ancient texts, including historical texts, promoted by the Renaissance of the twelfth century. Intellectuals emerging from the academic world also produced historical works, such as the important *Historia pontificalis* by John of Salisbury (v. 1115–1180), which dealt with the history of the Church and the papacy.

During the following era, however, the separation between history and other domains of scholarly culture widened. Not only was history not accorded a place in the curricula of new universities but the triumph of Aristotle's philosophy at the expense of grammar and rhetoric privileged a kind of thought in which an historical dimension was nearly absent. But even Roman law and Biblical exegesis—in our view, clearly historical disciplines—were almost never approached from a historical perspective in medieval schools. In any event, the fact remains that history was hardly present, except "ornamentally" in references and in *exempla*, in the great masters of Scholastic theology; and it had hardly any greater influence on the commentators on the *Corpus iuris civilis,* who took great pains to stress the immutable majesty of Roman law.

Yet the production of historical texts did not completely cease, though they did not take such ambitious forms as the vast theological histories and universal chronicles by Sigebert of Gembloux (v. 1030–1112) and Otto of Freising (v. 1111–1158). What we see in abundance, as often in Latin as in the vernacular, are national and regional histories, the lives of princes and popes, chronologies of reigns and tales of battles, not to mention compilations of ancient history such as *Ancient History to Caesar* (*L'Histoire ancienne jusqu'à César*) or *The Deeds of the Romans* (*Les Faits des Romains*) convenient accounts of Greek and Roman history composed at the beginning of the thirteenth century that remained popular until the end of the Middle Ages.

The authors of these histories and chronicles, often official historians paid by a prince or a city, continued to come largely from monastic milieus; but among the historians at the end of the Middle Ages we also find an increasing number of secular clerics (such as Froissart) and laymen, some courtiers, some diplomats or royal advisors, and still others officials or chancellery employees. Rarely were the historians university graduates or professors, though the latter were not indifferent to history. There are numerous extant inventories of the libraries of colleges and of college graduates—in particular, lawyers—showing that, though literature in the strict sense (poetry, theater and fictional narrative), whether in Latin or in the vernacular, was practically absent, history was present in a modest but consistent way. These inventories did not usually include works such as *The Deeds of the Romans,* which were more likely to be found in the libraries of the nobility, but rather, to name only the most commonly owned works, Valerius Maximus's *Memorable Acts and Quotations*, Vincent of Beauvais's *Historical Mirror*, Martin of Troppau's *The Chronicle of the Popes and Emperors*, and a few other works of the same kind, both ancient and medieval. From this we may conclude that without having formally studied history at school or at university, at least in the form of the history of events, most men of learning at the end of the Middle Ages had a minimal knowledge of political, military and ecclesiastical history from antiquity on and covering the principal countries of western Europe, no doubt along with a knowledge of geographical nomenclature. This historical knowledge that men of learning shared with the prince and the nobles of his entourage was for them a significant source of examples and arguments in support of the legal or political theses they were called upon to defend as part of their official functions.

Technical and scientific instruction was an even more significant victim of the narrowness of the scholastic and university curricula than was the study of literature and history. The disciplines comprising the *quadrivium* (arithmetic, music, geometry, astronomy) were supposed to have been taught at the faculty of arts; but in fact they must have been hurried through in a few lessons, reappearing later in the program only as optional courses that attracted groups of students particularly interested by such subjects. But since these disciplines did not lead to any definite profession, those who studied them tended to also study another discipline, such as law or medicine, in which it was easier to have a career. Even then, this was the case only in relatively abstract fields based on numbers and figures, and which involved neither equipment nor material contact.

On the other hand, disciplines that required direct observation of nature or, *a fortiori*, experimentation, never had a place in education and one could even say that they did not exist for cultured people in the Middle Ages. To satisfy a curiosity in chemistry, zoology, botany, mineralogy—areas considered frivolous hobbies—an educated person had to read Aristotle, while less educated people read popular encyclopedias such as those compiled by Vincent of Beauvais, Bartholomaeus Anglicus, or Thomas de Cantimpré—writers who generally did little more than repeat what their ancient predecessors had written and collect allegorical interpretations, rather than reporting on actual observation of the natural world.

The knowledge of artisans, engineers and architects (the most illustrious of whom enjoyed a certain social prestige from the thirteenth century onward) must have been transmitted largely through apprenticeships, from master to apprentice, from teacher to disciple, according to empirical and oral procedures that have left only faint traces in the documentation—for example, in the sketchpad of the French architect Villard de Honnecourt (middle of the thirteenth century), which is as well-known as it is unique. At the end of the Middle Ages, there was spectacular progress in some technical arts, for instance, mining, watchmaking and especially artillery (to say nothing of printing). These advances gave rise to genuine specialists, who were relatively well paid and whose level of knowledge certainly went far beyond that of simple artisans, yet these specialists were not able either to formalize or to disseminate their knowledge beyond the concrete practice of their skills, and thus did not transform them into a real scientific and technological culture.

However, the most common alternative to clerical learning had long been, not the culture of the *homo faber* but rather that of the knight. In theory, writing and *a fortiori* Latin held a very minor place in the culture of knights, who usually left these activities to some chaplain or other. The knight devoted himself chiefly to physical action and to military training, with some attention given to the social arts—singing, music and dance. Though a knight might enjoy hearing epic poems, tales of love or *fabliaux* recited, he seldom read them himself. This was, of course, an ideal. It is highly unlikely that all nobles had completely assimilated the refinements of courtly culture and, on the other hand, a knight who had some sense of literature—*miles litteratus*—was not altogether rare. Many knights knew how to read and write, and even Latin, at least the Latin of charters and the Church, was not necessarily completely foreign to them. Still, the idea that developing a well-rounded culture involved combining physical with intellectual exercises, familiarity with courtly values and aesthetic feeling with rhetorical expertise and the art of memory, and games with serious study, remained relatively foreign to men of learning in the Middle Ages. This ideal, that of the *païdeia* of the ancients, was not really accepted until the humanists of the sixteenth century popularized it, criticizing their medieval predecessors for their disdain of the body and, more generally, their neglect of the affective and moral aspects of education. The humanists' grievances were excessive in that they failed to take into consideration the pedagogic writings of some monks as well as the theories of education espoused by Ramon Llull (v. 1232–1315),[13] Pierre Dubois (v. 1250–v. 1320)[14] or Jean Gerson (1363–1429).[15] They did, however, clearly indicate the restrictive character of the conception of knowledge on which the medieval definition of culture was based.

The list of lacunae in the erudite culture of the end of the Middle Ages could be extended indefinitely (though not without risking anachronism), but we will limit ourselves to one last point: the absence of a knowledge of economics among the intellectual élites of this time period. This was not inconsequential during an era when taxes and tariffs had become permanent, trades and market fairs were increasingly organized and supervised, Italian banks were developing internationally and currencies were constantly changing. All this made it possible for princes and cities to pursue a genuine economic policy, whose effects were often unforeseen and poorly controlled. At least in pioneering regions, some European businessmen started to develop a true commercial and financial culture that went beyond simple oral traditions and empirical practices. In a few cities in Tuscany and Flanders there seem to have been schools for merchants' sons in which commercial arithmetic—the *abacus*—and modern languages were taught. "Commercial manuals" (*Pratica della mercatura*), exercises in mathematics and writing, accounting lessons, and bilingual or trilingual glossaries all attest to this type of education. Furthermore, businessmen were not adverse to purchasing books that would give their children, or at least their sons, grammatical and religious instruction, and they were quite willing to employ private tutors. Thus one can conclude that in these milieus there developed, during the last centuries of the Middle Ages, a vital and original culture, which was moreover essentially in the vernacular. Religious questions[16] were even debated, and *livres de raison*—volumes that combined autobiographical sketches, family chronicles, and collections of moral reflections and counsel—were composed. Studying "merchant writers" in Florence, Christian Bec points to the quality of their *libri di famiglia*, in which perceptive observations are conjoined with an acute sense of psychological and political realities in an effort to rationally explain the world.[17] One should not, however, base far-reaching conclusions on this example from Tuscany. Elsewhere, for instance in the area of the Hanseatic League, the culture and mental apparatus of merchants seem to have been much simpler and more archaic. In France, the perfunctory nature of merchants' commercial activities and their small interest in books and study—they had no personal libraries and did not found schools—does not allow us to include them in the group of men of learning as we understand the term here. We know virtually nothing about the culture of even the most well-known of these French merchants, Jacques Coeur (ca. 1395–1456).[18]

In any event, an almost unbridgeable gap continued to separate these modern but still embryonic forms of economic culture and the scholarly culture, fundamentally Latin, recognized by the Church and disseminated by schools and universities. Even in princely entourages, the two coexisted without melding. While men of learning increasingly monopolized administrative positions in the field of law, kings, in order to manage their finances, nonetheless availed themselves of the services of businessmen and financial experts, often Italians whose exceptional competence was known throughout Europe.

Nicolas Oresme's *Traité des monnaies*, written around 1357 in both Latin and French, is an original work, but it is too isolated and too much characterized by conservative and timorous notions for us to see it as the beginning of a true sense of economics among men of learning educated in the schools and universities.[19]

3. The Higher Disciplines: Theology, Medicine, and Law

We now come to the areas of erudite learning that the élites of the late Middle Ages most highly valued. The list is quite short; for all practical purposes, it corresponds to the disciplines that were actually taught in the schools, *studia*, and universities of the time. The universities, in fact, had only three faculties beyond the level of preparatory study: theology, medicine and law. It was therefore the mastery—more or less developed—of these disciplines that characterized men of learning in western Europe at the end of the Middle Ages.

At the highest echelon was, of course, religious learning (*sacra pagina, sacra doctrina*), which was more and more frequently called "theology," especially from the thirteenth century on. The theology taught had two branches: commentary on the Bible, and systematic study of Christian dogma, based on the teachings of the Church Fathers and on the reasoning and resources of philosophy (which ran the risk of heterodoxy). The four *Books of Sentences* Pierre Lombard wrote around the middle of the twelfth century remained until the fifteenth century the basic manual for theological study.

In theory, theology was the most privileged discipline, and this gave theologians a kind of supervisory role over other areas; Christian orthodoxy could thus be ensured. The preparatory disciplines in the faculty of arts, in particular dialectics and philosophy, were naturally the most vulnerable to possible censure. Practically speaking, however, no one imagined that theology was intended for dissemination to a large audience. Not only were lay people prohibited from studying it, but even among clerics, monks and other ecclesiastics, only a small minority received a true theological education, though it is true that it was conceived according to the most rigid standards. At the University of Paris, fifteen years was the normal time period required to complete the theological curriculum and doctorate. It was therefore out of the question to impose this kind of education on the whole of the clergy. In Mediterranean countries at the end of the Middle Ages, members of the mendicant orders were practically the only ones who studied theology. Elsewhere, a sizeable number of students were secular clerics but, in any event, this was never more than a small élite, and it appears they were never intended to occupy high positions in the Church; these were filled, as we will see later, by jurists. As for the theologians themselves, they were highly qualified intellectual specialists whose role was to cultivate and enrich this privileged discipline and also (at least so far as the mendicant orders are concerned) to devote themselves to a well-defined pastoral practice—preaching—for which a theological education seemed to adequately prepare them.

There were fewer physicians in medieval society than theologians, at least if we consider only doctors who had completed their studies and obtained university degrees, as opposed to, on one hand, healers, bone-setters and other empirical practitioners, and on the other, barbers and surgeons, who were perceived—particularly the former—as simple arti-sans, because of both their educational background and their practice.

Actually, medicine had a hard time being accepted as a real science. It was still not listed among the main areas of learning in the twelfth and thirteenth centuries; some people claimed it was merely an eighth "liberal art," (in other words, not a discipline in itself but rather a study preparatory to another), or even a "mechanical art," since it involved the care of the body and the search for material causes. However, professors of medicine in Salerno, and then those in Bologna, Padua, Montpellier and Paris were able to get medicine accepted as a scientific discipline. To their critics, they argued not only that medicine was socially useful, but also that it was based on philosophy. More than being therapeutic, medicine was above all presented as a theoretical discipline essentially grounded in Aristotle's natural philosophy and Galen's interpretation of it. It replaced the notion of man as the center of a created universe with the notion of man as subjected to the same principles of cause and change that apply to the physical world. Moreover, by adopting a strict code of medical ethics and subordinating the concern for bodily health to that of the soul's salvation, physicians were able to protect themselves from possible criticism from theologians.

Professors of medicine composed a social, as well as an intellectual, élite, and clearly had an eminent place among men of learning in the Middle Ages. We will return later to the successful political or ecclesias-tic careers some of them were able to pursue on the basis of their scien-tific reputations. The important thing to emphasize here is that some physicians were without a doubt among the most liberally minded and the most culturally open of their contemporaries. For instance, as early as the end of the twelfth century they taught Aristotle's philosophy, even before the Parisian philosophers did. In the thirteenth century, Arnaud de Villeneuve (ca. 1240–1311)—a truly exceptional individual who was a professor in Montpellier, a practicing physician, and an advisor and am-bassador for several popes and kings—was able to combine his thorough understanding of philosophical and medical texts in both Greek and Arabic with his interests in alchemy, astrology, religion and politics. In-fluenced by Joachimism, interested in millenarian notions, close to the theology of Spiritual Franciscans, and a tireless traveler, this cosmo-politan Catalan showed an active curiosity regarding all the issues of his day.[20]

Though today theologians and physicians may seem to us to have been the most creative individuals among medieval men of learning, the dominant discipline within the learned culture of this time, both by its magnitude and its social ranking, was law. The last centuries of the Middle Ages were a golden age for jurists. In some countries, in fact, this age extended to the end of the eighteenth century and beyond.

Because civil law and canon law emerged as academic disciplines at the same time, we have chosen not to differentiate between them here, though they obviously differ in content.

It is probably an exaggeration to say that Roman law was "rediscovered" in Italy in the last years of the eleventh century, on the basis of previously forgotten ancient manuscripts. As early as the year 1000, there were judges in the kingdom of Italy who, while using and commenting on Lombard law, seem to have had some knowledge of Justinian's legislation, in particular those in Justinian's Code,[21] and around 1100, Roman law began to be regularly studied in Bologna and several neighboring cities such as Ravenna, Modena and Piacenza. If we disregard Pepo's enigmatic work, we can say that Irnerius (d. 1125) wrote the first glosses; he re-edited in five volumes the *Corpus iuris civilis* (*Code, Digest, Institutes* and *Novellae*) that remained in use until the end of the Middle Ages. In the next generation, the school of Bolognese commentators was in full swing, and its students spread all over Italy and even over the Alps to Provence, Languedoc and Catalonia. Canon law became a true academic discipline in the latter part of the twelfth century, again in Bologna. Unfortunately we know almost nothing of Gratian who, around 1140 or a little earlier, compiled the *Concordia discordantium canonum* (better known as the *Decretum*), a collection of canonical texts of diverse origins. This work was of unprecedented scope, and was presented thematically, the apparent contradictions in sources being resolved by recourse to dialectical method. The *Decretum* was still only a "private" collection, even if it enjoyed an unprecedented authority. After the thirteenth century it was supplemented by official collections of pontifical decretals (Gregory IX's five volumes, Boniface VII's *Liber sextus*, Clement V's *Clementinae*, and John XXII's *Extravagantes*), which taken together constituted the ecclesiastical pendant to the *Corpus iuris civilis*. The parallel between the *Corpus iuris civilis* and the *Corpus iuris canonici* was all the greater because canon law compilers and commentators drew largely on concepts borrowed from Roman law.

Around the middle of the thirteenth century, a *glossa ordinaria* or "ordinary gloss" was added to these two *Corpora*. Franciscus Accursius was responsible for covering Roman law and Johannes Teutonicus for canon law. The "ordinary gloss" brought together over a century of Bolognese commentaries and became a kind of official *apparatus criticus* of scholarly law, which was taught on the same basis as the latter, and was thus known to all those who studied Roman and canon law. This did not put an end to the commentators' activities but rather redirected them henceforth toward writing either specific "questions" or long treatises with various titles (*Lectura*, *Summa*, etc.). The Italians did the lion's share of this work, whether they taught in Bologna or elsewhere. Pope Innocent IV (ca. 1190–1254) and John Andreae (1270–1348) wrote the most widely known commentaries on canon law, while Bartolus (1314–1357) and Baldus (1327–1400) were widely read on civil law. Other groups of commentators appeared outside Italy toward the end of the thirteenth century, the most productive emerging in Languedoc from the universities of Montpellier and Toulouse; other important authors came from Paris and Orléans. Elsewhere in Europe, however, no significant contributions were made to commentary on scholarly bodies of law until the fifteenth century. The various schools of commentators may have been different in some ways—in southern France they were less abstract and in Orléans more philosophical—but for the most part, the teaching of Roman and canon law was remarkably uniform throughout Europe until the end of the Middle Ages. This uniformity resulted from the uncontested superiority of Roman law and from the popes' influence on Church law after the Gregorian reform.

It is sometimes imagined that bodies of scholarly law could develop by contending with pre-existing, customary law of feudal, barbarous origin. The general population may have perceived Roman and Roman-canon law as basically foreign and imposed at the expense of ancestral customary law, but this view was certainly not shared by the jurists themselves. For jurists, scholarly law was the only possible law; it alone enjoyed a universal authority based both on antiquity and on its own rational structure. Customary laws, on the contrary, were diverse and empirical, though jurists did not fail to recognize their utility and made no attempt to abolish them in favor of Roman law. Instead, they sought to confer on law the dignity of a scholarly discipline and to require on all levels—from procedures to decisions—a scholarly spirit (*mens legis*) based on the rationality of its demonstrations and on the universality of principles.

This appeal to rationality also allowed jurists to overcome the Church's hesitations. In the twelfth century, the Church still claimed to see law as the very type of lucrative and deceptive knowledge. Holding out the hope of profit, it drew great minds away from sacred learning, and made it possible for clever minds to deceive the simple and chicanery to triumph over truth. Consequently, the Church forbade clerics and monks to study Roman law. Officially, this prohibition was maintained until the thirteenth century and even beyond. In 1219, in his bull *Super speculam*, Pope Honorius III forbade the teaching of civil law in Paris, for fear that it would compete with the schools of theology.[22] This prohibition was aimed in particular at members of religious orders, who were even forbidden to study canon law. Though this prohibition may have been respected in the mendicant orders, in the fourteenth century the Cistercians and Cluniacs received a special dispensation to study law when requested to do so by the leaders of their orders. Secular clerics were quick to take up the study of Roman law. In the fourteenth century, 40 percent of the cardinals in Avignon who had university degrees had specialized in civil law,[23] as had even greater number (46 percent) of the auditors of the Rota, the highest Christian court, at the time of the Great Schism (1378–1417).[24]

The arguments that had allowed jurists to mitigate the Church's opposition are expressed in various twelfth-century texts, one of the most explicit being the *Sermo de legibus*, written in 1186 and attributed to Placentinus, a well-known Italian jurist who taught at Montpellier.[25] Law, we read in the *Sermo*, is not a matter of opportunism and deception, but rather of reason itself (*ratio scripta*); the principles of human law contradict neither the laws of nature nor divine law but rather actualize them in given situations. Law is the supreme means by which society is regulated; it is knowledge of the just and unjust and is equivalent to fairness itself, rendering to each his due.

The canonists were able to demonstrate that Church law, far from opposing theology, was actually its necessary complement within the militant Church. They were furthermore clever enough to involve theologians in their teaching by making them responsible for commenting on decretals bearing directly on questions of dogma and rites.

We can see how these arguments had the double advantage of legitimizing law as a scholarly discipline in its own right and providing a basis for the jurists' claims to occupy high positions in society and in the Church as advisors to princes and prelates. Law professors soon applied to themselves the verse from Daniel (12:3) that St. Bernard had applied to teachers of theology: "And those who are wise shall shine like the brightness of the firmament; and those who turn many to righteousness, like the stars for ever and ever."[26]

That said, the social and intellectual prestige Roman and Roman-canonic law enjoyed in the Middle Ages was not uniform throughout the West. It was absolute in the Mediterranean countries, that is, in Italy, southern France and the Iberian peninsula. In this area, the number of law schools and scholarly commentaries had been increasing since the twelfth century. Charters show the social ascension of jurists (called *doctores legum, judices, causidici*, etc.). In thirteenth-century France, faculties of law were dominant in universities, where faculties of arts and of theology, when they existed at all, were relegated to a secondary or marginal position, along with their graduates. Jurists did not hesitate to describe themselves with the most flattering epithets: *circumspectus, venerabilis, magnificus, sapientissimus*, etc. In short, all signs of social

recognition and political prestige worked to their advantage by expressing the glory of the law in Mediterranean culture.

Though somewhat later and to the advantage of a more limited élite,
the Germanic countries of the Empire also welcomed Roman law and
jurists able to teach or practice it. On the other hand, Northern France
and England accorded less prestige, or at least a less exclusive prestige,
to scholarly law. In Paris and Oxford, philosophy and theology, long
reinforced by tradition, were held in high esteem. French customary
law did not mount a true and organized resistance to Roman law—in
fact, the former was influenced by the latter, as we see in Philippe de
Beaumanoir's *Coutumes de Beauvaisis* (thirteenth century). In England,
on the contrary, Common Law—which was nonetheless influenced
by Roman law, unified and systematized in the *Tractatus de legibus et
consuetudinibus regni Angliae*, reputedly by Ranulf de Glanville (end of
the twelfth century) and in a book of the same title by Henry Bracton
(ca. 1216–1268)—limited scholarly law, at least in the *Corpus iuris civilis*,
to the respected but marginal status of a foreign and strictly academic
discipline.

Be this as it may, at the end of the Middle Ages, the man of learning in
western Europe was very often a jurist. Granted, he was a good Latinist
and could read Aristotle and formulate syllogisms, but above all, he was
imbued with the two *Corpus iuris*, and his head was stuffed full of quotations from the *Decretum*, the *Code* and the *Digeste*. The Spanish canonist, Juan Alfonso de Benavente (1453) claimed in his *Ars et doctrina
studendi et docendi* that mnemonic devices, which were very popular in
medieval schools, enabled the man of learning to know by heart up to a
thousand titles of laws, which were then instantly available when he
needed to support an argument, enrich a report, or embellish a speech.

The considerable weight of law in the culture and mentality of people
living at the end of the Middle Ages cannot be overemphasized. It
was commensurate with the social and political success of the jurists
themselves.

4. Social Utility or General Culture?

The scholarly culture of the Middle Ages—even limited to those disciplines I have just discussed—did not hide its practical goals or its desire
to be of social utility. It would be anachronistic, of course, to conceive of
this social utility in terms of specific professional opportunities, and yet
the people of that time did indeed think that the knowledge acquired by
men of learning would naturally lead to socially valued roles and that the
quality of a person's performance in these roles would be commensurate
with his level of scholastic competence. After all, theology was studied

in order to preach, medicine in order to heal the sick, and law in order to become a judge or lawyer. Only the liberal arts did not clearly define their social function (although Masters of Arts could at least become school teachers or secretaries), and this was because, at least in theory, the liberal arts were considered preparatory to more advanced study. The idea of disinterested learning that had no goals other than the development of one's personality and the pure joy of knowledge for its own sake was completely foreign to the intellectuals of this time. Individual success was not a question of education and learning but rather of faith, of submission to God, of the practice of virtues and good works in the hope of obtaining salvation. The aesthetic pleasure associated with art or knowledge was considered suspect; better to limit that kind of pleasure to entertainment—at best inoffensive, at worst dangerous. For this, the social arts and literature in the vernacular would amply suffice. Scholarly culture was considered too serious to be left to itself. "Who would want knowledge with no practical application? *Sciencia abscondita et thesaurus invisus, que utilitas in utrisque*? In an address given in 1405, Jean Gerson noted: "I do not learn merely in order to know but to teach and to work; what good is knowledge that cannot be applied, that is not useful for one's salvation and for society at large?"[27] The man of learning expected his own social usefulness to be recognized and rewarded for what it was worth, that is, that he be recognized as belonging to the élite—and more precisely, as we will see later—that he be recognized as belonging to the nobility, at least personally and for his own lifetime.

This utilitarian aspect of scholarly culture during the last centuries of the Middle Ages often led it, out of concern for social efficacy, to give priority to concrete and technical procedures at the expense of intellectual elegance and curiosity and thereby contributed to the misunderstandings that would soon oppose medieval scholarly culture to that of Renaissance humanists. Even if modern historians no longer share the humanists' biases, they may be tempted to attribute to this notion of knowledge an insufficiency of critical thinking and an almost total absence of the spirit of discovery which appear, at least in hindsight, to be major traits of medieval scholarly culture. This is, of course, only a generalization. Many indications of intellectual progress are evident in the writings of various authors, ever since Bernard de Chartres coined, at the beginning of the twelfth century, the famous maxim about "dwarves, perched on the shoulders of giants," who could see much farther than their living pedestals. But such references are infrequent and limited largely to the twelfth and thirteenth centuries. After 1300, a more conservative and obstructionist notion of knowledge seems to predominate.

However, the view of medieval culture we are outlining encounters two objections. The less pertinent is that the social benefit or function of erudite culture was far from being generally and unanimously recognized. No role in medieval society (with the exception of some kinds of medical practice) was ever strictly accorded to holders of this or that degree as much as intellectual competence, birth, seniority, or simply chance were often the deciding factors in procuring positions and promotions. Medieval society was never a true meritocracy. The men of learning were themselves well aware of this and did not hesitate to exploit all the resources of chance, nepotism, and connections to obtain what their knowledge alone should have been able to confer upon them. The essential point, however, is that from the twelfth century on, the idea that intellectual competence could be a regulating factor in society—an idea practically unknown in the early Middle Ages—never ceased to advance, though it never succeeded in shaking off entirely the weight of competing factors.

A more serious objection is the fact that the principal disciplines comprising scholarly culture, as they were practiced and taught at the end of the Middles Ages, hardly seemed in conformity with the notion of social utility. What could there be in common between scholastic theology, with its rebarbative abstractions and endless distinctions, and delivering sermons to ordinary people, or between the theoretical discourse of physicians and the real needs of patients? What possible good did it do for a jurist called upon to judge according to customary law to have spent years interpreting Roman law, already several centuries old and inapplicable as such to particular cases in medieval society?

Even at the time, people were aware of such disparities. It is likely that in their everyday practice both teachers and students often tried to promote simpler and less formalistic forms of teaching, simplifying traditional programs and introducing into schools exercises and texts, indeed whole disciplines, that were not originally part of the curriculum. Unfortunately, these initiatives, which were little coordinated and often ignored or even fought by the authorities, left few traces in the archives. A few projects of reform and college statutes probably reflect them. In one form or another, we find in them the same tendencies to rehabilitate grammar, to give up certain disputations, to work in small groups, to introduce simplified manuals, to shorten the length of study, and to give greater attention to Biblical study in theology, to clinical internships in medicine, and to modern customary law in law schools. Nevertheless, few seem to have dared to suggest that the vernacular be substituted for Latin.

Here and there, on the fringes of the old universities—and often under their control—new kinds of schools were created. In Oxford, a network of high quality grammar schools were developed alongside the faculty of arts. In Bologna, schools for notaries appeared in the shadow of the university law schools. Elsewhere as well, schools for surgeons, more or less supervised by the faculties of medicine, were founded. In

Salamanca, degrees in music were accorded, while in the faculty of law Castilian royal legislation—*Siete Partidas* and *Fuero real*—was taught alongside the *Corpus iuris civilis*. In England Common Law became a subject of study, but it was taught completely outside the university in special, private schools—the Inns of Court—that appeared in the fifteenth century in London. In them future lawyers were trained; they combined magisterial lectures given by practicing lawyers with internships in court. One could give other examples as well. The curricula that were developed, especially in the fifteenth century, within some university colleges seem to reflect a common uneasiness brought about by the rigid and ill-adapted character of university teaching.

Overall, however, these innovations did not go very far. The authorities—"ordinary" university professors and public officials—generally combined their efforts to contain these innovations and maintain the *status quo*. It must be acknowledged that these innovative tendencies were not of great cultural import. One may even be tempted to conclude that those who tried to slow their development were justified in doing so. Resulting less from a general reflection on the nature of the disciplines than from the pressure exerted by students and their families, which were concerned about deriving the most from their educational investment, the efforts to promote a more practical and less formal approach to academic disciplines could well have ended up exacerbating the most questionable tendencies of medieval culture: the primacy of authority, the dread of heterodoxy, the substitution of anthologies, summaries and handbooks for original texts, and the overdevelopment of memory.

The defense of traditional disciplines and methods was clearly and above all the effect of a corporatist reaction on the part of teachers, experts sure of their knowledge and little disposed to diminish their own authority and prestige. But it also revealed an awareness of the specific values of medieval scholarly culture. The latter was neither free, disinterested, nor dominated by the spirit of discovery, but it did claim at least to be based on broad knowledge and on "authorities" that could give students a knowledge which went beyond mere technical expertise. In the Middle Ages an educated person was recognized by his mastery of a whole disciplinary field, by his ability to reason, solve problems, analyze texts, conduct a discussion, and derive universal principles that made him capable, within a given discipline and even beyond it, of assuming a variety of related social roles. Intellectual disciplines and processes were certainly rigorously and even rigidly defined, yet within this framework men of learning in medieval societies—which were still largely "international"—could see themselves not only as capable of accomplishing tasks they considered socially and politically useful but also as forming a cultural community defined by common references.

This is not to imply that there was no crisis of the scholarly culture at the end of the Middle Ages. This crisis had begun in Italy in the middle of the fourteenth century, and it became perceptible in France around 1400; elsewhere it made itself felt only in the last decades of the fifteenth century. The obsolescence of some subject matters and the discovery of new texts made it necessary to reexamine the definition and even the canonical list of the disciplines. Literature came once again to the forefront, and Plato reemerged to compete with Aristotle. But the most significant change was no doubt the decline in the utilitarian perspective we have just outlined. The notion of culture—which in the Middle Ages was strongly linked to that of work, as Jacques Le Goff has persuasively argued—gradually, though not without debate, became more closely associated with leisure and disinterested activities, with the result that professional knowledge tended increasingly to be strictly functional.[28] This shift occurred slowly, but it reflected in a purely cultural domain the social and political changes that marked the passage of European societies into the modern era.

5. Scholarly Culture, Popular Culture

A final question remains to be explored. The scholarly culture we have been discussing was clearly an elitist culture. It is clear that men of learning never represented more than a small minority, primarily masculine, of the overall population. Their culture was composed of particular disciplines that were at first difficult, if only because they required a strong command of Latin. Lengthy study was almost always necessary, as well as the purchase of costly books. A strong awareness of their merit and value characterized these men of learning; modesty does not seem to have been their dominant character trait. In short, were not all the conditions fulfilled for the establishment of a closed caste defined by the possession of kinds of knowledge that were inaccessible to the common man?

The answer to this question is above all social. Clearly a caste of men of learning can be more easily established if the members constitute a fairly inbred group characterized by specific functions and a specific lifestyle. Conversely, when men of learning remained isolated individuals in families whose other members continued to be involved in other activities, they probably remained closer to the preoccupations and perceptions of society at large.

However, the question is also cultural. Did these men of learning and the rest of the population really constitute two culturally distinct universes? Were not some aspects of the knowledge of educated people disseminated to other groups? And, conversely, beyond the knowledge that was specifically their domain, didn't educated people also share with their contemporaries a significant number of beliefs and kinds of knowledge, explicit or implicit, which belonged to what we would call "popular culture" (an ambiguous term we use for lack of another)? These are issues that are difficult to grasp precisely, since this "popular" culture has, by definition, left far fewer written traces than scholarly culture.

A question as fundamental as the rate of literacy in the Middle Ages is beyond our power to determine. Naturally, this rate must have been quite low but, at least starting in the twelfth and thirteenth centuries, it may not have been as low as was once thought. In numerous regions, in towns and even in the countryside, small grammar schools were able to reach a relatively "popular" audience. From the thirteenth to the fifteenth centuries, the number of English localities that had one or several schools of this kind went from thirty-two to eighty-five.[29] Other regions, it is true, were probably less well provided for. However, even if children who attended such schools acquired only an ability to understand simple texts (accounts, letters of credit, rental and sales contracts, statements of arbitration, marriage licenses, and testaments), they nonetheless gained some familiarity with the administrative and legal practices that regulated everyday life.

Michael T. Clanchy has shown that at the end of the Middle Ages, many English peasants had titles of property and legal rulings in their strongboxes and that they were able to understand and use these papers in their litigation with their lords or with royal officials.[30]

Was England, illustrated by these two cases, an exception? Anyone who has done research in the registers of notaries in Mediterranean countries, and has had to deal with a mass of transactions that are often minute and with contracts between the commonest sort of people concerning what seem to be utterly futile matters, cannot help thinking that, in these regions as well, most of the inhabitants were able to understand the gist of written documents and that they were as likely to put their faith in the legal system as were jurists themselves. Finally, the extraordinarily litigious character of medieval men is well known; they constantly overloaded the existing courts and often adroitly took advantage of the overlapping and possible competition of various judicial authorities.

This would seem to imply the presence of a kind of popular legal culture. Ordinary people brought before the courts obviously did not have the knowledge of professional lawyers, but they shared with them a certain idea of the power of law and of its main principles. The lawyers would not have been able to attain the rank and prestige they enjoyed at this time had there not been a general consensus about their legitimacy and the efficacy of their discipline. The consensus was widespread; princes, townships, religious orders, etc., all employed lawyers and legal advisors whose aid seemed indispensable in defending the "freedom and privileges" without which institutions as well as individuals felt deprived of their legal existence and thereby vulnerable to all sorts of demands and even to violence.[31]

It would be difficult to make the same argument for other areas of learned culture (philosophy, theology or medicine). The gap was undoubtedly greater between the specialized knowledge of the élites and the general knowledge of the populace. The trial of Joan of Arc, apart from its political ramifications, remains a famous example of the difference in theological understanding that could exist between a devout woman of the people and the doctors of theology at the university.

Was this difference in understanding reciprocal? Had popular culture itself become impenetrable to educated people enclosed within the logic of their disciplines and the certitude of their intellectual superiority? There is no simple answer to this question. There may be as many answers as there are personal cases, especially since we have brought under the rubric "men of learning" individuals having quite varied levels of knowledge and social practices.

There was, however, one area common to all: that of Christian faith. This was, after all, an age of religious unanimity, but does this mean that everyone's religious culture was the same? Let us set aside the case of theologians, whose education was rigorous but who were not a large group, as well as monks and friars, who were supposed to derive something from the daily lectures (*collationes*) given by their abbots. As for the others—laymen and even simple secular clerics—the medieval Church did not provide a specific kind of religious education. The Church relied on families, and particularly women, to inculcate children with the rudiments, and especially the main prayers. The Church offered the faithful, without distinguishing between ages or sexes, only a more or less intelligible message in the liturgy, in iconography (the decor of the churches) and especially in vernacular preaching. Did men of learning benefit from these teachings more than the simple people? That is possible. Some left marks of their piety. The personal libraries of those who sat in the Paris Parlement, including lay councilors, contained spiritual works alongside their law books.[32] But at the end of the Middle Ages the development of lay devotion was a general phenomenon that affected men and women of modest means and of little education as much as the highly educated. Conversely, we know nothing about the level of knowledge and religious culture of men of learning. Apart from a few introductory formulas invoking God, their writings, which are too technical, have little to say about religion or, more generally, anything that would indicate their interest in the popular, oral or folk culture of their contemporaries. A few proverbs and personal reflection do not suffice to answer our questions.

The *exempla* (moral anecdotes) with which preachers, including eminent theologians, peppered their sermons have often been mentioned by scholars contending that these might be conscious borrowings from popular culture (reinterpreted according to religious orthodoxy), used to better hold the attention of listeners.[33] In fact, even if we set aside the fact that many *exempla* are actually of scholarly origin, their inclusion in sermons testifies to the theologians' knowledge of, but not necessarily to their participation in, the popular culture referred to in the *exempla*.

The same holds true for many judicial documents, notably those connected with the Inquisition. The canonists and theologians who needed to deal with cases of heresy and witchcraft—extreme manifestations of a popular culture at odds with the established order—often seemed not only malicious but also poorly informed. Their lack of understanding can be seen in the paradoxical character of their attitude, which consisted in describing heretics and witches as "rustic ignoramuses" and in trying to discern behind their practices the resurgence of erroneous doctrines earlier condemned by the Church Fathers (Manicheanism, Arianism, Sabellianism, etc.).

This issue comes up particularly in relation to the witchcraft trials that multiplied throughout Europe in the fifteenth century. Did the judges who interrogated and condemned the witches participate, as agents of repression, in a general movement of collective fear (which would last until the seventeenth century)? Did they "believe," as did everyone else, in the witches' sabbath and nocturnal horse rides? Or instead should we see in this demonological flare-up the sign of a break between a popular culture that had long been tolerated but was henceforth to be rejected and an erudite culture, that of the jurists and the men of the Church, that was incapable of understanding and accepting cultural expressions that had become completely foreign to it?[34]

I do not intend provide a definitive answer to an issue on which specialists are divided. Instead, I will merely point out that although specific aspects of the culture of men of learning are relatively easy to determine because of the numerous texts bearing witness to them, it is far more difficult to discover what these educated men of learning had in common with most of their contemporaries, which is obscured by official language and specialized kinds of knowledge. Political and sociological studies and—insofar as they are possible—studies of behavior may perhaps reveal what those concerned would undoubtedly have preferred, consciously or unconsciously, to keep hidden.

CHAPTER II

Education

At the end of the Middle Ages virtually all men of learning had pursued studies of an academic sort, often for prolonged periods. Although the existence of self-taught men cannot be excluded, neither the social and political context nor the material conditions of access to culture were favorable for autodidacticism. The latter's modern form is probably a consequence of the printed book.

In the Middle Ages as in any other period, school was first of all the place where one acquired knowledge. Schools inculcated in their pupils, in accord with the pedagogical principles of the time, knowledge and methods of reasoning and working that would constitute the core of the intellectual baggage each would carry with him for the rest of his life. But school was far more than that, even if in the Middle Ages it claimed less than at other times to undertake the complete social, moral and religious training of individuals. School was a place of sociability and discovery. There one learned to behave, to assert one's personality, and to compare oneself with others while at the same time adapting to a collective discipline. Long-term friendships were forged; an individual became integrated into a group or clientele. This existential experience, inseparable from the acquisition of knowledge, doubtless contributed to the collective profile of the educated in the Middle Ages.

In short, given the recognized function of education, school was important politically. There were certainly forms of education and even schools that were essentially familial or private, but in general, the Church's various authorities (the pope, bishops and religious orders), cities, and rulers went to great lengths to establish and control schools. The political goal was above all ideological: to guarantee the preservation and dissemination of certain kinds of knowledge while at the same time monitoring orthodoxy and opposing the development of other kinds of knowledge considered illegitimate or dangerous. But it was even more a matter of creating favorable conditions for training the educated, competent individuals whom the Church, towns, and rulers thought they needed to serve them either directly or at least by contributing to the harmonious functioning of society.

Educational networks in the last centuries of the Middle Ages were neither complete nor perfectly coherent. Depending on the country, they varied in density, followed different rules, and thus did not produce the same education. Overall, they were nevertheless much more uniform than they are today. For this reason we can study them all together, provided that we take into consideration regional and national particularities.

Three levels of educational institutions can be distinguished. First, the elementary level, which we can compare with only slight anachronism to the modern-day elementary, and to some extent, secondary schools. Relying principally on private or local initiative and receiving only limited social and political respect, these schools were the most diverse and the least coherent. Archival records relating to them are often scattered and scarce. Particularly at this stage in historical research, these schools are therefore by far the least well known to modern historians. A few regional cases have been the object of reasonably substantial monographs, but it would be premature to generalize their conclusions.

The key element in the medieval educational system was the universities, or as they were then called, the *studia generalia,* which date from the thirteenth century and whose functioning we will examine in detail later. The universities possessed by far the most solid institutional and economic infrastructure (which explains the abundant archives they left), and they enjoyed the greatest—and in fact, long uncontested—social and intellectual prestige, and they nearly monopolized the attention, and the favors of public powers, ecclesiastical as well as lay, though they also sometimes attempted to dominate the latter.

The first universities appeared around 1200 and were the direct heirs of the principal schools of the twelfth century. In 1300, there were in all of western Europe only about fifteen universities; two centuries later there were four times that number. In spite of such rapid growth—revealing the popularity of the institution—it is clear that medieval universities, which moreover varied considerably in size, never enrolled more than a small élite of students and conferred diplomas to an even smaller number. The "men of learning" are not identical with these recipients of university degrees, but the latter formed their central core and to a large extent their point of reference and model.

In spite of this, universities and their students did not escape criticism. This was more often implicit than overtly expressed. However, it resulted in the appearance of a number of educational establishments—and these constitute the third level of educational institutions—that offered an alternative to universities. These were often still newly established, local institutions of disparate character and varying success. Many of these new institutions were modest in caliber, while others were already providing some real competition for the universities in some areas of study. Taken all in all, they were harbingers of the colleges devoted to the student's overall development that would become a key element of European education in the modern era and would often even relegate universities to second place. Because of their importance, it is essential to examine these institutions at the time of their first appearance, that is, in the thirteenth or fourteenth centuries, or more often in the fifteenth century.

In the following sections, we will study successively each of these three kinds of educational institutions, in which most if not all men of learning were schooled during the last centuries of the Middle Ages.

1. Elementary Schools

Elementary education, beginning with reading and writing, took place in various settings. It might take place in the home itself, with the mother as teacher, if—and this was quite rare—she was literate, or with a tutor. Private tutoring certainly played an important role at the end of the Middle Ages, even among the urban patriciate, although the existing documentation gives us a clear picture of tutoring only in the highest echelons of noble and royal families. Even in the latter case, what we know is usually only the name of the knight responsible for the child's military and social education in his family or at the court, while intellectual education was left to some cleric or chaplain who very often remains anonymous.[35] With very few exceptions, before the fifteenth century a solid literary education was seldom considered advantageous, indispensable, or worthy of special attention for a future prince or young noble expecting to pursue a military career.

For all those who, while wanting to give their children some kind of literary education, were neither willing nor able to engage a tutor, there remained the possibility of Latin grammar school. Such schools were located chiefly in towns of some size, and thus we might be tempted to conclude that city dwellers were at a distinct advantage. It seems that most large cities boasted many schools. In greater Paris, for example, a document from 1380 lists the names of forty-one grammar school regents, both clerical and lay, as well as twenty-one female teachers for girls.[36] This list probably does not cover all Parisian schools, since it includes only those under the supervision of the cantor of Notre Dame, though other Parisian churches and abbeys must have also sponsored schools. In Genoa, the college of grammar teachers, which seems to have excluded both regents of Church schools and simple drill-leaders or teaching assistants working under a regular teacher, had thirteen members at the end of the thirteenth century and twenty-two at the end of the fifteenth.[37] In London, instruction in grammar remained more under the Church's control, but toward the end of the Middle Ages, in addition to the large old schools connected with St. Paul's cathedral and with the parishes of St. Martin's-le-Grand and St. Mary's-le-Bow there were two or three other Church schools, the mendicants' *studia* (which were no doubt open to external auditors) and an undetermined number of purely private schools.[38] Smaller cities often had only two or three schools, or even only one associated with the local chapter of canons. But practically no city lacked a grammar school, as Nicholas Orme has shown for the southwest of England and Giovanna Petti Balbi for Liguria.[39]

The rural population, though it had less access to schools than town-dwellers, was nonetheless not irremediably doomed to ignorance and illiteracy. Many villages had no school, of course, but others did, and in addition there was often some elementary instruction offered by the local priest. In towns of some size it was common to have a small school, though because they lacked continuous financial support, many of these schools functioned sporadically, and the level of their instruction was probably fairly low. Peasant children who displayed enthusiasm for learning could study in a city, provided they could find lodging. Until the end of the Middle Ages, a few urban monasteries seem to have boarded young pupils. For instance, a young peasant boy from the Ardennes who bore the name of his native village, Jean Gerson, is said to have started his studies at the monastery of Saint-Remi in Reims.[40] Elsewhere there were true colleges intended to house some of the students from the cathedral school. At the beginning of the thirteenth century there were two such schools in Reims offering some twenty-four rooms. In the middle of the fourteenth century the neighboring city of Soissons, though considerably smaller than Reims, had three colleges able to lodge as many as one hundred pupils.[41] Teachers in private schools also sometimes lodged and boarded pupils who came from outside town.

It is hard to determine with any certainty the size and density of the grammar school network in the fourteenth and fifteenth centuries. Large cities, as we have seen, had an ample number of schools. On a larger scale, there seem to have been significant regional differences. For instance, medieval England seems to have had a relatively large number of schools, even in the six southwest counties, which were sparsely populated and contained no large cities. In the study already cited, Orme found forty-four localities that had, at one time or another between the thirteenth and fifteenth centuries, some kind of school (not to mention the thirty-three monasteries, priories or convents that also had schools, usually for boarding pupils). In contrast, in medieval Champagne only one village out of ten had a school;[42] and in Liguria, G. Petti Balbi found that neither coastal fishing villages nor mountain communities were able to attract school teachers. These disparities are perhaps accentuated by the current lack of adequate documentation and research and should not be used to support sweeping generalizations. Both urban and rural grammar schools functioned under the auspices of various institutions. The oldest were the church schools that began operating in the early Middle Ages and were under the control of cathedrals, monasteries and abbeys of canons regular. Starting from the thirteenth century, many convents of the new mendicant orders had a *studium,* in which one or two tutors taught and which were initially intended for young friars. Auditors from outside the order, in numbers unknown to us today, may have also attended these *studia,* though it is an exaggeration to call the mendicant orders "teaching orders."

In addition to the Church schools, there were also purely private schools that operated with or without episcopal authorization, run by teachers with sometimes dubious credentials who collected fees from the pupils' parents. These grammar teachers were occasionally poor priests who were trying to supplement their insufficient prebends and chaplain's benefices. More often, however, the teachers were laymen. Apparently, they did not enjoy much social prestige; most were somewhat itinerant and spent only a few years at one school before moving to another. They certainly did not become rich.

At the close of the Middle Ages, this situation seems to have changed somewhat. In the middle of the fourteenth century, we find an increasing number of public and charitable schools that enjoyed stable financing (though not clean and suitable school buildings; teaching continued to take place at the teacher's house). This may have been due to the general economic crisis or, more likely, to the greater interest that the ruling classes and municipal élite showed in primary education.

In England, pious founders often established "chantries" combining a school and a commemorative chapel whose chaplain was also the teacher. Elsewhere, and in particular in the Mediterranean countries, municipalities took it upon themselves to recruit teachers, provide lodging for them, and pay their salaries in whole or in part. The Church did not always approve of this secularization of the school, and tried, as in Aix-en-Provence, to maintain the right to confirm the *magister grammaticus* whom the consuls had chosen.[43] This beginning of secularization sometimes offered an opportunity to modernize teaching by establishing a selection that made it possible to engage teachers with a humanistic orientation. Before the sixteenth century, however, both the audiences for these "public teachers" and the efforts made to remunerate them were too modest to attract candidates other than beginners or teachers of no stature.

For our purposes, information about the pupils, teaching methods, content and level of teaching, and the curriculum in these schools is even more important than knowing about their institutional framework. Unfortunately, our knowledge in these areas remains scant.

As for attendance in grammar schools, the documentation reveals sharply contrasting figures. Some urban grammar schools seem to have enrolled several hundred pupils of varying levels and ages. In 1469, the school of the old Saint-Gilles monastery in Nuremberg had no less than 230 pupils;[44] and similarly high enrollments are also found in some urban Italian schools. This would almost certainly require separating students into several classes, adding assistants, or perhaps establishing what was called, well into the nineteenth century, "mutual teaching," in which the older students would help the younger. Elsewhere enrollments were lower—seldom more than ten—and pupils could thus be taught in an almost individual or apprentice-like manner by one teacher or "grammaticus."

In all of these schools, the basic subject was grammar, in other words, Latin. Study was initially passive, and sometimes associated with singing; in the latter case, the teacher presumably did not hesitate to use the vernacular. Children learned texts by heart, notably those of the Psalter and other liturgical books that had the advantage of being accessible, even in the most modest schools, since they could be borrowed from the local church. Study then turned to grammar itself in the form of short exercises in translation or Latin composition. Donatus's old manual of grammar, sometimes supplemented by Alexandre de Ville-Dieu's *Doctrinale* or Évrard de Béthune's *Grecismus*, were basic books in the curriculum, along with several collections of simple short texts such as the *Distichs* attributed to Cato, the *Ecloga Theoduli*, the *Chartula*, Aesop's *Fables*, the *Floretus*, etc., in which the child found proverbs, fables and other little poems, elementary catechism, moral tales, and table manners.[45] This fairly heterogeneous pedagogic material, dating from the early Middles Ages or the twelfth century, hardly changed between the thirteenth and the fifteenth century, and it was surprisingly uniform in all the schools of western Europe, from England to Italy.

The quality of instruction no doubt depended in large measure on the teacher's qualifications. Apparently no serious attempt was made to check the teacher's credentials, even in areas where episcopal authorization or municipal examinations existed. University graduates—usually Masters of Arts—constituted only a small proportion of the grammar school teachers. Orme estimates the figure at 25 percent for England; and on the Parisian list of 1380 already mentioned, only 22 percent (nine out of forty-one) of the teachers are university graduates, despite the proximity of the largest university in the land.

The time pupils spent in grammar school, their expectations and, especially, those of their parents, are issues at least as important as the qualifications of the teachers. Pupils who started Latin grammar school at around eight or ten years of age and stayed only two or three years could hope to acquire only a basic command of reading (if not of writing) and a few vague religious and moral references drawn from the Psalter and from textbooks. On the other hand, those who studied for up to a decade could expect to attain a clearly superior level, and if their teacher offered them the opportunity, they might be able to study disciplines other than basic Latin.

This required, of course, a motivated student. The well-known humanist Enea Silvio Piccolomini (the future pope Pius II) deplored the lack of enthusiasm for study among the inhabitants of Genoa: "They are hardly hungry to learn; they study grammar only if it is indispensable and are little interested in other kinds of study."[46] In fact, in Genoa, school contracts required that children study grammar "as befitting a merchant," (grammatica ad usum mercatorum Ianue).[47] In this way, the study of grammar led directly to the business of contract-writing and accounting, the latter subject often being taught by a special teacher, an "abacus teacher" who was better paid than the regular grammar teacher. At the time it must have been thought that such an education would be sufficient for a future merchant who did not need more advanced study.

However, except in large commercial cities the study of grammar was more naturally followed by the study of the traditional academic disciplines listed in the old classifications of subjects. In that respect, the teaching in grammar schools resembled that in the universities and could even prepare the student for university. After grammar, logic and the classics were studied (from the fifteenth century onward, the influence of Italian humanism obviously strengthened considerably the emphasis on these subjects); moreover, the sciences of the quadrivium were not wholly neglected and occasionally, in Church schools adhering to their pre-university traditions, courses on theology and law were offered to students, or at least to future clerics. In these latter disciplines, however, university teaching was on the rise; what was learned elsewhere was not as highly esteemed, particularly since it did not lead to an academic degree. Only the mendicants, to whom we will return later, were able to create in their studia theology courses organized in a coherent curriculum at a level truly equivalent to that of the university. All this served to direct gifted students, those who wished to become recognized men of learning, toward the university.

However, the double role played by the grammar schools should not be underestimated. They offered something of a literary culture to a segment of the population and prepared the best and most ambitious students for the university. Some of these schools operated at a very acceptable level, especially those located in large non-university towns that had an old cathedral school and a solid tradition of teaching (e.g., Reims and London), particularly when compared to the second-tier universities. Moreover, some of their students were able to become true men of letters, provided they continued their education and subsequently engaged in a profession that kept them in the sphere of intellectual activities.

This was the case of many notaries, scribes, and chancellery secretaries. They belonged to milieus in which there were never many university graduates. Most of these men probably started with solid study in a grammar school, since they then went to work for a notary or else were hired as clerks in a court or in an office providing writing services. Here one of the older clerks would teach them the law forms as well as fine handwriting. Despite claims to the contrary, the latter was not systematically taught in the schools, whose slates and wax tablets were not well suited to the task.

2. The University

Of all medieval educational institutions, the universities left by far the richest archives (even if they do not answer all our questions), and those that have provided the basis for the most probing historical research. In a way, the abundance of these historical studies, which tend to be commemorative, itself bears witness to the enduring prestige of an institution that has long been recognized as one of the most original and fertile creations of Western medieval civilization. We will not try to sum up these many studies, which have, moreover, recently arrived at a synthesis to which we can refer the reader.[48] Instead, we will simply try to bring out the way in which, between the thirteenth and the fifteenth centuries, the institution of the university helped shape the contours, the composition, and the self-awareness of the men of learning who are the subject of this book.

The first universities appeared in Bologna, Paris, Montpellier, and Oxford in the first decades of the thirteenth century. Emerging from already existing schools (though not necessarily from cathedral schools), they were all autonomous organizations of a corporative nature. Being autonomous meant being able to control recruitment, to formulate their own regulations, and to impose on their members respect for collective discipline and rules of mutual assistance; it meant being acknowledged as a moral entity by external authorities, both ecclesiastical and secular. Finally, it meant being free to organize teaching, the very raison d'être of the university corporation, to determine curricula, the length of studies, and the modalities of both the examinations that evaluated students' achievements and the conferral of the degrees that rewarded success on these examinations. Universities were, in a way, federations of schools. Sometimes they taught only one of the disciplines that the preceding chapter defined as the superior disciplines of learned culture at the time: law in Bologna, medicine in Montpellier. Sometimes a single university might combine schools of different disciplines, distributed into different faculties. Thus in Paris and Oxford, there was both a preparatory faculty of (liberal) arts and advanced faculties of medicine, law,[49] and theology. In any case, it was certainly not possible to gain access to university faculties, even to the faculty of arts where there was one, without having previously received some kind of basic training, particularly in grammar. On the other hand, if the student's proficiency in grammar was sufficient, it could even make it possible—especially in Mediterranean countries where the faculties of arts were always mediocre—to move directly to a "superior" (i.e., graduate-level) faculty, particularly a faculty of law.[50]

Lacking historical precedents, the first universities were constituted in an empirical way and in accord with very diverse plans. It was only toward the middle of the thirteenth century that the papacy, which had from the outset supported the development of these new educational institutions, unified them under the concept of *studium generale*. The principal effect of this was to make them institutions of Christendom, conferring degrees of universal validity and directly protected, and at the same time overseen, by the Holy See.

As for the deep causes that are at the origin of the institution of the university, historians' interpretations vary.[51] Two basic theses have been proposed, more complementary than opposed. For some historians, the renewal of knowledge itself brought about by the discovery of Aristotle's philosophy and the intellectual enthusiasm aroused by these novelties, led teachers and students to set up these autonomous institutions, which alone could ensure the necessary freedom of expression and teaching. Other historians emphasize the social pressure exerted by those who aspired to obtain, under the best possible conditions, the qualifications and diplomas that led to the more and more numerous careers opened up by the reform of the Church and even more by the rebirth of the state. However that may be, one thing is sure: the appearance of the first universities was not a "spontaneous" phenomenon, a pure creation of teachers and students alone. Even if the personal involvement of teachers and students was indispensable, it was always supported by a political will that made it possible to overcome resistance (chiefly that of the local powers, the bishop and his chancellor in Paris, the commune in Bologna) and to grant the new institution its legitimacy and legal status. This political will was that of both the ruler (particularly visible in England, more discreet but real in Paris) and the pope (especially active in Paris and Bologna).

The support lent the first universities by superior powers, whether ecclesiastical or lay, was obviously not purely disinterested. They expected the universities to contribute to the development of the disciplines on which their own legitimacy was based. Roman law was an essential instrument of the rebirth of the state, and canon law and theology, as they were taught in the universities, emphasized pontifical *plenitudo potestatis* and helped the papacy stand up to the resistance of local churches, to the challenge of heretics, and to the secular princes' desire for independence. Moreover, the universities also trained competent men who could put themselves in the service of power and ensure the triumph of these ideas. The crucial test occurred, at least in Paris, when the papacy forced the university to accept within its structure the mendicant orders' schools of theology, Dominican and Franciscan. These newcomers, whose eminent role in the Church of the time is well known, put fidelity to the goals of their own orders and obedience to the pope before solidarity with the university. For this reason they were not always well received, but at the end of a crisis that reached its climax between 1250 and 1259, the university had to yield to the pontifical will.[52]

However, this episode did not compromise the success of the new institution. Still skimpy and vague at the beginning of the century, its organization gradually became tighter, detailed regulations were written, and new privileges were granted by the authorities. Precise figures are not available for the thirteenth century, but there is hardly any doubt that the number of teachers and students grew steadily, at least until the first half of the fourteenth century. New universities appeared; in 1300 there were about fifteen *studia generalia*, and more than twenty in 1346.

At that date the university was still primarily a Mediterranean phenomenon.[53] The southern *studia generalia* were almost always more or less modeled on the one in Bologna. From an institutional point of view, this means that students were responsible in whole or in part for organizing and administering the university. But especially, from a cultural point of view, it means that here we have universities in which the predominant disciplines were civil and canon law. Faculties of medicine also had a place in some universities (Montpellier, Padua, Bologna). On the other hand, in these universities instruction in the arts attracted only a minority of students, and consisted chiefly in instruction in grammar, often at a mediocre level, rather than in logic and philosophy. As for theology, it remained absent from these southern universities until the 1360s. In short, although they were under the Church's supervision, these southern universities already had a strong secular bent that was reflected in the content of their programs of study and in the kinds of careers for which they prepared their students.

Obviously, the situation was completely different in the northern half of Europe. There *studia generalia* were few in number and the Parisian model, rather faithfully imitated in Oxford and Cambridge,[54] had no rival. This model was that of the "university of masters," that is, of a federation of schools in which each professor retained full authority over his own students and in which all the administrative organs of the university were in the hands of teachers elected by their peers. But what was still more essential was the difference in intellectual perspective. In the Parisian and English schools, the teaching of law occupied only a limited place and was limited chiefly to canon law. Roman law, as we have seen, had been prohibited in Paris in 1219, whereas in England, the early existence of a unified customary law or "Common Law" had deprived it of part of its prestige and utility. These universities therefore retained a strong ecclesiastical bent by focusing on the study of theology, which was itself underpinned by the study of the liberal arts entrusted to a preparatory faculty that always had the largest enrollments. From the first years of the thirteenth century, under the impact of the massive dissemination of Aristotelianism, the faculty of arts nonetheless ceased to have as its chief vocation the more or less propaedeutic teaching of grammar and logic and rose to the level of a genuine faculty of philosophy in which students who had already received preliminary training in small pre-university schools were taught physics, metaphysics, psychology, and ethics, on the basis of Aristotle's works and Averroes' commentaries. This broadening—which was of scant benefit to the scientific disciplines of the *quadrivium*—naturally led, especially in Paris, to a demand for both intellectual and professional autonomy on the part of regents in arts, who wanted to comment freely on the whole corpus of philosophical texts, without being subjected to the theologians' supervision and possible censure. This trend, whose most determined representatives were designated by the pejorative and no doubt excessive term "Averroists," was participated in by a large number, and perhaps even the majority, of the faculty of arts in Paris in the 1260s. It even adumbrated a new social type, the professional intellectual, who, while certainly not anti-Christian, was nonetheless more secular; he was defined by the disinterested pursuit of his vocation as a thinker and teacher, and drew from the very exercise of this vocation a superior certainty of a kind of terrestrial felicity and of a natural aptitude for virtue. Initially benefiting from a certain tolerance, "Latin Averroism" soon aroused polemical reactions on the part of theologians (Thomas Aquinas's *Contra Averroistas* of 1270),[55] and then came the time of the ecclesiastical condemnations made by the bishop of Paris and the archbishop of Canterbury.[56] The Averroist trend was, if not destroyed, at least permanently weakened, but the problem of the relations between theology and philosophy remained, as did, on the social level, the problem of the relations between teachers in the faculty of arts and teachers in the graduate faculties (theologians and canon lawyers), whose authority was still not accepted without resistance by the former, particularly since neither they nor their students were necessarily going to pursue studies in a graduate faculty.

For a long time, historians, adopting the complaints humanists had been nurturing since the sixteenth century, contrasted the creative dynamism of the thirteenth-century universities (supposedly reflected even in their internal conflicts) with the decline that these same universities are said to have experienced in the fourteenth and fifteenth centuries. This decline is thought to have affected both the content of their teaching (in the aridity of their doctrines and the rigidity of the Scholastic method) and their institutional functioning. Geographical and social restriction of recruitment (regionalization and aristocratization), disorganization of the programs of study and subjection to the control of the princes won out, it is argued, over the old Christian universalism based on the high degree of autonomy that constituted the university's original strength.

Recent research has strongly challenged this way of seeing things. First, it suggests, we need to make a sharp distinction between the fourteenth century and fifteenth centuries. The fourteenth century remains in many respects a prolongation of the thirteenth, especially in Paris and Oxford, and seems to have marked the apogee of the medieval university in terms of both its intellectual influence and its enrollment, autonomy, and even its doctrinal, political, and moral authority. In the fifteenth century difficulties mounted for institutions struggling to deal with changes connected with the establishment of the modern state. Second, recent research indicates that we should contrast earlier historians' negative judgment with the obviously favorable image that, with rare exceptions, men of the time had of universities.

It is true that some contemporaries were aware of the tedium of Scholastic teaching. A stock of authorities that had become virtually immutable, an essentially oral and repetitive pedagogy, the exclusive use of Latin, very long periods of study (three or four years in arts, six in medicine, eight to twelve in law, as many as fifteen in theology), the increasingly high cost of degrees, especially in graduate faculties, where a doctorate in law or in medicine ended up costing a fortune, which no doubt discouraged candidates more than the very conventional examinations—all these were just so many factors leading some students to give up along the way and others to try to acquire the prized diplomas through special exemptions or even fraud. The disorganization of the program of studies, professorial absenteeism, the gradual abandoning of certain kinds of exercises (for example, disputations) are, especially in the fifteenth century, uncontestable realities.[57]

But this must not obscure the fact that in the great universities there was a genuine renewal of doctrines, at least until the beginning of the fifteenth century. It is not our purpose to make a detailed study of this question, which was mentioned in the preceding chapter. It will suffice here to recall the general tendency, in philosophy and theology, to criticize Aristotelianism and Thomism that is sometimes characterized, in a convenient but somewhat excessive way, as "nominalism." There was an analogous dynamism in the other faculties throughout the fourteenth century: in medicine, the works of the doctors in Montpellier and in Padua and, in law, both public and private, the works of the Italian commentators (John Andreae, Bartolus, Baldus) and the commentators in Toulouse enjoyed considerable and enduring success. They were found in all the European libraries, which shows that university teaching was far from having exhausted its fertility. It is true that the universities missed out to a greater extent on the beginnings of humanism, that is, the rediscovery of Greek and of Plato, the renewal of rhetoric, and, in the religious domain, the awakening of an evangelism based on returning to the original texts of the Bible. A few contacts made here and there, notably in the Italian faculties of arts, cannot conceal that in the course of the fifteenth century an increasingly broad gap began to open between the tradition of medieval culture maintained in the universities and new aspirations. But let us note that if this evolution led to men like Petrarch (1304–1374) and Lorenzo Valla (1407–1457), that is, to a few severe critics of Scholasticism, while at the same time promoting in other ways the appearance of a few new types of educational institutions (which we will discuss later), it did not succeed, either before or even after 1500, in seriously discrediting the old universities or in decreasing the prestige of the degrees they conferred.

On the contrary, documentation from this period clearly shows that those who held university degrees took care to mention them in an increasingly precise way in the documents concerning them. In Western societies of the end of the Middle Ages, there are many indications of the ever-greater social and political importance granted to universities and to those who had graduated from them. The first and most obvious of these indications is the number of new universities founded after the middle of the fourteenth century: ten between 1340 and the beginning of the Great Schism (1378),[58] ten during the Great Schism (1378–1417),[59] and about thirty more between 1417 and 1500.[60] Taking into account universities that were founded but more or less rapidly dissolved (failures are always significant, and there were some) and those whose university character is debatable, we can estimate that in 1500 there were sixty-three or sixty-four *studia generalia* actually operating in Europe.

The university map at the end of the fifteenth century, compared to that at the beginning of the fourteenth century, thus shows a much denser network. This obviously does not mean that this network was homogeneous. Not only were these universities based on extremely diverse institutional and cultural models (generally Bolognese in the south, Parisian in the north) but they were of very unequal size. The oldest universities (Paris, Oxford, Bologna, Salamanca), which, despite a certain decline, retained the greatest prestige, the widest influence, and the largest enrollments (on the order of several thousand students), were practically incommensurable with some recently founded, strictly local universities that vegetated with a few hundred or even only a few dozen students. There were some fine successes among the new universities (Prague, Cracow, Louvain, Cologne, Caen), but many of them, particularly in the Iberian peninsula, remained very modest, both in their enrollments and in the level of their teaching. In the Empire, some universities were essentially reducible to their faculty of arts, their graduate faculties often remaining skeletal.

In spite of these reservations, the universities founded in the fourteenth and fifteenth centuries had an important influence on the conditions under which the European intellectual élites were educated. They made general throughout the West an institution which, setting aside the cases of Paris and Oxford, was at first essentially southern European. To be sure, new *studia generalia* were established in the Mediterranean countries (especially in southern France and in Spain), but the chief beneficiaries of the new wave of foundations were the Germanic countries, which had up to that point completely ignored or rejected the institution of the university; in these countries, those who wanted to study had to undertake long trips to France or Italy. Let us also note the emergence on the map of the university of various somewhat peripheral kingdoms (Scotland, Scandinavia, Poland, Bohemia, Hungary), which signaled in this way their increasingly deep integration into the Western cultural arena.

The new universities generally offered, at least on paper, a more or less complete range of courses. Moreover, at this time some old universities were supplemented by the foundation of new faculties, notably in theology. However, faculties in medicine remained virtually absent from these newly founded institutions, while theology was more or less taken over by the mendicant orders. Thus it was in fact the faculties of arts, at least in northern Europe, and faculties of law everywhere, that were the largest. The consequence was a wider dissemination—even if at a lower level that had nothing in common with the level of the Parisian *alma mater*—of the basic literary and philosophical culture that we defined in the preceding chapter, along with an increase in the number of learned jurists, both canon lawyers and civil lawyers, but always imbued in some way with Roman law. In addition, regents in law, grouped into colleges, almost everywhere played the central role in running the new universities.

The advantage thus gained by legal studies allows us to see the political dimension of the movement. If in the Middle Ages no university could be founded and develop without the support of external powers, it was the latter that in the fourteenth and fifteenth centuries often took the initiative in operating them. We must add that henceforth these were chiefly princely or urban powers, the papacy no longer playing an important role, except at the request of the lay powers that wanted it to confirm, often after the fact, a newly founded institution and to certify its status as a *studium generale*. Naturally, as several failures and false starts indicate, political will was not enough; a favorable context was also required, that is, either a preceding academic tradition or a rather strong social demand.

Nonetheless, it became increasingly accepted that a modern state or principality should have its own university to train the religious and especially administrative élites it needed, without being dependent on foreign universities to provide such training. A 1427 document from Toulouse puts it this way: "Every prince must have a university in his lands,"[61] and Crown Prince Louis (the future king of France, Louis XI) clearly repeated the same conviction when he founded the University of Valence in Dauphiné (1452): "We consider it entirely suitable, indispensable, and normal to found a university in the countries and land subject to us . . . in fact, whereas there are few princes on whose territories no university has been founded, there was none in ours."[62] These princely universities were usually established in the capital cities of the countries or principalities, or at least in a city that was particularly connected with the prince. The statutes provided at their foundation, while endowing them with autonomous institutions, left open large opportunities for control and intervention on the part of the external powers and their representatives. The most evident of these was often that the professors (or at least some of them) were paid by the prince, who in return had the right to approve their appointment. In Italy, individual magistrates, the *Savi* or *Riformatori dello Studio*, were often named to deal with university matters.

The old universities did not escape this development, even if they resisted it to some extent. To limit ourselves to the French case, where an increase in royal power came particularly early, in the fifteenth century the old universities (Paris, Orléans, Toulouse) came under the supervision of the king, his Parlements, and his officials. Reforms were imposed in an authoritarian manner, royal tribunals henceforth dealt with all matters relating to teachers and students, abuses to which ancient privileges often gave rise were severely repressed, and the right to strike was itself soon challenged.[63] This crackdown did not prevent favors from being granted. "True students" continued to enjoy their privileges (especially relating to taxation) and the king of France since Charles V (1364–1380) had been accustomed to call the University of Paris his "eldest daughter." This acknowledged the latter's prestige and intellectual, moral, and political authority (which Gerson, its chancellor, still claimed in his address *Vivat rex*, delivered on 7 November 1405),[64] but on the condition that this authority henceforth be expressed within the framework of national institutions and of monarchical loyalism, and no longer at the universalist level where it had been placed by the original pontifical authorizations.

Statistical and social analysis of student populations confirms that it is difficult to speak of a decline of the institution of the university at the end of the Middle Ages. The still incomplete documentation (scrolls containing university petitions preserved in the Vatican in pontifical registers, since there are virtually no enrollment lists except for the Imperial universities) makes it possible to advance a few quantitative hypotheses.[65] At the beginning of the fifteenth century, despite the various crises that caused some foreign students to leave (war, plagues, the Great Schism), the University of Paris apparently still had about four thousand students, three quarters of them in the faculty of arts.[66] The main provincial universities (Angers, Orléans, Toulouse, Montpellier, Avignon), which taught chiefly law, must have attracted altogether about as many students, between five hundred and a thousand each.[67] In England, once the Great Plague of 1348 was over, Oxford University rapidly recovered its earlier levels of enrollment,[68] and even continued to grow, whereas Cambridge, gradually closing a century-long gap, reached an enrollment of 1300 students.[69] We do not have precise figures for the Mediterranean countries, but Bologna must have had two to three thousand students, while Padua, which flourished in the fifteenth century, approached an enrollment of one thousand.[70] Germany is the only country for which an attempt at a general assessment has been made. The results are impressive:[71] although universities were established in Germany only toward the end of the fourteenth century, for the next hundred years there was virtually continuous growth, although it was influenced by a rhythmical cycle that seems itself to have been connected with fluctuations in economic activity. From 1385 to the beginning of the sixteenth century, a total of nearly 250,000 students were enrolled in Imperial universities. Although the total population decreased until about 1450, and then stagnated, beginning to grow again only in the sixteenth century, the average annual enrollment increased tenfold in a little more than a century (from

300 to 3,000). Even if the great majority of these students did not go beyond the faculty of arts, and if many of them did not obtain a diploma, there was nonetheless a definite rise in the number of men of learning in German society (all the more because at the same time, the most ambitious and wealthy young German students continued to go to Italian universities, or sometimes to French ones).

On the whole, then, even if the old universities complained about the competition of the new ones (Paris condemned with particular vigor the foundation of universities in Caen and Bourges, which it deemed too nearby), it is entirely probable that at the end of the Middle Ages, despite the misfortunes of the time and the general demographic crisis, there was a major overall increase in the number of students. The possible stagnation—at a level that was, nevertheless, relatively high—of enrollments in the most venerable *studia generalia* must have been more than compensated for by the proliferation of new universities, even if many of them attracted only a few hundred students.

Thus the number of graduates emerging from the universities, especially in arts and—still more important for our purposes—in law, must have risen in comparable proportions, even if it seems clear that despite a general tendency to shorten the time of study, many students did not receive diplomas. In German faculties of arts, more than half the students left the university without having received any diploma, and in the graduate faculties of law and medicine, at least in Germany and in southern France, where a quantitative assessment has been attempted, the rates of elimination were on the same order: a third of the students received the baccalaureate, less than 10 percent received the *licence*, and, *a fortiori*, fewer still received the doctorate.

At the same time that they grew overall, did the composition of European university populations change in the course of the fourteenth and fifteenth centuries? Without allowing us to draw truly definitive conclusions, the results of recent research suggest that the double tendency traditionally diagnosed—regionalization and social closure—should be qualified in important ways.

The influence of recent universities was usually chiefly local or at most national. Moreover, the prince sometimes forbade his subjects to go to a university other than the one in his domains (the Seigneurie of Venice did so in 1444, requiring its subjects to go to the university in Padua after that city had been incorporated into its territories on the mainland). On the other hand, the old universities, even though the proportion of students coming from distant lands may have decreased, continued to be the intersections of an active *peregrinatio academica*. As in the past, the most mobile students were the Germans (and, to a lesser degree, the Slavs and Scandinavians), while the main poles of attraction remained on one hand Paris (complemented in civil law by Orléans), and on the other the Italian universities (Bologna, of course, but also, and increasingly, Padua, Pavia, Sienna, Pisa, Perugia, et al.). Starting in the 1440s, conditions became more favorable for travel, and the increasing attraction of Italian humanism made "travel to Italy" exceptionally popular. The Germanic students who traditionally went to Italy were henceforth joined by growing contingents of French, English, and Iberian students.[72]

This suggests that if the majority of the men of learning, henceforth trained in their own countries and at lower cost, must have had relatively limited geographical horizons and human contacts, there were still, at least in the form of an élite, individuals who in their youth had acquired through study abroad an openness of mind, a knowledge, and relationships that led people to speak, as early as the end of the Middle Ages, of a "Republic of Letters," at least in an embryonic form. Learned correspondence and diplomatic missions allowed relationships formed in this way to be maintained all over the Western world. In the France of Charles VI the milieu of humanistic notaries and royal secretaries, who were in constant contact with their Florentine and Neapolitan counterparts, in central Europe the cosmopolitan courts of Charles IV (1346–1378) in Prague, of the Habsburg monarch Frederick III in Vienna, of Matthias Corvinus (1458–1490) in Budapest, and of Casimir Jagiello in Cracow, where Italian humanists and local scholars trained at Bologna or Padua gathered, are a few illustrations of the universalist openness that the university network allowed its alumni to maintain over the course of their careers.[73]

Did university studies promote social ascent or did they instead hasten the formation of little hereditary castes of men of learning? Available sources provide only fragmentary information on this subject and seem to indicate that the situation varied from one university to another. For example, among the German students who attended the University of Bologna between 1400 and 1530, the proportion of nobles was about 18 percent, but in the universities of southern France around 1400 it had not yet reached 5 percent. Conversely, "poor" students (probably students who were temporarily unable to pay university fees as well as students of truly popular origin) represented on average 15 percent of the enrollment in the Imperial countries, with figures as high as 25 percent in Cologne, Leipzig, Heidelberg, and Rostock, but seem to have been very rare in Mediterranean countries.[74]

Individual examples showing a great diversity of situations could be multiplied. The universities' social recruitment remained open, but we cannot determine the precise proportion of each group or say whether this recruitment changed in a significant way over the long term. Until the end of the Middle Ages, it remained possible for young people of modest origin, especially rural, to achieve a fine career through study and diplomas; one thinks of Gerson. But it is also clear that in some families, particularly families of physicians or officials, pursuing an education seems to have become a normal practice in which sons followed in their fathers' footsteps to ensure the permanence of the family vocation. Finally, it is also very probable that education allowed some old élites—families of the old nobility or merchants who may have been struggling with the problems of the economic crisis—to guarantee that their social position would be preserved for their descendents through a shift in social status and integration into the rapidly rising group of the men of learning.

It is in any case certain that whatever their social origin, nearly all students were seeking a stable situation that would shelter them from certain risks by putting them directly or indirectly under the wing of the organs of political power. Among students, there were indeed some who were marginal or déclassé—such as the poet François Villon (who aspired at times to put himself under the protection of some prince)—but on the whole students at the end of the Middle Ages were socially conformist, respectful of the established order, and mainly concerned to find or to keep their place in it. In the history of university towns, incidents involving students and the urban population or students and royal sergeants tended to become fewer at the end of the Middle Ages. Usually attributable to the student's youthful excesses or to the increased requirements of a public order imposed by those in power, these incidents, which were generally resolved by a compromise achieved in court, did not question the fact that the universities were part of the established institutional order. At most, they reflected, in addition to a certain hardening of that order, the academics' will to make their specificity and dignity recognized in relation to possible competing groups. In Paris and Toulouse, the councilors of the Parlement, who were interpreters of the royal will but also defended their own caste interests (they all held university degrees), tried to put the university under their control. In Montpellier, the old merchant families sought to remove jurists from the consulate, while the patriciate in Barcelona resisted until 1440 the kings of Aragon's plans to create a university they feared would promote the rise of groups of clerics and officials, parvenus committed to the service of the prince and the Church and caring little for the old urban freedoms.[75]

In this will to become part of the leading groups in society, the practice of university studies played a very important role. First, because the disciplines studied in the universities all belonged to a legitimate order of kinds of knowledge, in complete accord with the dominant social and political order. Secondly, because the legal status of students and teachers made them privileged from the outset, and this was something of great value in the society of increasingly complex and rigid hierarchies that was then being established. At the end of the Middle Ages, no matter what one's previous status had been, becoming a student meant entering a privileged condition; one could escape taxes and the most rigorous forms of ordinary justice, apply for certain kinds of revenue (income from ecclesiastical benefices without residential obligation), and take one's place under the direct protection of the highest lay or ecclesiastical authorities, which intervened as "preservers of the privileges" of academics. Even before any degree was earned, simply enrolling at the university already constituted a kind of social promotion.

University life taught not only the enjoyment of privileges but also the demands of responsibility. It promoted the development of political individualism at the end of the Middle Ages. The decision to leave home "to study" was fundamentally an individual decision (or at least a family decision), and even if it promised a future rise in status, it also implied an initial risk and disorientation. For studies to be pursued successfully, passive listening to magisterial lectures had to be combined with a certain amount of personal work at home and at the university. The readings made by holders of the baccalaureate and participation in disputations accustomed students to expressing themselves and to taking positions in public, to confronting and if possible overcoming the arguments of possible adversaries. Let us add that in most universities, the students and younger Masters of Arts could take the floor in the deliberations of various assemblies and councils, exercise elective functions, and represent the university vis-à-vis the external authorities. Finally, the examinations, which were always oral, were relatively easy for the baccalaureate, but much more formal and solemn for the *licence* and the doctorate. They were perceived to some degree as individual feats in which each person had to display not only his knowledge but also his memory, his presence of mind, and his character, not to mention the generosity that had to be expressed in the celebrations that followed the examination. In lending importance to all these activities, the university contributed to shaping men of learning by endowing them not only with a certain amount of knowledge but also with a socially useful savoir faire and ease of manners.

Individualism, however, was not the only human experience acquired at the university; students also experienced a different kind of sociability, a deeper integration into the networks of alliances, friendships, and clienteles that so strongly structured the whole society of the end of the Middle Ages. Academic sociability was based first of all on belonging to the community of *scolares*, on the common enjoyment (and possibly the collective defense, by means of strikes or otherwise) of their privileges. But it was probably more fully expressed at the level of smaller units. The school, sometimes compared to a *societas* constituted by the teacher and his students, might be one of these units. A still more significant role was played by the faculty, which grouped together students in the same discipline, and especially the "nation," in which compatriots assembled, and which was responsible not only for administrative duties relating to new students but also for common entertainments, religious supervision, and mutual charitable aid. Thus the most brilliant or richest students might constitute little groups of friends and people who owed them favors, and who would remain faithful to them throughout their careers.

But at the end of the Middle Ages the site of academic sociability par excellence in most universities was the college. Even if the colleges never had more than a minority of the students (around 1450, one in ten in Paris and Oxford, one in six in Cambridge, one in four in Toulouse), their importance must be emphasized. In the fourteenth and fifteenth centuries they became more numerous, usually being founded by prelates, princes, or high-ranking royal officials. If we set aside religious houses, thirty-seven secular colleges were founded in Paris in the fourteenth century, compared to five at Oxford and seven at Cambridge. The development slowed in the fifteenth century, more through saturation than through the decline of the institution: five colleges were founded in Paris, three in Oxford, five in Cambridge. While it was not unknown, the institution of the college established itself less massively in the new universities in Germany and in central Europe. It also had some success in the Mediterranean region: at the end of the fifteenth century there were fourteen colleges in Toulouse, three in Montpellier, three in Avignon, and three in Bologna; there were also a few in the Iberian peninsula that were to have a bright future.

In theory, medieval colleges provided lodging for poor students, but in fact they were usually largely reserved for relatives or compatriots of the founder. They only gradually became teaching institutions that competed directly with the faculties, and at the end of the fifteenth century some of them still had not taken this step. But even without their own courses and staff of regents, the colleges developed a strong esprit de corps among students who had the good fortune to be admitted to them (and who remained for several years)—because they brought together all their members in the common life of a residential institution subjected to a rather strict discipline, because they were managed in a more or less collective way by the fellows themselves, and because they offered many opportunities for friendly or intellectual exchanges or for work in common (many colleges acquired a library very early on). Enduring friendships were formed, and in their later careers alumni had a tendency to favor those who had studied at the same college. The most flagrant example, which reached an apex in the sixteenth century, is that of the *colegios mayores* in Salamanca, Valladolid, and Alcalá (to which we may add the college of San Clemente or of Spain in Bologna), which became the sites where virtually all the administrative élites of the modern Spanish monarchy were trained. Analogous tendencies may be observed in Oxford, Cambridge, and Paris. At the University of Paris, the college of Sorbonne, a seedbed of important secular theologians that had a magnificent library and was careful to avoid getting too involved in the political vicissitudes of the time, was above all the site of an intense intellectual life. On the other hand, the college of Navarre (founded in 1305 by the queen of France, Jeanne de Navarre) and that of Dormans-Beauvais (founded in 1370 by Jean de Dormans, cardinal of Beauvais) maintained close connections with the monarchy and with its major administrative offices, the Chancellery and the Parlement. A large proportion of the political and intellectual élites of the time of Charles VI (notably "the first French humanists" such as Pierre d'Ailly, Jean de Montreuil, Nicolas de Clamanges and Jean Gerson) came from these last two colleges of the University of Paris.[76] A few decades later, the four great "pedagogies" of Louvain began to play a comparable role in the Low Countries.

However, while they increasingly tended to attract the élite of university students, the colleges also called into question some of the principles that had originally constituted the very spirit of the pedagogy practiced in medieval universities. They restricted the student's freedom by imposing on him a strict discipline and a certain control over his program of studies; to the university's old universalism they opposed the specific rules that governed each college's recruitment and functioning; they paved the way for interventions by the founders, principals, visitors, et al., who were generally external to the university but responsible for the proper operation of the collegial institution. In that way, while remaining within the university they were more closely related to other kinds of non-university educational establishments that began to flourish in the West at the end of the Middle Ages—new places where men of learning who were repelled by the tedium or the insufficiencies of traditional university studies could seek an alternative.

3. New Institutions

We will not attempt here to draw up an exhaustive list of initiatives that were in fact local and disparate. We will simply give a few examples of these new institutions, all of which offered, alongside the universities and without necessarily rejecting their whole heritage, forms of instruction open to new disciplines and new pedagogical methods that were supposed to be better adapted to the expectations and abilities of the students.

It is possible that the mendicant orders played a pioneering role in this matter. As early as 1220–1230 the Dominicans, a little later the Franciscans, and at the end of the century the Carmelites and Augustinian Hermits, all established coherent networks of conventual *studia* that were specially intended for young members of their orders who had shown genuine aptitude for study (although there may also have been a few external auditors). In each province these *studia* formed a hierarchized system within which students moved around in accord with their personal progress: they began by attending the grammar *studium*, and were then sent by their superiors to the *studia* in arts (for logic), natural philosophy, Holy Scriptures, and theology. Established in university towns such as Paris or Oxford and incorporated into the local faculties of theology, they had an opportunity to receive students from all the order's provinces and to confer on them not only the conventual title of *lector* but also genuine university diplomas, licentiates and master's degrees in theology. In spite of this, the mendicants' academic network was fundamentally autonomous, distinct from that of the universities. On the other hand, the kind of teaching dispensed in these *studia*, both the initial training in grammar and arts and the later training in theology, seems to have very quickly become just as thorough and modern as that in the universities.

Whether or not they were modeled on these *studia*, in the final decades of the fourteenth century there appeared here and there in Europe large colleges in which resident students were taught mainly grammar, arts, and philosophy. Their ostensible goal was to compensate for the too frequent shortcomings of the traditional grammar schools and the small number of university faculties of arts. Thus between 1363 and 1373 popes Urban V and Gregory XI founded in Provence and lower Languedoc, at Trets, Saint-Germain-de-Calberte, Saint-Roman-de-l'Aiguille, Gigean, Avignon, and Carpentras, very large colleges (some of them could accommodate up to two hundred resident students), financed by the Apostolic Chamber. These were intended to train pupils in arts and grammar in preparation for future study (presumably in law) at the universities in Avignon and Montpellier.[77] Despite considerable initial success, these institutions fell victim to both their high costs and to the epidemics that raged among their resident students, and soon had to close their doors.

In 1382 Bishop William de Wykeham, who was also Chancellor of the kingdom, founded a college in Winchester that had similar goals but was to last far longer. This powerful man, who had in 1379 founded the largest of the medieval colleges at Oxford (New College, with room for seventy students), wanted the college in his episcopal city of Winchester to prepare, under favorable conditions, future fellows for his university college. This ancestor of all the later English public schools was imitated a few decades later when King Henry VI founded Eton College in 1440.

Since no such institutions were founded in Paris, small colleges of grammar sprang up in the city. These were not directly connected with the university, though they were in its sphere of influence. In them, children between eight and sixteen years of age studied the rudiments of Latin before entering the faculty of arts proper. The College of Ave Maria, founded in 1336 by Jean de Hubant, the president of the Chambre des Enquêtes at the Parlement, is the best documented example of such an institution.[78]

However, that is not where we must look for the early harbingers of the modern college dedicated to the student's overall development, which seems to have a twofold origin. First of all, in the last years of the fourteenth century schools were founded in the Low Countries by the Brethren of the Common Life and the canons of Windesheim. These two closely connected religious congregations emerged in the 1380s, bringing together the devout and those attracted to simple mysticism; they were an expression of the religious trend characteristic of northern Europe at the end of the Middle Ages that is often called *devotio moderna*. Condemning both the pride of the university doctors and the abuses of the clergy as responsible for all the misfortunes of the time (we are still in the period of the Great Schism), the Brethren and the canons had recently established communities that combined the active life and the contemplative life. On the side of the active life, they soon took as their vocation, among others, to open schools for children in which, subjected to strict discipline and attentive religious supervision, they would be instructed in the elements of grammar and logic and at the same time trained for a more personal religious life based directly on Bible reading and prayer. The first great schools of the Brethren of the Common Life were established in Deventer and Zwolle; subsequently, they became widespread in the Burgundian states, and the Brethren also established themselves in university towns such as Louvain and even in Paris. Among their pupils were many of the future lights of northern humanism, first of all Erasmus. Despite the rather traditional nature of their teaching and the sometimes excessively austere discipline they imposed on the children, we can credit the Brethren of the Common Life with a number of pedagogical innovations. The most remarkable of these was probably the creation of genuine class levels: the old, essentially repetitive courses were replaced by a rational progression in which the child encountered texts and exercises that increased in difficulty as he grew older and achieved greater mastery of the disciplines. This system was generally adopted by other institutions during the sixteenth century.

The other cradle of the modern college was humanistic northern Italy. There a few pedagogues, of whom the most well-known is Guarino Guarini of Verona (1374–1460), perfected the system of the humanistic *contubernium*. A non-university residential school that charged high fees (thus guaranteeing that most of the students were aristocrats), the humanists' *contubernium* provided its pupils with a kind of instruction derived from that of the old grammar schools but enriched with new elements: the classics were studied at length for their own sakes, and included rhetoricians, poets, and historians; Greek, of which Guarino had complete command (in his youth, he had studied in Constantinople), was not neglected. On the other hand, the emphasis was put on developing the student's personality; physical exercises alternated with religious exercises, the master supervising each student personally and keeping an eye on his physical and moral equilibrium.[79] Guarino had a number of emulators, in particular Vittorino da Feltre (1378–1446), whose *Casa giocosa* in Mantua was another fine example of a humanistic *contubernium*.

The new schools that appeared in Venice in the fifteenth century were slightly different but nonetheless comparable to the *contubernia*. The school in the Rialto, opened shortly after 1400, was at first under the influence of the faculty of arts in Padua and its "Averroist" philosophers. But beginning in 1441, under the direction of Domenico Bragadin, a scion of one of the greatest families in Venice, and subsidized by the state, it became a center of humanistic studies for the Venetian patriciate. At about the same time (1446), the school of San Marco was founded to provide training in grammar and rhetoric for young people who would later be employed in the Chancellery.[80] Emphasizing the new disciplines, meeting the expectations and needs of the local patriciate, and emphasizing their civic purposes, the new schools in Venice thus clearly located themselves in the same cultural and political line as the *contubernia*.

Of course, the perspective in these Italian institutions was far more secular, if not worldly, than that of the schools founded by the Brethren of the Common Life, but at least both of them shared a common interest in returning to sources (in the former, the classics; in the latter, the Bible) and in taking into account the specific aptitudes of childhood and adolescence.

The Brethren of the Common Life and the Italian humanists were not in overt conflict with the university. They sometimes even ended up being incorporated into it. Jan Standonck of Malines (1453–1504), at the end of the fifteenth century the principal pedagogue of the *devotio moderna*, reformed the old College of Montaigu in Paris before going to Louvain to found the *domus pauperum* that later took his name (College of Standonck). In Italy, we may note, for example, that in 1442 the last *contubernium* founded by Guarino, in Ferrara, ended up being assimilated into the faculty of arts of the university that had just been reopened in that city. But in both cases it was nonetheless a matter of new pedagogical formulas that were intended, both in the level of their instruction and in their proclaimed social ambitions (to train future social élites, by further emphasizing religious education in the first case, and literary and civic education in the second), to contribute to the constitution and renewal of the group of men of learning.

Finally, we must remember that at the end of the Middle Ages a few areas of professional instruction began to detach themselves, in a very haphazard and even embryonic way, from the traditional system of learning, clearly moving somewhat closer to the practices and the level of the university, while at the same time remaining rather distant from them.

Since the time of the brilliant Pisan mathematician Leonardo Fibonacci (ca. 1170–ca. 1240), abacus teachers in Italian merchant cities were no longer limiting themselves to teaching—successfully—commercial arithmetic to future merchants. Some were already operating at a high level in arithmetic and algebra, and had no counterparts among the university teachers of the *quadrivium*.

The first real schools of surgery must have been established in Italy, under the influence of certain faculties of medicine. In the same country, there may also have been schools for training notaries (in France, they seem still to have been trained by apprenticeship).

The emergence of the English Inns of Court in the first half of the fifteenth century appears to be part of more or less the same trend.[81] The Inns of Court (so called because they were initially set up in inns) were four law schools established not in Oxford or Cambridge but in London, the kingdom's capital city, close to the main law courts. Alongside the Inns of Court there were about a dozen Inns of Chancery of lesser importance. In these various schools, future judges and lawyers came to study Common Law by listening to lectures given by practicing jurists and by accompanying the latter to the courts when they were in session. In the second half of the century, the Inns of Court in London seem to have attracted as many as two or three hundred auditors and a large portion of the royal jurists were trained in them, as many or more as from the university faculties where Roman law was taught. The teaching, at first fairly informal, was subsequently rigorously organized (except that no diplomas were given), and the students consisted chiefly of the sons of knights or squires of the gentry who were seeking professional training or at least useful relationships in court circles and in the capital's governmental offices.

Perhaps these few examples (among many others that might be given) suffice to show that in the fifteenth century, even though the traditional university model still had considerable weight everywhere, the opportunities for training offered future men of learning began to become significantly more diverse, no doubt in proportion to the steadily increasing size and complexity of the group constituted by these men of learning and to the social functions assigned them.

CHAPTER III

Books

---•─•─•---

Everything we have said in the first two chapters of this study clearly suggests that men of learning in Western societies at the end of the Middle Ages were men of the book, and more broadly, of the written text. Not, of course, exclusively; they also knew how to use the spoken word. Thanks to their knowledge of grammar, they could express themselves with equal ease in Latin and in the vernacular. Their studies of logic and rhetoric had given them the ability to reason correctly and to offer convincing demonstrations. Long training of their memories permitted them to summon up, without referring to written notes, the countless quotations of "authorities" that provided the basis for their knowledge.

As students, they had learned to follow the lessons of their teachers and to participate in discussions without using their pens. As professors, university regulations required them, at least in theory, to teach without limiting themselves to reading out a text written in advance. As clerics, they were used to preaching; as lawyers, they were used to pleading. As counselors, ambassadors, or members of some state assembly, they had to be able to address the prince or the crowd, to make themselves heard in the tumult or to whisper a few decisive words into the ears of the powerful.

It nonetheless remains that men of learning were fundamentally men of the book and of the written text, and first of all in the eyes of their contemporaries. This was, indeed, one of their most important specific characteristics, compared with other social groups. In the final analysis, it was from books that they drew their knowledge; they were almost alone in being able if not to read, at least to deal easily with books. Books therefore provided the very justification of their social role. It was in books and archives that they made, consigned, and preserved their decisions and opinions. Ordinary people knew this, and often, when peasants or urban residents rebelled, libraries, books, registers, and papers of all kinds were among the first targets of popular anger. For our subject it is therefore very important to try to assess the place the book held in the lives of men of learning.

1. Access to Books

Without recapitulating here the whole history of the medieval book, we must first recall that the production and circulation of books still encountered many obstacles that made access to them difficult. The first and principal obstacle was of an economic order. Books were expensive. Their cost resulted primarily from the price of the material they were written on. A book required a large quantity of parchment (depending on the book's format, one could get two to sixteen sheets per skin), and parchment was a difficult material to work with. The use of rag paper, documented in Spain in the twelfth century and in France in the thirteenth, made it possible to lower the price of books. Only in the fourteenth and especially the fifteenth century, however, was paper widely used in the domain of manuscript books. On the basis of French documents, it has been calculated that for the same amount of surface, paper could cost five times less than parchment in the fourteenth century and as much as thirteen times less in the fifteenth, thanks to the improvement of the techniques of paper production and the increase in the number of paper mills. Elsewhere, especially in Germany, the difference in price was probably less.

In any case, the savings on the total price of the book remained relatively limited, on the order of only 10 to 20 percent in comparison to works on parchment. The relative modesty of this gain allowed the parchment book to retain a fairly solid position, especially since many educated people seem to have had a prejudice against books on paper, which was seen as both less noble and less durable, especially in the case of important texts and works that the owner valued and wanted to hand down to his descendents.

In reality, the main factor in the high cost of medieval books was the cost of copying. Good copyists were rare. At the end of the Middle Ages, the monastic *scriptoria* had lost most of their importance and the majority of scribes were henceforth professional craftsmen located chiefly in large cities, especially in those that had a large potential clientele, that is, princely capitals and university towns. Even leaving aside the case of luxury volumes ornamented with miniatures, true works of art intended mainly for prelates, great lords, and kings, the production of a book took time. Good copyists worked slowly—about two and half leaves a day, on average. In other words, in a year a good copyist produced barely five books of two hundred leaves; or to put it another way, to provide a thousand books of this kind in one year, no less than two hundred copyists working full-time were required. In university towns, where teachers and students needed many books but had limited financial resources, efforts were made to reduce the price of books to the minimum: small formats, many lines packed onto the page, more cursive writing, and the use of many abbreviations made it possible to save parchment or paper and to shorten somewhat the time spent in copying. The adoption of the system of *pecia*, which accelerated the rotation of copies to be reproduced, also helped improve the productivity of scribes while at the same time preserving the quality of the texts put into circulation.[82] Given all this, it is easy to see why many people resorted to the least burdensome solution (but which no longer guaranteed the correctness of the transcribed texts), which consisted in going to some "amateur" copyist—a needy chaplain or a poor student, for example—or even copying the book themselves.

The problem of the actual price of medieval books is a real conundrum for researchers. If one wants to make comparisons from one country to another or follow developments over the long term, one has to adopt some monetary unit as the reference point or convert all prices into their equivalent weights in a precious metal. Moreover, one has to connect the *estimated* prices on inventories with the actual prices of sale or purchase. Finally and especially, one has to be in a position to take into account the material condition of the volumes, which we often do not know but which must have caused prices to vary considerably: parchment or paper, type of writing, the number of folios, the format, the presence of illustrations, the binding, etc. Two manuscripts, even of one and the same work, were never exactly the same.

A few relatively firm conclusions can nonetheless be drawn (here I leave aside, once again, the deluxe books in princely libraries). First of all, the price of books was extremely variable. The most expensive— generally large Bibles or glossed volumes of the *Corpus iuris civilis* or the *Corpus iuris canonici*—cost as much as thirty or forty *livres tournois* (to use a French monetary unit). But alongside these there were many small volumes, often in the form of simple unbound fascicles, which included "reportations" on courses, a few fragments of disputed questions, sermons, short practical treatises, etc., and which were sold for only a few deniers.

Prices of books seem to have varied by as much as 100 percent depending on whether they were new or used. The market for used books was in fact very active, particularly in university towns where it was fed by books sold by students who needed money or who were leaving the university, by pawnbrokers, colleges getting rid of their doubles, or heirs liquidating the library of some uncle who was a priest or canon.

Given these conditions, can one establish an "average price" of the medieval book? Basing their work on extensive documentation from

northern France in the fourteenth and fifteenth centuries, Carla Bozzolo and Ezio Ornato have proposed for this region average prices of
5 *livres* 10 *sous parisis* in the fourteenth century and 2 *livres 16 sous parisis* in the fifteenth,[83] the decrease being attributable both to the already mentioned advances in using paper and to the general economic
slump. These figures are clearly meaningful only for individuals who had
acquired or possessed a relatively large number of volumes. It is nonetheless interesting to note that in Paris, around 1400, the "average price"
of a book corresponded to approximately seven days of the "wages and
expenses" (*gages et bourses*) paid to a notary and royal secretary. If that
is so, one sees why such a person (and, as we will see, in the Paris of the
end of the Middle Ages notaries and royal secretaries were, along with
councilors in the Parlement and university professors, the main owners of private libraries) would scarcely have been able, even if he devoted a fourth of his income to book-buying—obviously an optimistic
hypothesis—to acquire more than two hundred and fifty volumes in a
twenty-year career. In reality, the largest private Parisian library at this
time whose composition we know, that of Nicolas de Baye, a clerk at the
Parlement, remained far short of this theoretical figure; in 1419 it contained 198 volumes, some of which may have been acquired as gifts or as
an inheritance.

By examining extant manuscripts or analyzing inventories and wills,
it has been possible to reconstitute a relatively large number of private
libraries at the end of the Middle Ages. In the case of France, studies
have been able to show that setting apart the king, the royal princes, and
the great lords, until the end of the fifteenth century our men of learning were virtually the only ones who had libraries of any significant
size. Once we leave this milieu, even among groups in which there must
have been literate individuals—the petty and middle nobility, merchants,
the lower ranks of the clergy—books are practically absent. Here we
find a fragment of a chronicle, there a book of hours or a saint's life, or
again a collection of synodal regulations—clearly, these cannot be called
libraries.

Among men of learning themselves, collections of books varied in
size. The library of even a well-off student seldom consisted of more
than a dozen volumes: basic textbooks on one hand, a couple of anthologies of religious texts on the other. Their professors, who needed a small
personal library to prepare their courses, had a few more books, pos-
sessing, in addition to the basic "authorities," a number of commentaries
and modern treatises, amounting in all to about thirty volumes. However, some teachers, who were wealthier or more intellectually curious,
owned libraries containing a hundred volumes or more.[84] The libraries
of those connected with the Parlement of Paris around 1400, to which

I will return later, also contained on average about a hundred volumes. This number was not exceeded, it seems, except in the case of genuine bibliophiles such as Nicolas de Baye (or, fifty years later, Roger Benoîton, a former notary and royal secretary who had become canon of Clermont, and who in 1470 proudly drew up a catalogue of the 257 books in his personal collection) and in the case of people who had risen to high office, for example, former professors of law or pontifical dignitaries who had become bishops or cardinals, such as Gaulcelme de Deux, a former papal treasurer who became bishop of Maguelone, who at the time of his death possessed at least 435 books, or Cardinal Piero Corsini, a former Rota auditor, who left 320 volumes at his death in 1405.[85]

Did the average size of libraries increase from the fourteenth to the fifteenth century? Without arriving at clear results, recent research does seem to indicate a tendency in this direction. To be sure, in the study already cited, Bozzolo and Ornato assumed that the production of new books had significantly decreased in France between 1350 and 1450, in connection with the general economic depression in the period, and this may well have been a tendency common throughout western Europe. But libraries did not contain only new books. The existence of an active used book market and the careful preservation of old manuscripts— the life expectancy of medieval books, especially the most useful and most expensive ones, was surely more than a century—made it possible for collections to grow through simple accumulation. However, this growth, if it occurred, was not very large. In a number of cases, it is the appearance of a few large libraries with several hundred volumes that seems to have raised the average, rather than a general increase in size.

The owners of libraries therefore considered them genuine treasures, which they treated with the greatest care. For a man of learning, the value of a book was both symbolic and material. Carefully preserved in a trunk or armoire, books showed their owner's knowledge. Often acquired from university booksellers, sometimes sent at great expense from Paris or from Bologna,[86] books were inseparably linked to studies and to diplomas. Wasn't the presentation of a book to the candidate one of the rituals of the ceremony honoring a new doctor? On the other hand, every library of any size had a considerable market value; it was a way of saving, and represented a form of capital both intellectual and financial that its owner wanted to hand on to his heirs, if they were themselves pursuing studies, or else to a college or a church. Men of law always fought to keep their books from being counted when tax officials came to evaluate their personal effects; in their view, this privilege was not only an appreciable fiscal advantage—for these books often represented half or more of their owner's capital (excluding real estate)— but also a public acknowledgement of the nobility of their knowledge and of the activities they pursued in function of their intellectual competence. A doctor's books should no more be taxed, they felt, than a knight's weapons.

Was the relatively small size of private libraries perhaps compensated by recourse to "public" or at least—the notion of public service obviously being anachronistic in this area—institutional libraries? In this period there were three types of libraries that could be seen as falling into this category.

First, princely libraries. At the death of King Charles V of France (1380), his library in the Louvre contained slightly less than 1300 volumes; in the fifteenth century, Philip the Good, the duke of Burgundy, had a library of about 880 books. For their part, the popes in Avignon constantly added to their book collections; they had more than two thousand at the death of Urban V, according to an inventory made in 1369, and in spite of the avatars of the Great Schism, when the last Avignon pope, Benedict XIII (1394–1423) died in exile in Peñiscola, he still had almost as many books in his library.[87] Were the libraries of princes and pontiffs open to the public? Their precise cataloging suggests that at least those close to the sovereign, his important visitors, and his political counselors had access to them.

Then there were libraries in cathedrals, monasteries, and convents. These were often old collections that—except for those of the mendicant friars—did not grow much at the end of the Middle Ages, but they were of considerable size. There were more than 300 volumes at Notre-Dame de Paris at the end of the fifteenth century, 486 at the cathedral of Reims in 1462, and even more in the monasteries: around 1450–1460, there were about 1600 volumes at Saint-Denis and at Clairvaux in France, 1100 at Monte Cassino in Italy, 800 at Melk in Austria, etc.;[88] the oldest manuscripts were preserved in these places. It was there, as the humanistic Italian editors of ancient authors were to find, that one had the best chance of discovering particularly venerable manuscripts, sometimes going back to the Carolingian period. But these ecclesiastical libraries were particularly rich in religious texts and liturgical books that were not necessarily of much use to men of learning. Moreover, it is not at all certain that they were freely open to readers other than the canons and monks that served these churches or monasteries.

The most "modern" libraries were, on one hand, those of the mendicant convents, whose resources were shared by students, convent readers, and preachers, and on the other, the libraries of colleges and universities. The main university colleges had libraries whose core was usually constituted by the library of the founder himself, complemented by later gifts from benefactors and former members of the college. Thus in 1338 the college of the Sorbonne had a library of 1722 volumes that was no doubt at that time the largest in France; the College of Navarre in Paris and the College of Foix in Toulouse both had about 800 volumes around 1500.[89] Other colleges had significantly smaller but sometimes precious collections: about 200 books at the College of Autun in Paris (1462), 150 at the College of Annecy in Avignon (1435), 78 at the College of Pélegry in Cahors (1395), etc. English college libraries seem to have been of comparable size at the end of the fourteenth century (500 books at Merton, 150 at Balliol, 100 at Oriel), and still more in the fifteenth century (369 in the initial endowment of All Souls in 1438, 800 given to Magdalen in 1480).[90] One of the most famous college libraries at the end of the Middle Ages was that of the *Collegium Amplonianum* in Erfurt, which in 1433 received from its founder, the former rector Amplonius Ratingk, a superb collection of 637 books, rich in classics, which made it one of the gateways for humanism in Germany.[91] On the whole, however, college libraries contained chiefly textbooks belonging to the disciplines traditionally taught in universities. These libraries were thus particularly well adapted to the needs of men of learning. It remains to discover whether the latter still had access to these libraries after they completed their studies; the extant regulations seem to suggest that outside visitors were not given free access to college libraries.

The same must hold true for university libraries, which were often smaller and were first established in the fifteenth century. The earliest university libraries in France, which had only a few dozen volumes, were in Orléans (founded in 1411), Avignon (1427), Poitiers (1446), and in the faculties of medicine (1395) and canon law (1475) in Paris. Only in Caen does an inventory—made in 1515, it is true—show a more substantial collection of 277 volumes.[92] Other universities had larger libraries; the growth of the library at Oxford, which was founded in 1412, was largely the result of gifts made by the duke of Gloucester (280 books between 1439 and 1447).[93]

On the whole, it is therefore likely that in their everyday professional or administrative activities men of learning, especially laymen, whether physicians, lawyers, prosecutors, judges, or royal officials, must have relied chiefly on the resources of their little personal library and of their memory, possibly aided by the small notebooks and personal repertories that some teachers advised them to begin composing while they were still in school and always to keep at hand.[94] Men of learning must have sought only on rare occasions to gain admission to a university, ecclesiastical, or princely library in order to consult some work in its original form. We can therefore easily understand the success enjoyed in the Middle Ages by the anthologies, repertories, dictionaries, and encyclopedias of all kinds that made it possible to alleviate, to some extent, the difficulties of getting access to books.

2. The Contents of Libraries

Despite their imperfections, inventories of old libraries, as well as extant manuscripts, give us relatively reliable information about the content of the books of men of learning at the end of the Middle Ages. It is in fact clear that men of learning owned the great majority of the books, at least those in private possession. Thousands of manuscripts relating to the disciplines of scholarly culture—grammar, logic, philosophy, law, theology—have survived, whereas many works of literature, history, or politics, even some of those that seem to us most remarkable, are known only in a small number of manuscripts or even a single manuscript, especially when it is a text in the vernacular.

Throughout Europe at the end of the Middle Ages, "scholarly libraries" have an unquestionable family resemblance, whether they are university libraries or the personal libraries of the men of learning that interest us more directly here. This further confirms the universalist character that had been retained by scholarly culture.

In these libraries one finds first of all the basic texts, the fundamental authorities in each discipline. Jurists had the heavy volumes of the two *Corpus juris*, along with their usual glosses; theologians had the Bible, often glossed as well, St. Jerome's and St. Augustine's exegetical commentaries, and, among modern writers, a few treatises by Hugh of St. Victor, Peter Lombard's *Sentences* and St. Thomas Aquinas's *Summa theologiae* or *Summa contra gentiles;* physicians had translations of Galen and the great Arab masters (Avicenna, Rhazes); finally, Masters of Arts had Donatus and Priscian plus a few collections of *auctores* on grammar, Aristotle's *Organon* on logic, and less systematically, a few other works of Aristotle on natural and moral philosophy (*De Anima, Physics, Metaphysics, Ethics*).

In addition to these fundamental, ubiquitous texts, there was also a varying number of modern commentaries, treatises, and "questions," along with a few manuals and reference works. These are more reflective of the owner's personality and financial means. Some libraries seem very traditional, others quickly incorporated new books. Some seem very neutral, others show a particular doctrinal bent. Some seem very academic, the direct products of courses taken or given, whereas others contain works completely foreign to teaching and obviously connected with professional practice.

Finally, there is the inevitable rubric "miscellaneous." In some austere libraries, it occasionally remains almost empty. In others, especially in private libraries, it may represent a considerable proportion of the whole, though always less than half. In such cases, it reflects, in addition to the accidental factors that determined a given collection, the personal interests and tastes of the owner, which are not necessarily limited to his domain of professional activity or the scholarly disciplines of schools and universities. Religious books (the Bible, religious treatises, lives of saints, books of hours) are a sign of piety and devotion, perhaps influenced by the mendicant orders. Other books signal their owners' interest in history (general chronicles, ancient history, or contemporary national history). Naturally, classics, and even some Italian authors—Dante, Petrarch, Boccaccio, and a little later on, Lorenzo Valla's *Elegantiae*—show that some of these men of learning, while trained in the pure Scholastic tradition, took an interest in the new humanistic trends. Finally, a small number of books in the vernacular, unfortunately often poorly represented by the condescending authors of inventories ("*Item,* a little book in Roman [i.e., a contemporary Romance language]"), or perhaps a collection of "prognostications," remind us that even those who had an essentially scholarly and Latin education were not necessarily ignorant of every form of vernacular literature, and even of popular culture.

A few examples borrowed from recent research illustrate this brief typology. Françoise Autrand has made a detailed study of libraries owned by those connected with the Paris Parlement,[95] who were the genuine élite of the men of learning in France at the end of the Middle Ages. Councilors in the Parlement were highly trained jurists; some were clerics and others were laymen, but almost all were licentiates or doctors, and in no way inferior to the best law professors in Paris or Orléans. Rich and often noble or at least ennobled, they belonged to the upper stratum of Paris society. Finally, constituting the supreme court of royal justice, and thus exercising in the king's name the regal function par excellence, they were situated at the summit of the hierarchy of state offices and duties.

The libraries of thirty-seven of these *parlementaires* are known to us, thanks to inventories or wills, for the period 1389–1419 (plus one from 1362). The group's homogeneity, particularly on the cultural level, is confirmed by strong resemblances among these various libraries. On average, they hold, as we have said, about a hundred books, with a slight tendency to increase as we move forward in time. A major component of each individual's possessions, these libraries were nonetheless first of all working libraries. That is why between a quarter and two-thirds of the volumes in them are law books. The library of the "bibliophile" Nicolas de Baye was unusual in having only 16 percent law books (32 out of 198). Somewhat more surprising is the fact that canon law, including not only the diverse volumes of the *Corpus iuris canonici* but also many recent commentaries, often written by authors from Italy or southern France, seems better represented than civil law. It is true that half of these councilors were clerics, who had to judge ecclesiastical as well as lay cases; moreover, when dealing with the latter, they usually made their decisions in accord with customary law and not Roman law. Professional concerns are reflected not only by law texts but also by a few political treatises, all favorable to the royal prerogative (such as John of Salisbury's *Policraticus* or the *Songe du vergier*, and even Marsilius of Padua or William of Ockham, both considered dangerous by the Church), formularies, a few collections of letters, and rhetorical manuals.

In the more personal part of these libraries, religious books are predominant, and not only among the councilors who were clerics: a few theological treatises, but especially Bibles, breviaries, and devotional and religious books. On the other hand, neither history nor the classics occupy an important place. Finally, let us add that works in the vernacular are virtually absent; these libraries were almost exclusively Latin.

The conclusion is clear: at a time when Petrarchizing humanism was making considerable inroads on the College of Navarre and on the milieu of notaries and royal secretaries (the "earliest French humanism"), when almost 60 percent of the books in the royal library in the Louvre were in French, the milieu of the *parlementaires*, which was homogeneous and bound together by a strong esprit de corps resulting from their having studied at the same colleges, appears as a culturally rather conservative milieu that still retained a strong religious flavor. It was a milieu of competent and austere jurists, in which a religiousness perhaps influenced by the *devotio moderna* that had come from the Low Countries provided the only counterweight to the crushing prestige of the law, perceived as both a scholarly discipline and a political vocation.

More summary investigations carried out on groups of cultivated clerics—41 libraries of canons in the fourteenth and fifteenth centuries, 68 libraries of French bishops and cardinals in the period of the Avignon papacy—yield similar results.[96] The former contain on average no more than 25 books, the latter 70 (and this confirms, *a contrario*, the *parlementaires*' high level of culture, with their libraries of a hundred books and more). Among these men who had often gone to universities and were entrusted with managerial tasks, law always had an enormous weight; in half the canons' libraries, it represented more than 50 percent of the books and fell below 20 percent only in a few exceptionally large libraries that reflected genuine literary and humanistic interests. But essentially, it was religious books—breviaries and other liturgical works, along with collections of sermons and theological treatises, more than the Bible and religious texts—that made up the rest of these libraries, which were also not very open to works in the vernacular.

Comparative study of these various libraries thus clearly shows the cultural homogeneity of the world of men of learning (whether clerics or laymen), at the same time as the limits of a culture in which the new currents of thought made their way only with difficulty. Still more remarkable, other studies suggest that the homogeneity of this culture—

juridical, academic, and Latin—is confirmed on the level of the Christian world as a whole. Everywhere we find the same tendencies and practically the same books.

Let us take the example of Sicily, located at the southern extreme of the western world in the Middle Ages. An old Roman law country, to be sure, but also a somewhat marginal zone at the end of the Middle Ages, dominated economically by businessmen from northern Italy, governed politically by Aragonese monarchs who did not succeed in establishing there a genuine central administration, lacking a university[97] and therefore forced to send its future jurists and physicians to the *studia generalia* of the continent (Bologna in particular).

Basing himself on a vast notarial documentation, Henri Bresc has listed and analyzed 247 library inventories or at least mentions of books for Sicily in the fourteenth and fifteenth centuries.[98] In 120 cases, these were private, individual libraries. Two characteristics strongly emerge from his study, which confirm in their own way the observations made regarding France in the same period. First of all, here too men of learning had a quasi-monopoly on the possession of books. Of the 2,341 volumes whose owners have been precisely identified, only one percent belonged to craftsmen or merchants, 9.2 percent to the urban patriciate or to the nobility; a clergy that was apparently not very cultivated and made do with the resources of church libraries owned only 3.2 percent of the books listed. All the rest belonged to men of learning. Among the latter, we may distinguish simple schoolmasters, notaries, surgeons, apothecaries, petty officials—in other words, those who had not gone to university and whose more modest libraries still accounted for only 12.6 percent of the books, from the doctors (in medicine and especially in law) who, although relatively few in number (27 out of 120 known owners of books), possessed no less than 74 percent of the books in question, with the best libraries having on average 65 volumes.

The composition of these libraries holds no surprises, either. To take the doctors' libraries first, books on civil and canon law are far in the lead (54 percent), with not only the two *Corpus iuris* but also a rich sampling of recent commentaries, most of them Italian but some from southern France, which testify to the quality of their juridical culture. Then come other academic disciplines, depending on their owner's specialization: Scholasticism (philosophy and theology) accounts for 12 percent of the titles, medicine 8 percent, grammar 5 percent. Religious works constitute only a limited section (9 percent), with the most banal—at least from our point of view—in the majority: liturgical books and sermon-books on the Bible alongside authentic religious treatises. Finally, and although Sicily was not one of the great centers of Italian humanism, the classics nonetheless make significant inroads, with 187 copies (8 percent of the total), essentially in the fifteenth century. On the other hand, recent literature (above all, Dante), with 3 percent of the total, and technical works (merchants' manuals), with 1 percent, clearly remain marginal.

Other studies of libraries in northern Italy, especially physicians' libraries, have yielded fundamentally similar results.[99] To be sure, more than on the other side of the Alps, we find here in the fifteenth century a certain growth of collections and inroads made by the classics and humanistic texts, but the largest part of these libraries—more than 75 percent—continued to be constituted of works on natural philosophy and medicine; in other words, a Latin, academic, and professional quality remained by far the major characteristic of the books owned by men of learning.

It is pointless to multiply examples. With a few regional nuances, the same observations are pertinent everywhere, testifying to the enduring unity of medieval scholarly culture and its strong conservative tendencies.

3. From the Manuscript to the Printed Text

Was this conservatism shaken by the invention of printing in the second half of the fifteenth century? Printing, which completely changed how fast and how much written information circulated within society, was certainly one of the most important technical revolutions in the history of humanity. Did it, however, make its effects immediately felt upon the milieu of the men of learning in medieval society?

Let us recall here—setting aside the problem of the Chinese antecedents—that it is difficult to assign to the invention of printing a specific date and inventor; the famed Hans Gutenberg (ca. 1400–ca. 1468) was probably only the best known of the fifteenth-century Rhenish craftsmen who succeeded in perfecting a new technique of printing with engraved moveable type whose material possibility and practical interest had been anticipated some time earlier by the vogue of xylographic images.

What matters for our subject is first of all to emphasize that the spread of printing was relatively slow. The first printed books of which copies are extant—the "42-line Bible," known as the Gutenberg Bible, and the Mainz *Psalter*—date from the 1450s. This was then an essentially German technique, established in Mainz, Cologne, Strasbourg, and Basel. Moreover, for another generation, printers throughout Europe were for the most part Germans. It was hardly before 1470 that they began to move in large numbers beyond their frontiers. At that time, there were only five or six printing presses operating outside Germany, and the only ones that were to produce anything important were those in Venice, where Johann von Speyer had established himself in 1469, and in Paris, where Ulrich Gering and two of his companions from Constance had come in 1470 to set up their workshop near the Sorbonne (if not within the college itself), at the request of two *socii* of the Sorbonne who were both strongly influenced by humanism, Guillaume Fichet from Savoy and Jean Heynlin from Basel.

During the decade 1471–1480, printing presses became more numerous in Germanic areas (in 26 new localities, including Switzerland and the Low Countries), and especially in Italy (44 new localities). Other countries had clearly not yet joined the trend; France had seven new presses in Albi, Angers, Caen, Lyon, Poitiers, Toulouse, and Vienne, the Iberian peninsula had eight, and, surprisingly, England only four: London, Westminster, St. Alban's, and Oxford. Between 1481 and 1500 twenty-eight new presses were established in France, nineteen in the Iberian peninsula—but none in England. Germany (21 new presses) and Italy (26 new presses) nevertheless preserved their advantage, and all the more clearly if we consider the quantity of books produced. Four-fifths of the overall production, which historians assess at some 27,000 editions before 1500, or certainly more than ten million books, came from Italy (44 percent) and Germany (35 percent); France accounted for 15 percent, and other European countries for the remaining 5 percent. Although a total of about 240 European localities had seen a functioning printing press in 1500, the map of European printing still had surprising gaps (Bordeaux and Montpellier in France, Cambridge in England), and in any case one should distinguish between localities served only by itinerant printers who moved around with their presses and type and whose modest activity did not result in regular production of books, and localities where print shops were permanently established because these places offered capital and guaranteed customers. Such permanently established presses were most common in the large German cities and in Venice; in France, Paris was by far the most important center of printing, with a production three times that of Lyon.[100]

The distribution of books interests us here even more than their production. German or Italian books could be imported into France or England to make up for the weaknesses of local printing. Conversely, the appearance of printing did not put a sudden end to the activity of manuscript copyists; even if the latter's production slowed everywhere after 1470, manuscript books continued to be transcribed until the beginning of the sixteenth century. And in any case, older manuscripts continued to be used and circulate. Those who had fine collections of manuscripts—and first among them were precisely our men of learning—had a tendency to keep them and only gradually replace them with printed books. The latter cost less, to be sure, but we are not well informed about the speed with which the gap between the price of manuscripts and printed books widened. We must not forget that the first printed books were often produced in very small numbers, sometimes on the order of a hundred copies, and were therefore not necessarily very inexpensive or very available.

Relatively precise studies suggest that around 1480 the proportion of printed books in French "scholarly libraries" was still only about 6 percent, and that it was only around 1500 that it rose above 50 percent. The development elsewhere seems to have been the same, about fifteen years earlier in Italy, and still slower in England.[101]

Were men of learning the main customers for this new invention? As has been long known, fifteenth-century printed texts were for the most part "medieval" texts that seemed certain to sell. But these were not necessarily the books that people wanted for scholarly libraries. They were first of all religious books, which constituted almost half the production of incunabula—Bibles, liturgical books (missals, breviaries, books of hours), treatises on spirituality, devotional books, lives of saints, etc.—in Latin or in the vernacular. Grammar books were also numerous, but they were elementary works (Donatus, Alexandre de Ville-Dieu's *Doctrinale*, Cato's *Distichs*, etc.) addressed to pupils at lower levels far more than to students at the faculty of arts; they could serve to improve basic instruction, but not to renew the cultural élites. Finally came profane literature, often in the vernacular: encyclopedias and anthologies, chronicles, more or less modernized versions of medieval epics or courtly romances intended, no doubt, for an aristocratic audience, accompanied by clearly popular works—almanacs and other "shepherds' calendars."[102]

On the other hand, scholarly books, of which hundreds of manuscript versions existed, especially in university towns, were printed only in small numbers and often after long delays. Neither Peter Lombard's *Sentences* nor the works of the great doctors of Scholasticism from Thomas Aquinas and Albert the Great to Gerson were printed in Paris before 1500; the few editions of these works printed after 1480 came from Germany or Italy. One could say the same of Aristotle or the *Corpus iuris* and commentaries on Roman and canon law. Juridical texts, which occupied such a place in the scholarly libraries of the Middle Ages, represented hardly more than 10 percent of the incunabula, and were produced chiefly in Lyon or in Italy. All things considered, it was the genuinely humanistic texts, that is, the classics (Latin and even, increasingly, Greek) and the works of recent Italian authors that were the printed books most often sought by educated people in both France and England, precisely because manuscript versions of these books were rare. The first books printed by Ulrich Gering (advised by Fichet and Heynlin) at the Sorbonne in 1470–1472 were almost all in this category. He began with an Italian manual on the art of letter writing, Gasparino da Barzizza's *Book of Letters*, and then published Sallust, Cicero, Persius, Juvenal, et al., together with modern authors (Lorenzo Valla's *Elegantiae* and Fichet's *Rhetoric*). We must also mention, however, that Gering left the Sorbonne in 1472, and having moved his print shop to the rue St.-Jacques, he went back to the most traditional university texts and especially devotional works.[103]

In short, we may conclude that from the first decades of its existence, printing considerably broadened the audience for written culture. Popular milieus, at least in cities, no longer remained completely separate from the world of books: lower-level officials (sergeants, notaries, et al.) and simple parish priests henceforth had an opportunity to collect a small library of a dozen volumes or so. Between 1480 and 1530, such "minimal libraries" (to use Pierre Aquilon's expression) were springing up everywhere.[104] On the other hand, printing certainly allowed great cultural advances in aristocratic milieus, where admirable libraries, composed principally of literary books in the vernacular, were assembled. Obviously, printing also resulted in a new growth of the great princely libraries as well.

As far as our men of learning are concerned, however (setting aside an élite of humanists—mainly Italians—who were on the cutting edge of the new ideas and always looking for new texts), it does not seem that the progress of the printed book before 1500 greatly changed either the size or the composition of their libraries. Michelet—unfair and perceptive, as always—discerned this initial ambiguity of printing: "If the great books of antiquity were published, those of the Middle Ages were published and republished even more, especially textbooks, summas, abbreviations, the whole doctrine of nonsense, confessors' manuals and books of casuistry; ten Nyders[105] for every *Iliad*, for every Virgil, twenty Fichets."[106]

More objectively, we can probably see in this an additional proof of the strength and coherence of scholarly culture at the end of the Middle Ages. Despite its limits and clearly perceptible signs of rigidity, it was still capable of providing a basis for the self-awareness of men of learning, which we must now see at work in the society of their time.

PART II

The Exercise of Competences

⎯⎯⎯•⚬•⎯⎯⎯

As we have seen, the idea of a disinterested use of knowledge, of a general culture whose goal is the full development of the individual personality, was quite alien to medieval conceptions of education. The Middle Ages were more attentive to the social purposes of knowledge, that is, to the practical uses that could be based upon acquired knowledge. According their nature, these defined the contours of specific competencies whose concrete efficacy was more or less generally acknowledged—even if in addition to intellectual abilities complementary or competing criteria such as birth, family relations, fortune, age, and experience were also taken into account when it came to designating those who were to exercise the principal social and political functions.

What were the domains in which the societies of the late Middle Ages attributed a special value—for lack of a true exclusiveness—to competencies based on the mastery of discursive modes of knowledge? Were these competencies limited to executive tasks or did they grant those who possessed them some role in the elaboration of the initial decisions and their ideological justification? Were they exercised only at the level of the highest authorities in medieval society—that is, did they come into play only in the hands and in the service of an élite—or were they, instead, diffused even in the broadest and most modest strata of the society? If the latter is the case, were they the instrument of a general process of putting things in order, or were they on the contrary, a possible factor of challenge and change?

Such are the main questions the chapters in this second part will seek to answer.

CHAPTER IV

In the Service of God, in the Service of the Prince

All the kinds of knowledge with which men of learning were more or less deeply imbued had practical applications that were scarcely separable, in the mentalities of the period, from the notion of service. In fact, people were averse not only to the idea of a personal and disinterested culture, but also to that of a kind of knowledge the possessor would use in his own way and for his exclusive, personal profit. *Scientia donum Dei est, unde vendi non potest*: Knowledge is a gift of God, and cannot be sold.[1] This constantly repeated medieval adage clearly condemned any "lucrative" use of knowledge, whether it involved instruction for a fee or legal, scientific, or medical consultations provided in exchange for cash. Theologians and canon lawyers ended up agreeing that it was normal that a man of learning should receive from society—that is, from the Church or from the prince, or if necessary, from the person who profited from his knowledge—a fair remuneration for his efforts, which was intended to allow him to live in a decent manner befitting the requirements of his status. On the other hand, it was reprehensible to derive a speculative profit from God-given talents, since this amounted to turning to essentially terrestrial ends money that would have been better employed helping the poor or supporting the Church.

Naturally, this theoretical position, laboriously developed by men caught between traditional Christian doctrine (supported by ancient maxims) and the concrete requirements of colleagues eager to gain esteem and social advancement, was often not respected in the Middle Ages. In spite of the suspicions to which I have just referred, many men of learning sought to derive the maximum profit from their intellectual competencies. Many of them set up shop on their own, at least in a provisional or episodic manner, in order to practice in the most lucrative way possible the activity for which they had been trained.

However, even in such cases men of learning hoped to be appointed, if only toward the end of their careers, to a post in which the exercise of intellectual competencies was no longer an economic obligation but a duty taken on in relation to the office conferred (*ex debito officii*).[2] It is therefore from the point of view of service that we may best approach the fields of competency that were open to them in the societies of the time.

1. *Docere aut applicare*

In one of his *Quodlibets* (I, 35), dated 1276, Henry of Ghent, at the time the most famous secular professor of theology at the University of Paris, asked himself whether it would be better for a young doctor in theology to remain at the university and devote himself to teaching or to leave the little, protected world of the *alma mater* and put the knowledge he had acquired in the service of pastoral and administrative activity directed to the salvation of the Christian souls entrusted to the Church (*Utrum melius sit stare in studio, spe plus proficiendi, sufficientur quam ire ad procurandum animarum salutem*). His answer was qualified, but on the whole, he thought it more useful that someone who was a gifted teacher remain at the university, where his words would have an infinitely greater impact than if he exercised his talents only at the level of an ordinary individual church.[3]

About a century later (1396–1388), we find a doctor at the University of Paris, Ameilh du Breuil—who was to become bishop of Tours—suing his colleagues on the faculty of canon law who were trying to remove him from the college of "ordinary professors" (*ordinarii*) of the university (and at the same time to deprive him of the rights and revenues that went along with that position), on the ground that he was not really fulfilling the obligations of such an office. Ameilh du Breuil replied that on the contrary, he should be praised for having managed, over the years, to alternately lecture at the university and work, sometimes in the service of the pope (hearing cases in the Apostolic palace) and sometimes in the service of the king (as *maître des requêtes*, an official in charge of hearing petitions).[4]

These examples remind us that at that time, all men of learning who had a university degree considered teaching the first and most obvious of their competencies, and it was therefore the form of service that most naturally occurred to them when they completed their often lengthy studies. Nonetheless, in the Middle Ages teaching positions were rarely perceived as excluding the simultaneous or successive exercise of other ecclesiastical or lay functions.

This was particularly true of Masters of Arts. Usually young (this degree was normally awarded at the age of about twenty), many of the Masters of Arts, especially those who were well off, taught for a few years after earning their degrees. Some of them became teachers in an urban or rural grammar school; others remained at the university and became regents of the faculty of arts. A Paris document from 1283 or 1284 suggests that there were then about 120 teachers *actu regentes* on the faculty of arts;[5] this figure does not seem implausible, but it is nonetheless clear that despite the regulations that theoretically required two years of obligatory service as a regent, all candidates who received the degree Master of Arts did not teach. In any case, there were very few who, like the famous Jean Buridan (ca. 1300–ca. 1360), regent of arts from about 1325 to his death, remained their whole lives in this situation. After a few years, having accumulated a small sum of money, most Masters of Arts left the university or registered as students in a graduate-level faculty; perhaps they still continued to teach for a while, but for them this was certainly no more than a provisional solution that guaranteed a supplementary income.

Graduate studies took a very long time to complete (between six and fifteen years, according to the statutory rules, depending on the faculty and the university in question), so that what was supposed to be only a period of training at the beginning of a career sometimes became, if not an end in itself, at least the longest phase in the life of some men of learning. While many of them gave up somewhere along the way or succeeded, more or less legally, in achieving their degrees in a shorter length of time, others prolonged their studies indefinitely, especially if they had been fortunate enough either to obtain a comfortable sinecure that did not require them to be in residence, or else a room and a scholarship in a college. Moreover, it was possible to interrupt one's studies for a time in order to perform an official duty, and then resume them so that one could take the examinations. In mendicant orders, the administrative authorities often called upon confrères who were pursuing advanced studies, asking them to give a series of sermons in various churches or to assume administrative duties.

Once they had completed their advanced studies, the men of learning who had achieved the highest degree, the doctorate, could look forward to remaining at the university as professors. This was, in fact, the original significance of university degrees. The baccalaureate recognized the progress made by advanced students, who were then allowed to give some lessons themselves. The combination of the *Licentia* with the Master's or Doctor's degrees, which conferred the right to teach (*licentia docendi*) and official incorporation into the teaching staff (in the form of an inaugural lecture), was originally intended to provide a supply of new professors. If later on university degrees assumed the broader value of diplomas that guaranteed a certain level of knowledge, and hence of intellectual and even professional competence, they nonetheless continued to serve as instruments for recruiting new teachers.

Unfortunately, there is much we do not know about the teaching staffs of medieval universities.[6] It is often difficult to determine the precise number of professors in the various faculties and universities, or the payment they received for their teaching (honoraria paid by the students, examination fees, salaries paid by public authorities). In any case, they seem to have had a high opinion of their own worth, while society, both at the leadership level and at broader levels, willingly granted them marks of esteem and consideration, if not truly generous remuneration. Perhaps we can generalize what Dante Zanetti said about the professors at the University of Pavia in the fifteenth century: "The university granted prestige, not wealth."[7]

On the whole, it is likely that only a small minority of doctors actually became professors, especially in law, where many other equally prestigious and more lucrative career paths were open to those who held the doctorate. The proportion of those who went into teaching was perhaps somewhat higher in theology, where the possibilities of a career outside the university were fewer, and also in medicine, where, at least for those who lived in a university town, teaching and medical practice were perfectly compatible. In Montpellier, for example, there were always at least a dozen regents in medicine for a student body that rarely exceeded one hundred. But in other domains, the teaching careers of such regents seems not to have been very long. In Paris, at the beginning of the fourteenth century, doctors of theology, although their situation was more stable than that of others, seldom taught for more than ten years.[8] Particularly if we recall that the latter figure is an average, this shows that after a few years of teaching, a significant number of university regents gave up their posts in order to assume other functions. In some cases—doctors who became bishops or cardinals—this was clearly a promotion; in others, however, the reasons for which regents left teaching are less clear, at least in terms of social prestige. Those concerned probably did not consider teaching to be a genuine vocation that could occupy the whole of one's life; rather, they saw their years as regents as associated with their studies, which they had ended in order to move into another phase of their lives or at least of their careers.

The picture changes little in the fifteenth century. In many universities—particularly secondary or recently founded universities—two sharply distinguished groups emerge. There is a small, stable group of "ordinary professors" (*ordinarii*) who undertook to administer the university, deliver magisterial lectures, and organize examinations. These ordinary professors were not numerous—in Avignon, for example, there were only four of them. They lived on the income they received for their teaching and tended to stay in their posts for a long time. Sometimes, attracted by a better salary, they moved from one university to another. Particularly in Italy, where salaried chairs were established by communes as early as the end of the thirteenth century, towns competed for the services of the best teachers. Elsewhere, professors, especially in the arts and in canon law, often remained clerics, an ecclesiastical benefice ensuring at least in part their subsistence. Toward the end of the Middle Ages, modestly paid but stable positions as college regents also began to be established.

Alongside these quasi-professional teachers, there continued to be a second, less stable group of "extraordinary" professors. Having recently received their diplomas, they had only certain less important or substitute teaching duties; they did not fully participate in either university councils or examination panels. Some of them were waiting for a place in the college of ordinary doctors to open, but many of them rather quickly abandoned teaching to occupy other kinds of posts.

What were the consequences of this development? It is possible, but not certain, that the emergence of little oligarchies composed of ordinary professors led to rigidity in teaching and that the extraordinary professors, who were younger and more flexible, were preferred by students. It is also possible, but not certain, that ordinary professors, who were older, more dependent on outside powers, and more closely tied to local notables, were less enthusiastic defenders of university autonomy. However that may be, it is clear that the professional teacher, with his own way of life, his linguistic tics, his own networks of professional and familial relations, became at the end of the Middle Ages one of the social types in which, in the view of contemporaries, the image of the man of learning was invested. But as we will see, this was far from being the only such image.

2. Men of Learning, Churchmen

All through the Middle Ages, most schools and universities in the West were ecclesiastical institutions or controlled by the Church. To be sure, the proportion of priests and religious was high not only in faculties of theology but also in schools of arts and canon law. In any case, both students and professors were tonsured, whether or not they had been ordained, and on the fiscal and judicial level, their status was regarded as similar to that of clerics. Therefore it is not surprising that until the end of the Middle Ages the majority of men of learning pursued careers within the Church.

One could almost maintain that all churchmen were men of learning and that the two groups were identical. But although this kind of schema was not entirely alien to the clerical ideology of the early Middle Ages,[9] in the period with which we are concerned here it no longer had much pertinence. Paradoxically, however, there were surely fewer wholly ignorant clerics and religious in our period than in the early Middle Ages or even in the twelfth and thirteenth centuries. But the educated man was henceforth not defined by the simple fact that he was a member of the clergy or by elementary skills (reading, writing, singing) that any priest or monk was supposed to be able to master; he had to possess a superior level of knowledge and intellectual techniques that were no longer exclusively ecclesiastical in nature. There were now a great number of educated lay people, at least in some countries. The group of men of learning thus bridged the ancient cleft between clergy and laity; it was represented among both, constituting, beyond the line of demarcation between personal standings, an intellectual élite that was relatively homogeneous and perceived as such by contemporaries. To put the point more simply, one can imagine that at the end of the Middle Ages, a canon with a law degree was—and felt himself to be— both socially and intellectually closer to a lay graduate in civil law than to a simple country priest.

We must therefore try to determine here, within the clergy itself, the group of men who by their culture, their studies, their diplomas, their libraries, their competencies, their functions, and even their ways of expressing themselves and behavior, distinguished themselves from other clergymen or religious who were defined solely by their membership in the ecclesiastical order, their liturgical obligations, and their sacramental powers.

Overall, the proportion of men of learning within the Church itself increased greatly in the last centuries of the Middle Ages. But the size of that proportion varied considerably depending on the categories of clergy in question, and it grew with varying speed and intensity depending on the country.

Naturally, the presence of men of learning was most prominent by far in the upper strata of the clergy. Today, we have enough prosopographical studies to be able to offer some significant numerical data.

Toward the middle of the twelfth century clerics trained in the schools of Paris and Bologna began to play a role in the Roman Curia—a role that continually increased and culminated in the period of the Avignon papacy (1305–1378). Many studies have demonstrated the complexity and efficacy of the administrative and fiscal apparatus the Avignon papacy was able to establish—to the detriment, to be sure, of its spiritual influence. This apparatus was solid enough to survive even the Great Schism of 1378 and to allow the rival pontiffs to maintain their authority for almost forty years, each with his own obedience, before they had to yield to the general Council held in Constance.

An overall evaluation of this question makes it possible to gauge, at least approximately, the role that men of learning played within the central government of the Church at the apogee of the administrative papacy in Avignon, that is, at the time of the popes Clement VI (1342–1352), Innocent VI (1352–1362), and Urban V (1362–1370).[10] At that time about forty doctors and licentiates, almost always in law, directed the chief bodies of the Curia (the Chancellery, the Apostolic Chamber, the Penitentiary, the Apostolic Court of Justice or "Rota"), even if among them were a few prelates from the high nobility and close relatives of the pontiff.

At the subordinate level, the personnel of the pontifical administration amounted to about three hundred people. It is harder to assess the place of graduates and former students; at least for the Chancellery, 20 to 25 percent seems plausible. And in any case, it is likely that even the pope's treasurers, notaries, and secretaries, who had not pursued university studies, can be considered "men of learning," in view of both the complexity of the tasks they assumed and the well-informed, cosmopolitan, and cultivated nature of the curial society in which they lived.

This society was not in fact limited to the official organs of the administration. If the properly domestic or military services of the pontifical palace probably did not include many educated men, the latter were not lacking in the personal entourages—the *familiae*—of the cardinals and of the pope himself. In the cardinals' entourages, graduates and former students represented on average about 20 percent of the staff (to be sure, only a third were licentiates or doctors from a graduate faculty). Perhaps still more important for explaining the high level of the Avignon Curial culture (a high level that clearly did not prevent a certain timidity with regard to new ideas, particularly in relation to humanism), was the permanent or episodic presence in Avignon of prelates and ambassadors, of papal physicians or cardinals (who often came from the nearby university of Montpellier), of Franciscan or Dominican doctors of theology convoked by the pope and entrusted with looking into certain delicate matters, etc.

If we try to define more precisely the outlines of the group of men of learning who gravitated around the Avignon Curia, two characteristics leap to the eye. The first is the large proportion of jurists (civil as well as canon lawyers), at the expense of theologians and mere philosophers or rhetoricians from the faculty of arts. The second is the fact that most of these men were of French origin; more precisely, they often came from the Limousin or from Languedoc, even though it was not unusual to find among them Italians and even a few Englishmen. The graduates thus came chiefly from the universities of Toulouse and Montpellier, and to a lesser extent, from the universities of Paris or Orléans. It is clear that in accord with a movement that had begun in the thirteenth century and continued until the beginning of the fifteenth century, the papacy drained off a significant proportion of the intellectual élite of the French clergy. One can therefore see why the French clergy recalled with nostalgia this source of remunerative and prestigious positions which had seemed inexhaustible, as they watched it dry up after the Schism.[11] The French clergy now had to turn with gloom toward purely local careers or seek from the king of France and his court, at the price of being politically docile, the favors previously dispensed by Avignon.

Naturally, that does not mean that the popes of the fifteenth century no longer sought the advice of the men of learning. But the papacy's loss of influence outside Italy must have increasingly limited access to curial careers to the Italians themselves. Studies on the Roman Curia in the fifteenth century are not, so far as I know, sufficiently advanced to allow us to refer here to overall data, as we can in the case of the fourteenth century. Let us mention only that beginning with the pontificates of Nicholas V (1447–1455) and Pius II (1458–1464), a number of humanists, particularly from Tuscany, began to find positions at the pontifical court, such as Lorenzo Valla (1407–1457) or Platina (1421–1481), who held the office of abbreviator in the Chancellery and then became the papal librarian. Thus the pontiffs did not cease to employ men of learning. But they did not all look with equal favor on new ideas—Paul II (1464–1471) was even violently hostile to them—and on the whole, it is very difficult to say how, setting aside a few brilliant individuals, one should describe the general cultural level of the Roman Curia in the *quattrocento*.

If we now pass from the pontifical level to that of the local churches, major national or regional disparities appear, accented perhaps by the unequal progress of historical research.[12] It was probably in England— which, though sparsely populated and little urbanized, already possessed in the Middle Ages a remarkable network of schools, universities, colleges and Inns of Court—that the most learned clergy was found. Fifty-one percent of the bishops in the thirteenth century had studied at Oxford or Cambridge, and the proportion rose to 70 percent in the fourteenth century and 91 percent in the fifteenth century. These graduates were mostly in canon law, but we should note the significant presence of doctors of theology (40 percent in the fifteenth century). These elevated percentages of educated clerics are found not only among the canons—80 percent of the canons in York in the fifteenth century were graduates—but even, at a more modest level, in the ordinary parish clergy. At the beginning of the fourteenth century, depending on the diocese, 7 to 26 percent of the those in pastoral service had studied at a university, percentages that may seem low but which were in reality exceptional for the medieval period. To put the matter in a still more striking manner, we may point out that between 1451 and 1500, at least 40 percent—and perhaps in reality considerably more—of the alumni of New College, the principal college at Oxford, pursued a career in the parish clergy.

If we now move to the Continent, we can contrast, in the heart of western Europe, old countries with younger and somewhat more peripheral countries. In the old countries—basically, Italy and France—the existence of ancient educational traditions allowed the relatively early promotion of genuine men of learning within the clergy, at least in the upper clergy. In the younger countries, archaic ecclesiastical and social structures were preserved for a long time, and the lag in the intellectual training of churchmen was closed only at a later date, and even then not completely; here we are speaking chiefly of Germanic, Slavic, Hungarian, and Scandinavian countries.

The French clergy long suffered from a significant backwardness in comparison with the English clergy, and this is all the more surprising in view of the fact that a large proportion of the English clergy had been trained in the schools of Paris and Orléans. At the time of King Philip Augustus (1180–1223), scarcely 20 percent of the French bishops and even fewer of the canons in a chapter as important as that of Laon were *magistri* (at a time when the English chapters commonly included more than 40 percent of canons who had graduated).[13] It was only after 1250, in the time of St. Louis, that the men of learning seemed to have gotten a firm foothold in the French upper clergy; the proportion of bishops who were *magistri* rose to 41 percent, and it became common for diocesan tribunals to be presided over by a licentiate or even a doctor's degree in canon law.

Soon the establishment of the papacy at Avignon further strengthened the position within the French clergy of the clergymen who had come from a university. Twenty-five percent of the pontifical provisions and expectations of benefices distributed in France by Pope John XXII (1316–1334) went to clergy holding university degrees; under Benedict XII (1334–1342), the proportion rose to 33 percent. Naturally, this does not correspond to the proportion of graduates among the French clergy as a whole, since the percentages just cited concerned only ecclesiastical benefices conferred by the pope, but because they concern several thousand individuals, these elevated numbers allow us to presume that the policies of the Avignon popes with regard to the distribution of benefices did a great deal to promote educated men within the French clergy. It is true—and this is the other side of the coin—that the graduates designated by the pope in this way often increased the ranks of the non-resident clerics who accumulated benefices and who were disliked by the simple faithful because they preferred to pursue their studies, gravitate in the orbit of a cathedral chapter, or look for a position in an Avignon office rather than occupy the pastoral office to which they had in theory been appointed.

We do not yet have systematic studies on the recruitment and training of the French episcopacy in the fourteenth and fifteenth centuries. So far as cathedral chapters are concerned, a few good monographs—whose conclusions must not be generalized without precautions, however—allow us to follow the inexorable rise of men of learning in the little world of the canons. In Laon, in one of the most powerful secular chapters in northern France, the percentage of graduates rose from 45 percent at the end of the thirteenth century to 65 percent a century later, reaching a high point of 86 percent in 1412, at the end of two centuries of steady progress.[14] Equally significant figures have been established for Tournai (64 percent of graduates in 1330–1340). In some chapters in southern France as well, one finds in the time of the Avignon papacy 30 to 60 percent of graduates and former students,[15] figures that are all the more remarkable because these are chiefly jurists, whereas in the percentages in Laon and Tournai, at least half the graduates were simple Masters of Arts.

We do not have equally precise information about Italian cathedral chapters at the end of the Middle Ages. A few very partial studies mention amazingly low figures (less than 20 percent of graduates in Parma and Pavia at the end of the fifteenth century). In Rome, graduates seem to have found it difficult to make a place for themselves among the youngest sons of noble or patrician families; in a chapter as prestigious as that of St. Peter, 80 percent of which was composed of nobles, between 1277 and 1500 only 15 percent of the canons had attended a university, and among them only 9 percent had graduated.[16]

Although it was comparable, the development occurred somewhat differently in the Germanic countries of the Empire as well as on the northern borders of medieval Europe (Scotland, Scandinavia, the Slavic countries and Hungary). Here, the Church long retained "feudal" structures and the offices of the upper clergy thus remained the exclusive prerogative of the high nobility, with the result that in these countries there were for a long time very ignorant bishops and canons who led a life that was little in conformity with the obligations of their condition. As for those who wanted to acquire a good intellectual training (and there were some), lacking local universities, they had to become expatriates and go to obtain their diplomas in Paris or especially in Bologna, where throughout our period they constituted prosperous and well-organized "German nations." The appearance at the end of the fourteenth century of universities in the countries of the Empire and of central and northern Europe changed the situation only gradually. The nobles who still monopolized the most important posts continued to go to study, if they did study, in France or Italy. As for the indigenous universities, they trained chiefly very modest Masters of Arts, many of whom could not hope to become more than simple parish priests. Thus there was certainly an improvement in the average intellectual level of the European clergy in the center and in the north, but this improvement did not bring about profound changes in either social recruitment or the cultural practices of the upper clergy. In Roskilde, in the main chapter in Denmark, the proportion of canons who had gone to university rose from an average of 55 percent between 1367 and 1430 to an average of 76 percent between 1431 and 1493, but this usually amounted to no more than a thin veneer of culture: less than half of these former students obtained even a simple Master of Arts, and almost none had studied in a graduate-level faculty. Less precise studies have yielded similar results for certain German chapters; in Mainz, for instance, between 1260 and 1503 42 percent of the 415 canons identified went to university, but only 38, or 9 percent, took a degree.

To complete this survey, we would have to be able to take the situation in the Iberian peninsula into account. The available information, at least what is accessible in France, is unfortunately rather slight. It seems to reflect a situation intermediary between the English and French models on one hand, and the German model on the other. Let us take for example Valladolid, a city that did not have a bishopric but did have a university, and which was the de facto capital of the Castilian monarchy until the sixteenth century. Among the canons there were, between 1369 and 1425, only 5 percent of graduates, all of them in law; between 1425 and 1480, this proportion jumped to 22 percent, while the principal parishes in the city were served by priests holding the baccalaureate.[17] We will encounter this development—an initial lag which was tardily and incompletely but rapidly closed—again when we discuss the *letrados* in the service of the monarchy; it can probably be considered characteristic of the Spanish situation in general.

What we have said up to this point concerns chiefly the secular clergy and some urban chapters of regular canons. The situation was entirely different in the world of monks and mendicant friars, more homogeneous perhaps at the level of Christendom but showing stark contrasts from one order to another.

All through the early Middle Ages, monasteries had sheltered in their libraries and their *scriptoria* most of the men of learning of their time. But of this ancient monopoly, which had long been outdated, very little survived at the end of the Middle Ages. It would surely be excessive to believe that monasticism was in complete decadence in the fourteenth and fifteenth centuries, and that the old abbeys no longer admitted anyone but the least presentable rejects of aristocratic families. Some monasteries, particularly the Chartreuses, were still capable of producing spiritual authors of great loftiness. Others, such as St. Alban's in England or Saint-Denis in France, remained places where monarchical historiography was generated. A man like Michel Pintoin, the recently identified author of the *Chronique du Religieux de Saint-Denis* and our best narrative source of information about the reign of Charles VI (1380–1422), manifests both a mastery of writing and an acuity of judgment that bear witness to a high level of literary, historical, political, and religious culture.[18] While nothing suggests that Michel Pintoin himself had studied at a university, the principal monastic orders nonetheless eventually opened up to the new scholarly culture, which was still very foreign to their traditions. From the middle of thirteenth century onward, the Cistercian and then the Cluniac monks established colleges in Paris so that they could send a few young monks to take courses in the faculty of theology—or even canon law, though they were theoretically forbidden to do so. Other monastic colleges appeared in subsequent years in Paris, in Oxford, and in Toulouse. Their existence remained difficult, however; there was not enough money and despite urging on the part of the popes, especially Benedict XII, abbots and chapters showed little eagerness to develop modern studies within the orders themselves. The proportion of graduates in monastic orders seems rarely to have exceeded 3 to 4 percent of the membership, and the principal abbots continued to be recruited among the high aristocracy rather than among the doctors.

The situation of the mendicant orders was, at least in appearance, completely the opposite. From the outset, St. Dominic had made the study of grammar, philosophy, and theology an essential part not only of the training of young preaching friars, but also of his order's spirituality, and after a few hesitations, the Franciscans followed him in this. Preachers and Minors were endowed with a complex, hierarchized network of *studia* whose most important elements were included within the university faculties of theology. Priors, chapters, and provincial and general ministers carefully managed these teaching institutions in matters concerning financing, the choice of students, and the appointment of professors. At the end of the century, the Carmelites and the Augustinian Hermits adopted an analogous system. Even if by the end of the Middle Ages hundreds of students had been taught in these *studia*,[19] we cannot conclude that all the mendicant friars in this period were first-rate intellectuals. In every order there must have been a majority of *fratres communes*, who had received only the minimal training provided in each house by the conventual lector. But it is true that mendicant spirituality always prized education and considered doctors as the ornaments and natural leaders of the orders. As André Vauchez has shown, before the fifteenth-century movements insisting on strict observance, among the mendicants the simplicity of the ignorant *idiota* was never considered a merit and still less a virtue.[20] The officials of the mendicant orders (priors, ministers, definitors, general preachers)—whatever their social origin, which was in any case often rather vague—were always recruited almost exclusively from the ranks of the doctors and licentiates in theology. The contributions of mendicant authors to the theological production of the late Middle Ages are well known; at Paris and Oxford, they produced 63 percent of the extant Biblical commentaries written in the thirteenth century, and 83 percent of those written in the fourteenth century. It is true that their share of such works dropped to 67 percent in the fifteenth century; the reasons for this decrease are complex and probably include a decline in the mendicant orders themselves, or at least the rise within them of "observant" tendencies that were less oriented toward scholastic production, as well as an incontestable revival of secular theology.[21] Their role was equally important in the domain of preaching: they represented 85 percent of the preachers shown to have been active in northern France in the fifteenth century.[22]

In the Middle Ages, few milieus within the Church or even outside it accorded scholars and educated men such an important role. Nonetheless, they were far from exercising the kind of quasi-monopoly in this area that had been enjoyed by the monks of the early Middle Ages. Serving the prince as well as God henceforth required the competencies possessed by men of learning.

3. A Golden Age of Jurists?

The opposition between serving God and serving the prince—or if one prefers, the state—is far from coinciding with the opposition between clerics and laity. While in the Mediterranean countries the political and administrative personnel employed by cities and princes was to a large extent already laicized in the last centuries of the Middle Ages, this was not the case in northern Europe. Educated lay people were still not numerous enough for such a development, and since the secular power found it convenient to call upon clerics who were paid by the Church, many of those who served the state were churchmen, canons, bishops, or abbots. We must emphasize that the Church and in particular the papacy seem not to have opposed this situation, even though it ran counter to ancient canonical prohibitions against clerics practicing profane disciplines. It even seems that from the thirteenth to the fifteenth centuries, the popes gladly conferred ecclesiastical benefices on clerics who were already involved in the service of princes and recommended by them. One might wonder about the causes of this generosity: did the Church see this as a way of influencing the new state apparatuses that were being constituted? Or was it, as Hélène Millet has suggested, a veritable "challenge to the nobility"[23] that traditionally held political power, and if so, why? However that may be, it is not difficult to demonstrate the importance of the aid the Church thus provided to the state, virtually without cost. The service rendered the princes and cities was of several kinds. These included both domestic and personal service that retained a certain religious aspect (confessors, chaplains, companions) and service that clearly belonged to the public, lay sphere (judicial or financial officers, ambassadors).

It was in England and France that clerics held for the longest time an important place among the servants of the monarchy, especially in the central offices of government. This tradition of clerical service to the state did not completely disappear in these countries until the *ancien régime* itself disappeared.

In England, not only was the royal chancellor almost always a prelate, usually the archbishop of Canterbury, but the central offices of the monarchy, the chancellery, the king's bench (the supreme court), and the exchequer, were staffed largely by clerics, at least until the end of the fourteenth century. In the fourteenth and fifteenth centuries, even in chapters rather distant from the capital such as Exeter and York, a high proportion of canons (32 percent in Exeter, 53 percent in York) held public offices.[24]

A prosopographical investigation into the staff of the central organs of government (including the Hôtel and the administrative services) in the France of Philip the Fair (1285–1314) has shown that 273 of the 1884 officials identified, or 15 percent, were canons (plus a few bishops and religious).[25] Canons were present everywhere, and not only as chaplains or confessors; in fact, they represented more than half of the notaries and secretaries in the chancellery, of the *maîtres des comptes*, and of the councilors in the Parlement. Subsequently, these percentages decreased, but slowly; in the Parlement, the parity between clerical councilors and lay councilors was strictly maintained until the middle of the fifteenth century. At the beginning of the fifteenth century, half the canons in Laon combined their sinecure with an office in the service of the king or a royal prince; moreover, the canons thus employed were generally those who had university degrees.

These graduate clerics and servants of the state suffered little from the "Gallican" policy (withdrawal of obedience to the pope in 1398 and 1408, the Pragmatic Sanction of 1438) that deprived the pope of the right to distribute French ecclesiastical benefices: the king and the great nobles, who largely regained this right, did not forget them when distributing favors and incomes.

In Italy, on the other hand, the staffs of the chancelleries, administrative offices, and courts of law were laicized very early on. In 1224, Frederick II, without calling on the Church, founded in Naples a *studium* of rhetoric and law intended to train the officials he needed for governing the kingdom of Sicily. In the fourteenth and fifteenth centuries, the chancelleries and courts of law in Italian cities seem to have been essentially the domain of lay secretaries and judges who had studied in Bologna and other schools of law in the Italian peninsula. Clerics were almost systematically excluded from political and administrative offices.

Even at St. Peter's in Rome—despite the fact that in the pontifical state service to the Church could hardly be distinguished from service to the state—only 19 percent of the canons were given public offices, and of these hardly one percent were strictly lay offices.

In any case, whether we consider clerics or laity, the number of government servants grew everywhere at the end of the Middle Ages (although there were great geographical and chronological gaps), and that is a major fact of the social and political history of this time. This phenomenon was so spectacular that contemporaries tended to exaggerate its importance and rapidity. Periodically, the Parlements or general assemblies denounced the excessive numbers of officials and the heavy burden they imposed on urban or princely finances; a few reforms were then undertaken to limit the number of officials, but their numbers soon began to rise again, because in reality states at the end of the Middle Ages, especially the great national monarchies, were still notoriously under-administered and could not get along without the services of these jurists and men of finance who were, or were at least reputed to be, devoted and competent.

Around 1350, the central administration of the kingdom of France, if we set aside the Council (a political institution), the Hôtel (a domestic institution) and the command of the army, employed scarcely more than 250 persons (a hundred or so in the Parlement, sixty in the Chancellery, and the rest in various financial and monetary offices), and this figure did not rise significantly before 1450 and the end of the Hundred Years' War.[26] It is true that most of these officials, except for the finance specialists working in the *Chambre des Aides* or the Treasury, deserved to be described as "men of learning"; almost all of the councilors of the Parlement and the *maîtres des comptes* were licentiates or doctors of law. Many of the king's notaries and secretaries held the same degrees, or at least a Master of Arts. In any case, simply having spent a long time in court and palace circles (and cathedral circles, for these were often clerics) had generally given them an opportunity to acquire a good acquaintance with both law and rhetoric. From Gervais de Bus, who wrote the *Roman de Fauvel* around 1314, to the "first French humanists" in the time of Charles VI, there were many chancellery officials who played an important role in the development of French literature and political thought.

In sum, the kingdom's central administrative offices, which were concentrated on the Île de la Cité in Paris, represented a milieu of high culture at the same time as a prestigious and remunerative outlet for the best graduates of French law schools. It is understandable that they should have done everything they could to monopolize it for their own benefit and that of their relatives and friends. At the end of the fourteenth century, personal relations had become the completely indispensable complement to a diploma for a successful career in the service of the king, and the *homines novi* soon became scarce in the central institutions of the monarchy.

The picture is slightly different when we consider the provinces, that is, the officials of the royal domain and of the administration of the offices of bailiff and seneschal. These represented groups of several thousand persons. For a long time, there were few in these groups who deserved to be called "men of learning." Bailiffs and seneschals, nobles and military men, tax farmers and tax collectors, finance men who were often efficient, the mass of sergeants, practically illiterate and whose job consisted chiefly in seizing property and persons, even the petty hacks and scriveners in the offices of the royal administration—all these were hardly competent to do more than keep their own accounts.

The district of the bailiff in Senlis, modest but close to the capital, and which has been studied in an exemplary way by Bernard Guenée, offers an image that can perhaps be applied to many other regions of France.[27] Until 1450, we find no doctor of laws in this district; at best a dozen licentiates, usually lawyers, a few of which succeeded in becoming bailiffs or the bailiff's lieutenants, royal lawyers or prosecutors. The rest were simple uncultured practitioners, sergeants or prosecutors from obscure backgrounds. Between 1450 and 1500, when the country was being reconstructed, officials became more numerous, but there were now twenty or thirty graduates who were sometimes obliged to accept, at the beginning of their careers, the rather humble posts of court clerk, provost, or keeper of the seal. Moreover, this development continued: around 1550, there were eighty to a hundred licentiates in law in the Senlis bailiff's district, a little world that was overstaffed with provincial law officials with a calm life and blocked ambitions. The growth of the state, by increasing the number of offices, stimulated the production of men of learning, but what should be emphasized here? The capillary diffusion of scholarly culture toward the humblest levels of provincial society, or rather the depreciation of diplomas and the frustration of graduates doomed to a life of morose leisure and intellectual routine with no future?

The king was not the only one in France who employed officials and who offered jurists possible careers. The princes (who had the prerogative of royal blood or held major fiefs), prelates insofar as they were temporal lords, and the communes also had at their disposal a governmental apparatus that reproduced on a smaller scale that of the sovereign, with the same tripartite structure (domestic services or *hôtel*, council, and administrative services; the latter themselves being classically divided into chancellery, courts, and financial offices). The chief difference is that here the individuals involved numbered in the dozens rather than in the hundreds, and that the role accorded cultured people, alongside relatives, friends or simple practitioners, was often of rather slim dimensions. Until the end of the fifteenth century, even principalities as large as the duchy of Brittany still had quite minimal institutions that were in the hands of a political staff of limited competence. Only the dukes of Burgundy were able to construct a genuine state capable of offering a considerable number of positions to graduates in law from the universities of Orléans, Dole, and Louvain.[28]

What we have just said about the French monarchy can probably also be applied, *mutatis mutandis*, to the English monarchy. For our purposes it is more interesting to ask what happened in the same period in the Mediterranean countries. Since the twelfth century, the latter had been the cradle of the renascence of Roman law and a geographical and cultural area in which jurists had won an important place on the social and political scene. But at the end of the Middle Ages these countries had not been able to establish governmental structures as solid as those in France and England.

In southern France, jurists (*jurisperiti, causidici*) and *professores legum* are first mentioned in the second half of the twelfth century, in the feudal principalities as well as in consular cities and cathedral chapters. A solid native curriculum in Roman law had been established in this part of France in the thirteenth century. At the beginning of the fourteenth century, when these areas had entered the orbit of the Capetians, there was an impressive number of lay jurists who were licentiates or even held university doctorates earned in local schools or in Italy. Joseph R. Strayer counted 189 of them, including at least 98 doctors or *jurispérits*, in Languedoc at the time of Philip the Fair (1284–1314). Some of these, like Guillaume de Nogaret, Guillaume de Plaisians or Pons d'Aumelas, were able to pursue brilliant careers all the way to Paris.[29] Similarly, Jacques Chiffoleau was able to count 272 judges (excluding other categories of men of law) in Avignon and the Comtat Venaissin, almost all of them graduates, in the century of the Avignon papacy.[30] But later on, once the papacy had returned to Rome and access to the central organs of the French monarchy had been monopolized by graduates of Paris and Orléans, the possibilities of a career for men of learning in southern France became more aleatory, and this was no doubt one reason for the relative decline of faculties of law in that area in the fifteenth century. Provençals and Languedocians were reduced to pursuing relatively mediocre careers in the administration of seneschalties or in urban consulates. In the service of the latter, they occasionally became effective agents of resistance to the progress of royal authority. But this nonetheless remained a rearguard action incapable of satisfying their ambitions. Serving the king without betraying the traditions and special characteristics of the *patrie de Languedoc* corresponded more to their expectations, and in this respect, the appearance of provincial Parlements

(Toulouse in 1443, Grenoble in 1453, Bordeaux in 1463, Dijon in 1476, Aix-en-Provence in 1501) and of the prestigious posts they offered to the best local jurists were particularly welcome.

In the same period, Italy and Spain underwent contrasting developments. In northern Italy and in Tuscany urban seigniories and city-states won out, and in their service we find side by side humanistic secretaries and doctors of law who were sometimes related to old families of commercial patricians, and sometimes came from more modest families that had recently immigrated from the neighboring *contado*.[31] At this same time in southern Italy and in the Iberian peninsula, after a long period of wars and troubles, the Catholic Monarchs began a campaign of territorial and monarchical unification (1479—Castille, Aragon, the two Sicilies) that was still not complete in 1500 but already required the creation of a modern administrative apparatus. It was in this context that there appeared in fifteenth-century Spain the figure of the *letrado*, who was destined to have a brilliant social and literary career. In reality, the *letrados* were a rather heterogeneous group. At its apex were the high officials of the monarchy, often working in Valladolid: judges of the *Audiencia real*, *contadores mayores* who supervised the state's ordinary and extraordinary revenues, secretaries of the chancellery, referendaries of the Cortes. Other *letrados*—and sometimes the same ones—occupied the principal municipal magistracies (*alcaldes*, *regidores*, and *corregidores*), practically all of which, in Castille, were appointed by the king.[32] Finally, the great aristocratic families had their own notaries and secretaries (*escrivanos*), who were often at the same time part of their domestic clientèle of proteges or *criados*. The rise of the *letrados* was particularly noticeable in Castille, which suggests the political preponderance that this kingdom was soon to exercise within a unified Spain. On the other hand, in Aragon and Catalonia, where the representatives of the states of the realm always vigorously opposed the progress of royal authority, the *letrados* had a much less important place, while in Navarre much more limited institutions simply appealed to a handful of licentiates and holders of bachelors' degrees.[33] In Portugal, finally, the lay jurists represented no more than 18 percent of the officials of the central administration in the fourteenth century,[34] but their rule must have increased in the fifteenth century.

A similar rise of men of learning in the service of territorial princes and cities can be observed in northern Europe, where political structures that had long remained archaic were now being modernized. Local administrations offered a fairly wide range of positions, from humble jobs as secretaries in small towns, to which Masters of Arts might aspire, to posts as counselors to the Imperial tribunals that went to doctors of law who had often graduated from Italian universities.

In sum, all over Europe, princes and cities, without yet welcoming men of learning as warmly as did the Church, employed an increasing number of educated people, particularly jurists. The level of these men's competence varied, as did their prestige and remuneration, but exercising a public office constituted for all of them a common point of reference around which began to crystallize the feeling of constituting a specific social group, the one that in France would soon be called the class of the *robe*.

4. Conclusion: A Few Necessary Qualifications

The reader will no doubt have garnered from the preceding pages a fairly simple schema that is, all things considered, predictable. It could be summarized as follows: At the end of the Middle Ages, we find two phenomena that mutually fueled each other, the transformation of the Church into a centralized administrative monarchy and the birth of modern secular states. Since it could not be satisfied with the support of the traditional dominant groups, namely the clergy and the "feudal" nobles, the Church and states increasingly called upon new categories of servants whose unconditional loyalty was accompanied by technical competencies based on mastery of writing and the disciplines of scholarly culture. This promotion of men of learning naturally caused in turn the growth of their group itself and of the educational institutions where they were trained. In view of this fact, the principal task of the historian of the political societies and cultural élites of the end of the Middle Ages is to reconstruct, using prosopography, and if possible in a quantitative manner, the parallel rise of religious or secular administrative apparatuses and of the educated people who provided a foundation for them.

This general schema is not false. It corresponds, moreover, to the ambition declared by the political powers of the time, for example when they established new universities whose purpose was to train the jurists and men of letters they said they needed. Confirming in 1413 the foundation of the University of Aix, the Count of Provence declared that his goal was to ensure that "educated men full of knowledge and virtue might at last serve the state and look out for its interests."[35] However, the somewhat mechanistic view of social and cultural evolution suggested by such a schema requires a few qualifications.

First of all, what precisely was the nature of the "services" rendered by men of learning to God and to the prince, to the Church and the state? They served them, to be sure, but were they not making use of them as well? Even if they accorded special value to theoretical notions and gauged the power of ideas more accurately than others, the men of learning of the Middle Ages must not be considered as abstractions defined solely by the conjunction of a competency and an office; they were flesh-and-blood people who had their own ambitions, interests, and friendships. We have to take all these factors into account in order to judge fairly their role in the societies of the time.

A second qualification to keep in mind: was there necessarily a functional connection between the intellectual competence of the men of learning and the tasks they accomplished? The answer is clearly negative. I am not referring here to the previously mentioned gaps between the disciplines in which they studied—Roman law, scholastic theology, Galenic medicine—and the later social practices of these men.[36] We can say that at that time people thought that by providing access to the very spirit of the disciplines, a high level of training, even if relatively abstract, could then be retailed in various kinds of concrete practices that were both customary and empirical. On the other hand, I wonder about the type of competence that was thought to be possessed by all those— certainly the majority of the men of learning, at least in the northern half of Europe—who had been trained only in grammar and logic, and at best crowned by a Master of Arts.[37] In itself, the Master of Arts led to few specific outlets: it allowed one to become a schoolteacher (and even then, as we have seen, many schoolmasters did not possess even a Master's); and if necessary a scribe, secretary, or *escrivano*. But otherwise it simply guaranteed a good knowledge of Latin, some idea of logic and philosophy, a certain aptitude for abstract thought and for the manipulation, active or passive, of written texts, and finally, a particular kind of sociability, that of schools, colleges, and universities. Yet this kind of training, to which two-thirds of the students in Paris and at least four-fifths of those in German universities limited themselves, was perceived as constituting an intellectual competency, even though it was without any technical or professional dimension. The rest—for example, a knowledge of religion or law—could be acquired on the job, gradually and empirically.

Thus we must beware of certain documentary illusions. It is true that jurists and, in an accessory manner, theologians, occupied the front of the stage, with their fine-sounding titles and beautiful diplomas— we think of the sumptuous parchments, decorated with paintings, that were delivered by the universities of Bologna and Padua in the fifteenth century. But behind the great, proud figure of the doctor, the medieval man of learning was much more often a humble Master of Arts, or the simple *magister*—a title whose ambiguity was rightly emphasized by Konrad of Megenberg in his *Yconomomica* III, 3 (ca. 1354)[38]—whose rather elementary knowledge nonetheless constituted a recognized acquisition that provided the basis for a specific social practice.

This social practice—and this is the third qualification of the general schema mentioned above—did not always lead to service to the Church or to the secular authority. Whether because of their spirit of independence, the pursuit of profit, or the lack of available positions, many men of learning in medieval society opted for a private practice, sometimes directly connected to their earlier training, and sometimes not (and thus difficult to discover). This individual and private use of intellectual competencies must also be taken into account by anyone who wants to reconstruct in a complete way the role of men of learning in medieval societies without reducing it to the *cursus honorum* of ecclesiastical and political careers, no matter how brilliant they may have been.

CHAPTER V

Knowledge and Power

————•◦•————

We have just reviewed the principal functions that Western societies of the end of the Middle Ages most often assigned to men of learning, though they did not, apparently, reserve them exclusively for the latter. We must now look into the precise nature of these functions.

At first sight, it seems that these were relatively technical functions, corresponding on the practical level to the intellectual disciplines that men of learning had previously assimilated. Only the case of Bachelors and Masters of Arts, whose training in grammar and logic did not correspond to any immediately usable know-how, was somewhat more complex. But other men of learning were expected, in one way or another, to put things in writing, to judge, to manage. They wrote letters and regulations, preached and argued court cases, rendered justice, audited accounts and administered the temporal affairs of churches and princes. In other words, it was always a matter of serving a master, of shaping or applying decisions or regulations made by those who actually held power.

Was the role of men of learning no more than that? Didn't they have a certain range of freedom? Weren't they ever associated—at one level or another—with the making of decisions, with the definition of regulations, in short, with the exercise of power? Didn't they have an opportunity to interpret, use their initiative, and act independently? While serving the interests of their master, didn't they also have a chance to defend their own interests? The goal of this chapter will be to answer these questions.

1. Knowledge and Ideology

In medieval societies—as in every other period of history, no doubt—almost all of those who held power, whether religious or lay, felt the need to accompany their action with an effort to legitimate and justify it ideologically. Many instruments could be put in the service of ideology and political propaganda: art in all its forms, public rituals, vernacular literature both oral and written, and history. In the Western Middle Ages, the idea of drawing on the resources of learned culture, and therefore of calling upon men of learning in this effort of ideological production, developed especially from the twelfth century on. The *Policraticus* (1159) represents an important stage in this development. In this work, which was the first major treatise of the Middle Ages to deal specifically—if not in lay terms—with political philosophy, John of Salisbury explained that the prince, if he wanted to provide for the good government of his lands, must not yield to either the intrigues of courtiers or to his own whims, which would lead him only to tyranny, but on the contrary he must follow the advice of "philosophers," that is, the doctors who were educated in the schools and were imbued with every good discipline, belles lettres, dialectics, law, knowledge of Scripture. It was John of Salisbury who popularized the adage "An uneducated king is like a crowned ass" (*Rex illiteratus est quasi asinus coronatus*), which was until the end of the Middle Ages one of the most commonly repeated commonplaces in political literature.

In this domain as in others, it was probably the Church that showed the way for the secular powers. From the end of the eleventh century, the quarrel regarding the priesthood and the Empire had led the popes (and hence the emperors) to seek in theology and Roman law a justification for their pretensions to supreme authority. The intense production that resulted from this in the two camps continued into the twelfth century, with Pope Alexander III (1159–1181) and Emperor Frederick Barbarossa (1155–1250), and then in the thirteenth century, at the time of the battles between Frederick II (1220–1250) and the popes Gregory IX (1227–1241) and Innocent IV (1243–1254). In the course of this final phase of the conflict, mendicant theologians joined the Roman law canonists in supporting the cause of the pontifical *plenitudo potestatis*. In the fourteenth century, the relative retreat of imperial power and the too-well-oiled functioning of the Avignon popes' administrative machine put ecclesial reflection on the back burner, but the latter returned to prominence with the Great Schism of 1378 and the conciliary crisis that persisted, because of the endless prolongation of the Council of Basel, until the middle of the fifteenth century. Philosophy, theology, and law were once again required to provide the partisans of the various popes, as well as those who belonged to the preeminence of council, with arguments that could provide a foundation for the cause they supported. On all sides, whether in the universities, in the entourages of princes or rival pontiffs, treatises and pamphlets "on the schism," "on the council," or "on the pope" proliferated.

Among the secular powers, beyond the pro-imperial literature already mentioned, the advances in political ideology accompanied, and probably even preceded, those of the actual renascence of the state and the prince's sovereignty. The English Plantagenet kings were the first to turn, as early as the twelfth century, to authors such as John of Salisbury himself, Giraud de Barri, or Gautier Map, all three of them pure products of the schools of their time, and theoreticians of the monarchy at the same time that they were bitter critics of courtiers and uncultured nobles.[39] In France, the dynastic cult and historiography were for a long time the chief ideological supports of Capetian politics. It was under St. Louis that a few jurists, such as Pierre de Fontaines and Jean de Blanot, began to use Roman law to support the assertion of the sovereignty of the king, "emperor in his kingdom." Twenty years later, political Aristotelianism, interpreted in the most monarchical way possible, provided a second, philosophical support for the construction of the modern state. Philip the Fair (1285–1314), who in his youth had had among his tutors one of the great teachers of philosophy and theology in the University of Paris, the Augustinian Giles of Rome, the author of *De regimine principium* (On the Government of Princes), was no doubt the first to decide to make systematic use of the resources of learned culture in the service of the monarchy's political action. His long and victorious dispute with Pope Boniface VIII, in which he sought to affirm the total independence of the king in temporal matters, was accompanied by the publication of a number of pamphlets arguing in favor of the royal prerogative.

The ideological orchestration of royal politics was pushed to the highest level in the time of King Charles V (1364–1380). His byname "the Wise" shows that his contemporaries noticed this aspect of royal action. Charles V was surely a man of culture. He created and installed in the Louvre a "royal library" in which national history, public law, and political philosophy found their place alongside religious books and vernacular literature. He liked to surround himself with a circle of intellectuals, who often came from the University of Paris, and whom Françoise Autrand has called "the king's club."[40] This was a genuinely informal organ, not for making decisions (that role was still reserved for the Council), but for general reflection on the nature and goals of the state and of political action. This circle often gathered around the king for conversations that were simultaneously erudite and amicable. It also produced, certainly in response to the king's direct command, a certain number of high-quality works in which were expressed in a very complete way the political conceptions (sovereignty of the state and the inalienable character of the crown, the necessity for counsel and consent, the election of officials, the full autonomy of the political with regard to the religious, etc.) that Charles V tried to put into practice in the government of his kingdom. Among these works, we have already cited Nicolas Oresme's translations of Aristotle and Evrard de Trémaugon's *Songe du vergier*; we may add Denis Foulechat's translation of the *Policratus*, Raoul de Presle's translation of the *City of God*, and so on.

Theoretical treatises, whose dissemination must have been limited, were not the only vehicles for political ideology. We must add, on one hand, pamphlets and propaganda tracts, and on the other, diplomatic texts.[41] The latter—preambles for charters and regulations, explanations of the grounds for decisions, letters of commission given to investigators or reform commissioners, etc.—were composed with care in the chancelleries, since they were by their very nature able to reach a vast audience and to explain in concrete terms the most classic themes of royal propaganda. Frederick II and the thirteenth-century popes had already shown the amount of ideology that could be packed into such formulas; the princes of the late Middle Ages did not forget that lesson.

During the reign of Charles VI, except for Philippe de Mézières (1327–1405), whose self-taught knightly culture does not allow us to count him among the men of learning in our sense, the propaganda effort was taken over by the French princes, who were struggling for the power that the king's folly had left in their hands. The dukes of Burgundy and Orleans competed for the services of the most prominent intellectuals. The duke of Burgundy also obtained the support of eminent university professors such as Jean Gerson as well as that of semi-professionals like Christine de Pisan, one of the rare women in the Middle Ages whose acquaintance with scholarly disciplines was such that she can be associated with the men of learning. Some men of letters remained faithful to the Burgundian cause, while others ended up detaching themselves from it, especially after the assassination of the Duke of Orléans (1407), to join either a rather illusory reformist third party or the Armagnac clan. For example, it was the latter that attracted the humanist secretaries at the Chancellery in the early fifteenth century, such as Jean de Montreuil (1354–1418), whose political treatises (*A toute la chevalerie, Traité contre les Anglais*) strongly supported, in opposition to England, the "nationalist" politics of the Orleanists. Their commitment gradually became explicitly anti-Burgundian, and when the duke of Burgundy seized Paris in 1418, most of them were executed or sent into permanent exile.

This break did not, however, completely interrupt this ideological trend. While the duke of Burgundy, Philip the Good, resorted to forms of propaganda that were simultaneously more literary and more traditional (chronicles and chivalric literature),[42] beginning in the 1430s King Charles VII again called upon political authors capable of elaborating the philosophical and juridical arguments necessary to establish his legitimacy, and then to justify the increasingly authoritarian, indeed, almost "absolutist" policies he had adopted in order to reconstruct the monarchical state at the same time that he successfully pursued the reconquest of the territories occupied by the English. Specialists in the field generally judge this work rather harshly, maintaining that crude argumentation in the service of shameless propaganda was increasingly substituted for the acute juridical and political analyses of the preceding century. Only Jean Juvénal des Ursins (1388–1473), the austere royal attorney who wrote various "propositions," "exhortations," and other "deliberations" dedicated to Charles VII, is treated relatively favorably by these historians, who are particularly severe in their judgment of Jean de Terrevermeille, another royal attorney (in Beaucaire), whose *Tractatus contra rebelles suorum regum* (1419) has been described as "an apology for the obligatory obedience of subjects . . . in relation to the omnipotent king," Robert Blondel, the tutor of Charles VII's second son (*Les droits de la Couronne de France*, ca. 1450), and, at the end of the century, the humanistic chancellor Guillaume de Rochefort, who praised in 1484 "the tireless readiness to obey" of the French people."[43] Should we see in this an early example of the "betrayal of the intellectuals" [*trahison des clercs*] in the long and difficult history of the relations between intellectuals and political power in France?

However that may be, for our subject it is important to determine the precise sociological origin of these men of learning for whom service to the prince, which was often quite well paid, took the form, not (or at least not only) of performing some administrative function, but rather of elaborating a state ideology whose purpose was to justify, in the guise of a "reformation of the kingdom," the decline of ancient freedoms and a steadily increasing acceptance of royal sovereignty. Many did not put their names on their works; one might wonder about the reasons for this discretion. Some of them probably acted spontaneously, moved by sincere "patriotism" or "royalism" (to use a somewhat anachronistic vocabulary), or else in order to attract the prince's attention and his favors. The latter was no doubt the case for Pierre Dubois, a former student in Paris and Orleans who had become a rather obscure lawyer in Coutances, in Normandy. Between 1300 and 1310, he produced a dozen short treatises in which he supported without reservation Philip the Fair's attacks on Boniface VIII and the Templars and his plans for a crusade (or at least the plans Dubois attributed to Philip). But he received no reward for his unfailing loyalty to Philip; perhaps the king never knew about Dubois's works.[44]

Other authors came directly from the university; Christine de Pisan tells us that "King Charles [V] clearly demonstrated to his beloved daughter, the University of clerics in Paris, that he loved knowledge and study. . . . He had great reverence for the congregation of clerics and for study; he often summoned the rector, the teachers and the most renowned clerics, of whom there are many, in order to hear their wise teaching, and made use of their advice regarding spiritual matters, and honored and supported them in everything."[45] Other authors already belonged to one administrative body or other when the prince called upon their writing talents. Obviously, in considering their decision to accept such tasks, we do not know the relative weight of considered self-interest and sincere conviction—a conviction that was itself based, if not on a common consensus, at least on a powerful current of opinion. Neither do we know how far the royal sponsor determined in advance the outline of the commissioned work, or on the contrary, left the author a certain degree of freedom that might allow him to anticipate his master's desires and to elaborate arguments or even concepts of which he had not yet thought.

To answer these questions, we would have to determine in a direct way the personality and culture of the prince himself. The "wise king" at the end of the Middle Ages was certainly not the *rex illiteratus* mocked by John of Salisbury, but since for this period there are very few extant, authentic documents that were actually written by the prince himself, it is difficult to say to what extent he could converse on an equal footing with men of learning, or instead preferred to leave them a free hand to develop their ideas, provided that this development followed the general line he had laid out.

I have discussed in some detail the French example, with which I am more familiar, but in most of the European monarchies we would also find, between the thirteenth and the fifteenth centuries, one or more "wise" princes who had succeeded in surrounding themselves with men of letters whom they ordered to compose ideological or propagandistic works intended to promote their efforts to modernize their governments.

In the 1260s the king of Castille, Alfonso X (1252–1284), also called "the wise" (*el Sabio*), had jurists trained in Bologna compile the famous *Siete Partidas*. This collection of legal documents was strongly inspired by Roman law and quickly became the basis for Spanish public law even before it was promoted in 1348 to the status of the official legal code and taught as such in universities. Other Iberian princes of the end of the Middle Ages were able to get the doctors in Salamanca and Coimbra to justify both the strengthening of the state and the first projects of maritime expansion; for example, King Edward I of Portugal (1433–1438), the author of great legislative compilations (*Ordenaçoens do Senhor Rey D. Duarte* and *Livro das Leis e Posturas*), and his younger brother, Henry the Navigator (1394–1460), whose interest in mathematics, astronomy and geography is well known.

In the Empire, imperial propaganda, which was still active in the time of Henry VII, Louis the Bavarian (the probable initiator of and model for the *Defender of the Peace* composed in 1324 by Marsilius of Padua, himself a former rector of the University of Paris who had become the imperial vicar in Italy), and Charles IV of Luxemburg, afterward declined. But the territorial princes, both Italian (the Medicis in Florence, the Sforzas in Milan, the Estes in Ferrara, Alfonso V in Naples) and German (the dukes of Bavaria, the Palatine Electors, the margraves of Baden), even when their power took the form of a brutal tyranny or did not extend beyond a relatively modest local level, often took care to surround themselves with doctors and men of letters in their service. In this context, one can see why the debate between defending civic freedoms, which had been rediscovered by reading Cicero, and rallying to princely patronage was one of those that most troubled the world of the Italian humanists, especially the Tuscans, in the fifteenth century.[46]

We could give further references taken both from English history— for example, in the time of Richard II, who tried to get jurists in his entourage, such as Robert Tressilian, the chief justice of the King's Bench, to justify his policy of personal power in opposition to the Parliament and the great barons[47]—and from the histories of more distant countries such as the Poland of Casimir the Great (1333–1370) or the Hungary of Matthias Corvinus (1458–1490), with its humanistic chancellors John Vitez and Peter Váradi, who had graduated from the universities in Vienna and Bologna.[48]

Naturally, the learned disciplines did not provide the only basis, and perhaps not even the principal one, for the ideological legitimation of the modern state. In France, as elsewhere, all sorts of traditional elements, borrowed in particular from the earlier chivalric culture, were also brought in, at the same time as more popular religious, moral, historical, or mythic beliefs that were well suited to arousing peoples' affective adherence to the idea of a nation and to the dynasty that incarnated it.[49] It remains that at the end of the Middle Ages at least some of the men of learning were able to inaugurate a new intellectual form of political engagement that went far beyond the exercise of the usual judicial or administrative functions.

2. From Service to Counsel

In a presentation copy of Nicolas Oresme's translation of Aristotle's *Ethics* (folio 1 of manuscript 2902 in the Royal Library in Brussels), an illumination shows the translator kneeling before Charles V. The king is seated in majesty, his crown on his head, under the royal canopy; Oresme respectfully offers the book he has just written "at the command of the very noble and very excellent prince Charles, by the grace of God king of France." Even if he has accomplished a task nobler than that of a simple scribe, even if he enjoys a certain freedom of inspiration, the ideologist who puts his talent in the service of his master's political choices and expects to be rewarded for doing so is still in a dependent position. His knowledge and competence are recognized, but used for ends that are imposed upon him.

Did the men of learning at the end of the Middle Ages go beyond these subordinate positions? Did they participate personally and directly in the exercise of power? The answers to these questions are not simple, and we must once again make a sharp distinction between the Church and the secular states.

For the Church, the answer is incontestably yes, at least from the middle of the twelfth century onward. To be sure, until the end of the Middle Ages many popes, cardinals, bishops, and abbots were recruited from the highest levels of the aristocracy. However, mastery of theological or juridical culture, which from the thirteenth century onward was demonstrated by the possession of university degrees, also became an effective criterion for promotion within the upper clergy. Pope Alexander III (1159–1181), though no longer identified with the canonist Rolandus, was the first of a long line of learned popes who had graduated from the schools in Bologna. Others, like Innocent III (1198–1216), had studied theology in Paris. The most eminent in this regard was no doubt Innocent IV (1243–1254), a renowned canonist who prepared the definitive edition of his *Apparatus in quinque libros Decretalium* after he became pope. The popes of the second half of the thirteenth century, like those in Avignon, although they had less brilliant personalities, were almost all former doctors of law or theology.

The rise of men of learning in the College of Cardinals is also easy to follow from the twelfth to the fourteenth century, though it was not entirely linear, since some popes were clearly more well-disposed toward scholars than were others. But there were already ten *magistri* among the thirty-four cardinals appointed by Alexander III, and in the period of the Avignon papacy at least half, and probably more, of the members of the College of Cardinals were licentiates or doctors.[50]

The role of men of learning in the papacy and the Curia may have somewhat declined in the fifteenth century, since the Italian high aristocracy made a strong comeback in the leading offices of the Church. However, even in this period there was no lack among the pontiffs and cardinals of well-known jurists, eminent theologians (Nicholas of Cusa), and prominent humanists, who were often collectors of fine Greek and Latin manuscripts or authors (Popes Nicholas V and Pius II, Cardinal Bessarion).

I will not discuss again here the equally important place occupied by graduates in the episcopacy, including those who directed the most important sees. It suffices to recall, for example, that from the twelfth to the fourteenth century important men of letters such as Anselm of Aosta, Stephen Langton, Robert Kilwardby, John Peckham, and Thomas Bradwardine served as archbishop of Canterbury, and thus as head of the Church of England. The mendicant orders were led by teams of doctors of theology. Only traditional monasticism escaped the graduates' takeover of the leading functions.

No doubt the promotion of these men of learning was greatly aided by their intellectual training (though it was not sufficient in itself, for social origin, political affinity, and personality also played a role), but can we conclude that it was as men of learning that they went on to govern the Church (or the local churches entrusted to them)? Men of knowledge who had become men of power, they henceforth made their decisions and executed them chiefly by means of the authority and the pastoral responsibilities invested in them, as these were defined by canon law. To a certain extent, their weapons were those of learning—breadth of knowledge, pertinence of judgment, the ability to convince—but they were also those of power—the arsenal of canonical sanctions, the temporal riches of the Church and its means of coercion, including military means, legitimated by law or custom. To put the point more concretely, can one say that it was the fact that they had been eminent professors of theology in the schools of Paris that explains why Stephen Langton led the English barons who revolted against King John in 1215, or why as archbishop of Rouen (1248–1275) Eudes Rigaud proved to be a particularly effective manager of his ecclesiastical province? The medieval Church certainly put a large part of its destiny in the hands of learned men, and the pious, mystics, and heretics occasionally reproached it for doing so. But for all that it was not a "republic of professors" or a modern technocracy.

The temptation nonetheless existed, at least at the time of the conciliarism crisis. The bankruptcy of the pontifical magisterium and the retractions of the College of Cardinals convinced a certain number of university teachers, in particular the theologians in Paris, that it was up to them to take into their own hands the resolution of the crisis, and indeed, in the long run, at least part of the government of the Church. Ecclesiological reflection on the role of the Council, which was itself supported by the rise of political Aristotelianism, provided a certain foundation for these claims. The University of Paris (despite the opposition of the University of Toulouse; all the universities were not conciliarist) began by intervening on its own to impose on the royal government and on the Church of France the "withdrawal of obedience" with regard to the pope in Avignon (in 1398 and in 1408), and then support for the general Council. Within the latter, in Pisa (1409) and especially in Constance (1414–1417), those who were present as delegates of the universities were very active in the assemblies and commissions, and sought to influence both the choice of procedures and the preparation of conciliary legislation. These efforts were redoubled at the Council of Basel (1431–1449), where the gradual withdrawal of a large number of bishops left the field open for the doctors' reformist ambitions and maneuvers.

The functioning and the work of the councils of Constance and Basel have been differently judged by historians. Those attached to an ultramontanist religious and cultural tradition are much more severe than liberal and/or Protestant historians. So far as the councils of Pisa and Constance are concerned, their relative success (they overcame the Great Western Schism) is generally attributed to the bishops, who were able to make realistic political decisions when necessary, rather than to the university men, who soon became frightened by their own bold plans for reform and were, moreover, uneasy about the possible financial consequences of the disappearance of pontifical provisions in the matter of benefices.[51] Conversely, the Council of Basel produced, under the leadership of theologians from Paris, an abundant and often interesting body of legislation, but it was not able to avoid political paralysis. Should we therefore conclude that the divided assembly was a failure, powerless when confronted with the double movement of the reestablishment of pontifical authority and the takeover of the national Churches by princely power? English and German historians nonetheless emphasize the fecundity of the ideas put forward at Basel, and the discredit—which was definitive in some countries—the council cast upon the centralizing papacy that had resulted from the Gregorian Reform; another Reform of the Church was henceforth possible and was not far off in time.[52]

The secular states were probably never seriously tempted to adopt government by an assembly of doctors. If some individuals were able to exercise certain forms of power, they could do so only as the prince's councilors. In the Middle Ages, the council was a basic given of political life. The word itself designated both one of the mutual obligations that linked the lord and his vassal (the vassal was supposed to counsel his lord as best he could, and the lord was not supposed to make any important decision without having asked his men's advice), and the body, whose composition was very flexible and varied in size (the great council, the limited council, the secret council), within which were examined all the issues concerning which the lord or prince requested his vassals' advice. Among the vassals, a distinction was drawn between the vassals proper and simple officials or friends whom the lord called "to the council" and to whom he might delegate, in a provisional or permanent way between two meetings of the vassals' court, the examination of certain questions and the judgment of certain lawsuits. Naturally, it was in relation to this second category of councilors that the men of learning might be called to the prince's council. I set aside here the specialized bodies (the Exchequer and the King's Bench at Westminster, the Chambre des Comptes and the Parlement in Paris), which were detached from the Council in the twelfth century in England, and in France at the end of the thirteenth century; these bodies had a chiefly administrative role and we have already discussed them. Here I focus on the Council proper, as the main body for political deliberation within which the most important decisions were made "by the king and his council." Except in periods of political crisis, during which the delegates of the aristocracy or the cities were able to attempt to take control of the composition of the Council itself, the prince normally called upon it when he wanted to. Were the men of learning present in it?

They could be consulted as a body, particularly in the case of university professors. It was Philip the Fair who became accustomed to consulting the University of Paris as a "new source of authority," asking it to examine certain questions, to formulate opinions, and ultimately to support royal authority. Thus in 1303, the Parisian masters had to make a statement about the conflict that opposed the king and Pope Boniface VIII, and in 1308 another about the Templars. The custom persisted, and even at the end of the Hundred Years' War the university played a significant role; particularly during the Great Western Schism it endeavored to impose on the royal government the "withdrawal of obedience" and its solution to the conciliarist problem, and then, its majority having rallied to the Burgundian cause, it approved the Treaty of Troyes (1420) and the double Anglo-French monarchy and later made an important contribution to the condemnation of Joan of Arc (1431).

Outside Paris, the main example of an important political role played by university men as such is that of Prague. John Hus and his reformist friends came from the Prague university milieu; after his death, the masters in Prague for the most part joined the most moderate trend within the Hussite revolution, the one which, while combating both Taborite extremism and the imperial armies, constantly sought to reestablish unity with the Church (1436). All through the crisis, the Prague university men thus served as interpreters of the Czech nationalist and reform movement at the same time that they served as natural counselors and political inspiration, first for the king, and then for the aristocracy and the patricians who had assumed power in Bohemia.[53]

There is no need to add that in Paris as well as in Prague, in the political domain as well as in the religious, the political ambitions of the universities came to a sudden end after the middle of the century. The end of the Schism and the Hussite wars, and the restoration of royal authority in France, allowed the sovereign, at the same time that he reduced the privileges of the university, to do without the counsels that the latter, as an independent institution, might claim to give him.

In a more everyday and common manner, the men of learning might also participate in the Council on a personal basis. But I know of hardly any examples of university people being directly called to take their seats on the Council. When graduates played a role on it, it was usually, especially at the beginning, as ecclesiastical councilors. A few prelates almost always sat on the Council, and they were usually doctors of theology or law as well. In the Empire, in France, and in England, during the twelfth and thirteenth centuries, ecclesiastical councilors had great influence. When he left France on his last crusade (1270), St. Louis left the government of the realm in the hands of a layman, the lord de Nesle, and two clerics, the abbot of Saint-Denis and the bishop of Paris.

Starting at the end of the century, the percentage of laymen among the king's councilors regularly increased, although churchmen were not entirely eliminated. Philip the Fair's celebrated "légistes" are well-known; for the most part, they came from the law schools in Orleans and southern France. In addition to the fact that not all of them were laymen (and conversely, some of Philip the Fair's important councilors, such as Enguerrand de Marigny, were not jurists), we must clearly distinguish, as F. J. Pegues and J. Favier have shown,[54] "jurists-administrators," simple officials attached to local or central administrative bodies, from "jurists-politicians" who, like Pierre Flote and Guillaume de Nogaret, actually sat on the Council. The latter were able to exercise a significant influence but were never dominant for an extended period of time, being in the minority in relation to the king's relatives and the great nobles.

The King's Council retained this type of composition, with varying proportions, until the end of the Middle Ages: a few councilors who were clerics, a few major officials who had generally studied law, like the chancellor or the president of the Chambre des Comptes (though Jean Coitier, who held this office under Louis XI, was a physician), and a majority of men of action, either belonging to the royal family or to the high or middle aristocracy. Moreover, the almost constant state of war in England and France from the 1340s on favored councilors who were competent in military matters, that is, certain bailiffs or seneschals, the constable, the marshals, the admirals. Some graduates, clerical or lay, were able to play an important role at one time or another—such as Guillaume de Melun, archbishop of Sens, Jean d'Angerant, bishop of Chartres, Jean de Dormans, bishop of Beauvais and then cardinal, Jean de la Grange, abbot of Fécamp and then cardinal, or under Louis XI, the bishops of Angers and Albi, Jean Balue and Jean Jouffroy, and a few *parlementaires* such as Hélie de Tourette, Mathieu de Nanterre, and Jean Dauvet.[55] However, there is no doubt that the nobility was then and for a long time to come the politically dominant class in France as in the other Western monarchies. It was the nobility that was really responsible for important decisions and that drew the greatest advantage (in the form of prerogatives, titles, pensions, etc.) from its proximity to the center of power. Even the university-educated clerics and the jurists who were appointed to high offices or seats on the Council were themselves often noblemen.

P.-R. Gaussin's analysis of the Council's composition under Charles VII between 1418 and 1461 clearly illustrates our point. Among the 238 individuals who sat on the Council at one time or another, setting aside fifteen cases (5 percent) that are difficult to identify, we see the primacy of the nobility: fifty-eight from the high and very high nobility (20 percent), eighty-seven from the low and middle nobility and courtiers (31 percent). While the fifty-nine prelates (21 percent) and sixty-five officials (23 percent) constitute a substantial minority, we must remember that many of them were also of aristocratic origin.[56]

Naturally, the great lords and royal princes who made up the king's immediate entourage had their own counselors and clients, who often included men of learning whose advice they asked and whom they generously placed in chief offices of the royal administration when they were themselves in a dominant position on the Council. Raymond Cazelles has demonstrated the succession of various clans—Burgundian, Norman, etc.—that succeeded each other in royal favor at the time of Philip VI and John II;[57] a number of prelates and graduates were included in each of these, but they rarely exercised power directly.

Let us glance briefly at the other European principalities and kingdoms at the end of the Middle Ages. It is true that in England the chancellor was almost always a graduate of Oxford, but a few high barons who were often related to the king usually dominated the Council. At the same time, the influence of the *letrados* in the Iberian peninsula was rising rapidly in the central offices of the monarchy. Some of them, such as the *contadores mayores* of Castille, Fernán Alfonso Robles and Alfonso Pérez de Vivero, both of them from modest backgrounds, achieved at the beginning of the fifteenth century successful careers as well as a spectacular rise in society.[58] But very few of them really reached the summit of power, as did João das Regras, a doctor from Coimbra, who was chancellor and principal councilor to the "master of Aviz" crowned king in 1385 under the name John I.[59]

The same was true for the cities, particularly in the independent city-states of Tuscany, in northern Italy, or in the Hanseatic world of Germany. In Florence, for example, while graduates and educated clerics filled posts in the chancellery and various other administrative offices of the commune, it has been calculated that at the beginning of the fifteenth century men of law and notaries represented only 10 percent of the political personnel who were really influential in the councils.

Moreover, many of these were themselves related to the families of bankers and merchants who constituted the core of the dominant oligarchy.[60]

In the simple communes and other "good cities" of the kingdoms of France and England, where municipal government consisted chiefly in exercising a fiscal and juridical autonomy that was carefully overseen by royal officials, access to the offices of magistrate and consul was open to men of learning in a more or less restricted way. While all cities were inclined to call upon jurists to act as judges, legal counselors and prosecutors, as ambassadors, and as assessors entrusted with one technical function or another, some did not allow such men access to the leadership of the city itself. The main pretext for this restriction was that they did not belong to the oldest families in the city and were suspected of not being sufficiently attentive to the city's interests, a suspicion that was encouraged by the fact that many of these jurists sought to combine or alternate municipal functions and offices in the service of the prince. The kingdom of France in the fifteenth century offers the whole range of possible solutions. In Montpellier, the consuls who came from the world of commerce and crafts obstinately refused until the end of the Middle Ages to admit representatives elected by "jurists, lawyers, or notaries."[61] On the other hand, in Toulouse, which was the capital of a seneschalty and later the seat of a Parlement, men of law made their way into the municipal magistracy as early as the fourteenth century, even though they generally remained in the minority (about 22 percent in the time of Charles VI).[62] In Lyon, in contrast, the great families of men of law succeeded after 1450 in almost completely supplanting the heirs of merchants as consuls of the city.[63] Finally, in Paris the provostship of the merchants and the magistracy, held in the fourteenth century by businessmen like Étienne Marcel, passed after 1412 into the hands of men of law connected with the court and the royal administration. Between 1420 and 1500, among the twenty-four provosts of the merchants, we find no more than two money changers and one merchant, the others coming from the Parlement (12), the Chambre des Comptes and other financial offices (7), or the Hôtel (2); sixteen, in particular all those from the Parlement, held university degrees.[64]

3. Esprit de Corps

Especially if we limit ourselves to laymen, and set aside a few exceptional individual successes, we can say that men of learning did not really arrive at supreme power at the end of the Middle Ages. Professors and officials were sometimes made councilors, but they rarely made the decisions. However, the direct exercise of high-level political responsibilities was not the only way in which they could operate in order to influence the evolution of society and the state.

In their simple role as officials and councilors, even while presenting themselves as faithful executors of princely policy, they could in reality exercise a certain influence through the internal solidarities of the groups they formed, their esprit de corps, and the stability and continuity they had managed to acquire, which allowed them to discreetly turn certain developments in the direction most in accord with their ideas and the most favorable to their interests. The idea that the administration was not neutral, that the prince's servants—and chief among them, the graduates—not only exhausted public finances by their great numbers but were also, through their daily practice of business and the jurisprudence of the courts, insidiously leading the state toward a constant strengthening of the prerogatives of the officials at the expense of the ancient freedoms of the country (that is, of the nobility and the cities), appeared vigorously in France during the great political crisis of 1356–1358. In the Estates General, the "party of the officials" was loudly and strongly denounced, and these officials had to make some sacrifices, though a few years later they recovered most of the positions they had lost.

This kind of attack was repeated several times. In 1380, on the pretext of the urban revolts, the uncles of the young king Charles VI dismissed Charles V's councilors. The latter returned to power in 1388 at the beginning of the personal reign of Charles VI; these *Marmousets* [grotesque figurines], as their detractors derisively called them, tried to revive the politics of the "party of the officials," which since the middle of the century had sought to strengthen monarchical sovereignty and to rationalize royal administration and justice. As early as 1392, however, the *Marmousets* had to cede power once again to the dukes' supporters. The latter all had supporters of their own in the various bodies of officials and men of law, but it was doubtless the Duke of Orléans who most took under his own wing the centralizing and authoritarian policy of modernizing the state that had earlier been promoted by Charles V's councilors. It is therefore not surprising that the criticism that there were too many officials and that they abused their offices became one of the leitmotifs of Burgundian propaganda and, in 1413, the leading principle of the "ordonnance cabochienne," a confused and backward-looking project of reform that was never applied.

The very repetition of the attacks on the party of the officials ultimately reveals their ineffectiveness. To the versatility of the assemblies and political intrigues that periodically changed the composition of the Council, the servants of the state could oppose the internal solidarities of their group as a guarantee of its stability.

This sense of solidarity often went back to the officials' early years and their school days. Men of learning were trained in the same universities and, in Paris, in the same colleges. I have already pointed out the essential role the colleges of Navarre and Dormans-Beauvais, and to a lesser degree, the colleges of Montaigu, Presles, and du Plessis, played in the training of the servants of the French monarchy at the beginning of Charles V's reign. Those who had graduated in civil law had also studied at the University of Orléans, where an effective system of "nations" strengthened solidarities among the students from the same geographical origin. In England, a college like King's Hall (Cambridge) seems to have been a similar site of privileged training for many of the crown's officials. In Flemish and Germanic countries, the links that had been earlier forged by traveling to study abroad and the memory of common experiences in Paris, Orleans or Bologna provided the glue that held together certain groups of graduates and jurists. Thus in Ypres there was a confraternity of alumni of the University of Paris that undertook, among other things, to pay for scholarships for their young Flemish compatriots who had gone to study at the same university.[65]

The relationships formed while studying at the university were continued throughout life. Constantly meeting at the same offices and courts and daily exchanges ensured that people would acquire the same mental habits, the same ways of living and experiencing, the same tastes, the same devotions. Institutional bonds were often reinforced by family connections and affinities with clients. In many groups of officials, at the end of one or two generations most of the families had become associated by marriage, and newcomers, without having completely disappeared, became increasingly rare. In the Paris Parlement, Françoise Autrand sees the "time of jurists and lawyers" who owed their promotion to their personal competence and their devotion to the service of the state, as being succeeded by "the time of allies" who persuaded the king to grant them the right of co-option, mutually supporting each other, and sealing their agreement by marrying their children to each other, and then by "the time of heirs," which is that of victorious family lineages in which hereditary transmission of offices by "resignation" and then by venality gradually became the rule.[66]

The example of the Paris Parlement, which is no doubt an extreme case, should not be rashly generalized. Other groups of officials, such as those concerned with finance, did not achieve the same stability. Still others, although coherent on the cultural and social levels, did not succeed in constituting themselves as equally effective political pressure groups. To limit ourselves to France, in the fifteenth century neither the university people, who suffered from the king's mistrust after 1440, nor the jurists in the south who were dismissed from the central offices of the monarchy and reduced to cultivating their powerless nostalgia for a past that was no more, that of the independent consulates and especially of the Avignon popes who had liberally distributed offices and sinecures to them,[67] were able to derive any political advantage from their institutional solidarities.

Everywhere, people connected with the Parlements, who had become the manifest élite of those who combined knowledge and power, were in sole possession of the field. The king had handed over to them the supervision and regulation of the privileges that founded the universities' autonomy, thereby acknowledging their victory over potential rivals. In the south itself, the local graduates soon saw their only salvation in the creation of provincial Parlements that would finally reopen to them careers in the service of the prince that they regarded as having a sufficient degree of dignity.

This development did not necessarily entail the deterioration of the intellectual competence of officials or of their sense of the state and public service; the election and co-option of officials not only guaranteed that the interests of families would be respected, but also provided protection against arbitrary appointments. But they surely strengthened the officials' esprit de corps, and gave rise to as many castes clinging to their interests and privileges as there were judicial or administrative offices within the governmental machinery. The constitution of the great governmental bodies, all of whose members were united by the internal solidarities I have just mentioned, made it possible to reduce to the minimum the effects of the purges that followed struggles between the opposing clans even at the very pinnacle of the state. Above all, this constitution made it possible to elaborate, if not a political theory, at least a political practice that was ultimately to be applied with relative constancy throughout the fourteenth and fifteenth centuries to the end of regularly strengthening the monarchical state.

Princes, great lords, and military leaders, grouped into leagues and parties, might well busy themselves at the front of the stage, confronting one another in bloody clan struggles and interminable vendettas (Armagnacs and Burgundians, the aristocratic revolt against Charles VII's military reforms and the Guerre du Bien Public in France, the Wars of the Roses in England, countless dynastic conflicts, civil wars and aristocratic revolts in Spain) or dream of chivalric exploits and crusades. But in the background the jurists and officials, who were henceforth convinced that they were "members of the king's body," participated in some way in his majesty and were protected in the exercise of their functions by his special support, obstinately if not silently pursued the "public good," that is, the construction of the modern state. They did so all the more stubbornly because they felt they were putting into practice the theories that their studies of philosophy and law had taught them were superior, and because they believed they were thereby gaining for themselves the maximum advantage, in terms of wealth and social prestige, from this development of which they were the instruments and, in large part, the creators.

CHAPTER VI

The World of Practice

The preceding chapters may have given the reader the impression that in the societies of the late Middle Ages, men of learning, and in particular those who held university degrees, were clearly situated on the side of the social and political élites. Filling the ranks of the upper clergy and the top-level offices of the royal administration, they seem to have had as their principal function—and their principal ambition—to serve the Church and the state and to exercise a more or less direct influence on the leading groups in society. They were able to enjoy a certain amount of intellectual freedom and to claim a real autonomy for the social group they constituted, but they nonetheless were tied to the leading groups of the society and were thus more inclined to put their culture in the service of the established order—and of its possible modernization—than to challenge it.

The practical execution of the decisions inspired or shaped by the men of learning seems to have been handed over, not without disdain, to relatively uncultured practitioners who were scarcely able to read or write: the lower clergy and ignorant monks, crude sergeants, unscrupulous provosts, rapacious tax collectors, scriveners who were barely capable of tirelessly copying the same formulas, barbers and surgeons who relied on random experience, etc.

Without being completely false, such a view of things caricatures them insofar as it presupposes, on one hand, that "practice" was completely alien to men of learning, and, on the other hand, that scholarly culture was completely alien to "practitioners." In the following pages I will try to rectify this double prejudice.

1. Scholarly Culture and Private Practice

It would be very difficult—and no one, so far as I know, has made the attempt—to calculate, except on a strictly local level, the relationship between the number of men of learning and the positions available in the employment market of administrative and ecclesiastical careers at the end of the Middle Ages. From the thirteenth to the fifteenth century, the increase in both areas must have been roughly parallel, but with significant distortions. At some points, especially in the thirteenth and fourteenth centuries, the competencies sought were sometimes lacking; bishops complained that they could not find, at least among secular priests, the theology teachers they needed to staff their cathedral schools, and many lawyers were still without any theoretical training whatever. Conversely, in the fifteenth century, the proliferation of new universities seems to have sometimes created a threat of saturation, and some graduates had to accept relatively humble posts: licentiates in law sat on secondary tribunals, and bachelors of theology became parish priests in the countryside.

In addition to the difficulty of getting an office or a benefice, many other factors helped convince some men of learning to devote themselves to private activity. Despite the social prestige of public offices or ecclesiastical degrees, one cannot exclude the possibility that for some it was counterbalanced by the attraction of a degree of personal independence or the hope of large profits to be derived from a private clientele. In any case, private service and public service were not necessarily incompatible; in many cases, one could probably engage in them successively, alternatively, or even simultaneously: the lawyer became a judge, the professor of law or medicine supplemented his income by acting as an arbitrator or a consultant.

Like public activities, the private activities open to men of learning were connected with the disciplines they had studied, and this limited *ipso facto* the field, for as we saw in the first chapter, many kinds of knowledge that were useful in the private domain, especially technical or economic knowledge, were not taught in the schools or universities. Limiting ourselves to the canonical disciplines of scholarly culture, grammarians and masters of arts, whether clerics or laymen, could become tutors or schoolteachers, and jurists could become lawyers or prosecutors; physicians treated their own patients. Only theologians, all of whom were priests or members of religious orders, remained outside the area of liberal activities.

It is hard to determine the number of people involved in these professions, which were not necessarily grouped into organized vocations, and whose members, who were sometimes exempt from taxes, did not always appear as such in fiscal documents. But at least in the cities, they seem to have sometimes brought together relatively large groups. Seats on the royal tribunals supported a certain number of attorneys, sometimes very comfortably; there were about a dozen in Toulouse, all of them licentiates in law, in the second half of the fifteenth century, after the creation of the Parlement.[68] A simple bailiffry such as Senlis had almost as many—eleven in 1465, of whom nine were licentiates in law, for only a few thousand inhabitants.[69] Doctors of medicine did not all find university regencies or pensioned positions in the entourage of some great aristocrat; they therefore had to set up on their own or negotiate a contract with one of the communes that generally employed one or two municipal physicians, in accord with a well-established custom, particularly in areas around the Mediterranean.[70] Studies on various cities in Italy, France, and England have arrived at much the same result: about one physician for every thousand inhabitants. Nonetheless, this rather low rate—which doubles or triples, however, if surgeons and barbers are also counted—corresponds to the presence of several dozen practitioners in all the large cities.[71]

There is another point that we must keep in mind when we attempt to gauge the place and the influence of men of learning in the society of their time. The activity and the social role of these men was not limited exclusively to "professional" practice, whether religious or lay, public or private, based on their intellectual competence. Although this practice was governed, like that of university men or judges, by a theoretically immutable calendar (working days, holidays, vacations) or adapted in accord with the varying degrees of urgency of the needs, the man of learning always had some free time to share the everyday life of his contemporaries.

As a consumer, he negotiated his purchases of grain and fabric with the merchant. As a property-owner, he managed his houses in the city and his lands in the country, and supervised his renters and tenants. As an investor, he used his money to buy shares of flocks, mills, or ships. As a religious person, he participated in the life of his parish or his confraternity. And as a city-dweller he participated in urban festivities and the municipal administration, though perhaps not in the defense of the city, for his privileged status often exempted him from the duty to bear arms and take his turn on the watch. Thus he took his seat alongside his fellow citizens on the councils and assemblies of his city and his neighborhood, and often held, as we have seen, communal offices.

The available documentation does not make it easy to say how our men of learning behaved in such circumstances. Did they conform, as soon as they were no longer performing their functions, to the most common manners of feeling and acting, or did they continue to distinguish themselves in some way by their attitudes, their language, and even their ways of acting? Without pretending to settle a complex question, we can at least formulate the hypothesis that in all aspects of everyday life they were able to discreetly, if not unconsciously, inject something of their culture and their way of thinking (confidence in the power of writing, legal perspective, rationality, etc.).

2. The Intermediary Intellectuals

Thus far, we have focused on men of learning in the relatively strict sense that we defined in the introduction to this book, and that corresponds well to a specific perception shared by people of that time. However, to stick rigorously to this delimitation of our subject would be to run the risk of seriously distorting our perspectives.

Behind this relatively limited group, which almost always came from the universities or schools at an equivalent level (mendicant *studia*, the English Inns of Court, and the Italian humanistic *contubernia*) there was the probably more numerous mass of far less cultivated individuals who possessed only a meager and fragmented knowledge they would no doubt have been quite incapable of teaching to others, at least in a discursive manner, but whose activity and social position were nonetheless defined, at least in part, by this intellectual aspect of their competence.

Sociology long ago discovered the existence, in very diverse societies, of what it calls "intermediary intellectuals" or, following Gramsci, "organic intellectuals." These are neither creators nor true transmitters of knowledge, but rather relays that are indispensable for disseminating on a sufficient scale, either by refraction or by ricochet, a certain number of elements proceeding from scholarly culture and for ensuring their social efficacy. Their role is obviously difficult to grasp and sometimes even indiscernible when documentation is lacking, as is often the case in the Middle Ages. However, we must attempt to bring together a few facts that allow us to perceive the role played by such intermediaries and to glimpse its importance.

These intermediary intellectuals did not go wholly unnoticed by their contemporaries. In his *Quolibet I,* question 35, Henry of Ghent refers to "*doctores rurales* ['village intellectuals'?]—and preachers [a theology teacher, he was concerned chiefly with the problem of pastoral activity] who were often ignorant of the principles of what they were teaching or preaching but pursued their work with confidence because they knew that what they were teaching had been received from their [university] professors."[72] One could not put the point better.

It is easy to draw up a list of all those who might come under the rubric "intermediary intellectuals" in medieval society. Let us consider first all the former students who had left the university without a diploma—or, at best, with a simple baccalaureate or a modest master's in grammar or in arts—often after only a few years or even months of study. That was no doubt the fate of the majority of students, that is, of thousands and thousands of individuals.[73] A few may have failed examinations, but most of them gave up out of discouragement or for lack of the money necessary to continue; it may also be that some never did intend to spend more than a short time at the university in order to acquire a vague familiarity with scholarly disciplines (without mentioning the attraction of traveling to study and the privileges connected with being a *scolaris*). Unfortunately, these ephemeral students escape almost completely the historian's scrutiny. Even when they were registered at the university, it is almost impossible to find them again after they leave because in subsequent documents their names are not accompanied by a university degree that would allow us to identify them with certainty. For example, it is only because he happened to be involved in a trial that we learn of the complaint, at the beginning of the fifteenth century, voiced by Jean de Roiax, the scion of an impoverished ancient family of Toulouse patricians who had become a simple country priest. He complained bitterly that he had been forced to leave the university prematurely and accept this subordinate position because his tutors refused to finance his studies appropriately.[74] But how many others in comparable situations left no trace at all in the documents!

However, it is unlikely that all those who had received a minimal university education in this manner, even when not crowned with a degree, and who perhaps still possessed a few books acquired at the beginning of their studies, derived nothing from it at the level of knowledge, cast of mind, or social relations. These former students who had never gone beyond the level of elementary training in grammar probably filled the ranks of the professions that interest us here: schoolteachers, many of whom had not even passed through the faculty of arts, surgeons and barbers, prosecutors and even some lawyers, especially in small towns, rural parish priests, and *a fortiori*, vicars and chaplains, scribes of all kinds, scriveners and notaries. Among the latter, a few might have a Master of Arts degree but very few of them had even a baccalaureate in law; they got their training essentially by apprenticeship in the office of an already established notary. But concerning the rest, one should not underestimate the importance, not only social but cultural, of notaries, at least in areas of written law. As early as 1327, there were twenty notaries in Sisteron, not to mention the six hundred notaries registered in 1338 in the *Arte dei Giudici e Notai* in Florence, which was then at the height of its power.[75] Toward the middle of the fifteenth century, in a far less favorable period, there were still twenty-two notaries in Arles for a population of about five thousand, and seventy-eight in Lyon, for a population of about fifteen thousand.[76] The mass of notarized registers in the fourteenth and fifteenth centuries that have survived in southern archives, and which are nevertheless only a small part—25 percent at best—of what must have existed, suffices to allow us to imagine the omnipresence of these individuals in Mediterranean countries, drawing up formal documents right and left in the smallest circumstances of life, constantly forcing on everyone reference to the written document and the rule of law.

It was by way of these men, whom no reverential distance separated from the rest of the population, that the majority of people were able to hear an echo, though much diminished, of the scholarly culture of their time and to experience in their everyday lives some repercussion of the practical application, which had been determined at the upper echelons of the Church or the state, of theories that were based on that scholarly culture.

The notarized document, and more generally any form of legal or regulatory document, provided a discreet vehicle for both the form and the content of certain elements borrowed from Roman law. The role of notaries did not stop there, since they commonly combined their main activity with more or less temporary offices such as bailiff, clerk, prosecutor, secretary, etc. in the service of individuals or rural or urban communities.

In an entirely different domain, ordinary preaching relied on collections of *exempla* and Dominican or Franciscan model sermons and took at least its basic notions from Scholastic philosophy and theology. Finally, the practice of surgeons and barbers was never so empirical that it did not imply at least an implicit recourse to one concept or another derived from Aristotle's physics or Galen's physiology.

3. The Social Scope of Knowledge: Challenge or Inclusion?

Thus the question of the political and social efficacy of the knowledge formulated and disseminated among the cultivated élites was most crucially raised at the level of these "intermediary intellectuals." There is hardly any doubt that the latter wanted to be included. Not that they necessarily represented tranquil and rigorously conformist milieus. It is well known that in university towns, and especially the largest ones such as Paris, Bologna, Oxford, Toulouse, or Orléans, conflicts between "town and gown," though not constant, were far from unusual. The professors trained a changing body of young, single men, almost always from outside the city. The students were proud of their knowledge and privileges, which they saw as guaranteeing their impunity, and did not hesitate to raise a ruckus in the streets and in the taverns, and were always ready to pick a fight with the sergeants of the guard, shopkeepers, or valets of aristocratic or patrician houses. These brawls, which were sometimes bloody and even resulted in deaths, often ended to the detriment of the university men, but the latter generally took their revenge by appealing to the courts, whether ecclesiastical or royal, where they usually won. In the fifteenth century things changed somewhat; royal judges were less inclined to excuse excesses that appeared increasingly incompatible with the stricter political order that the modern state was beginning to impose on all the subjects of the realm, whatever their personal status and whatever the collective privileges to which they might appeal.

In any case, one should not interpret these disorders as being subversive. When not the result of mere youthful exuberance, they were almost always an assertion or a defense of academic fiscal or judicial privileges. Thus they did not constitute a challenge to established authority; on the contrary, they expressed the *scolares'* desire to show that they belonged to the privileged strata of society and not to let themselves be reduced to the rank of simple bourgeois or, worse yet, to that of the foreigners (*aubains*) who were at the mercy of the local authorities. The latter and the urban populations from which they were drawn recognized this, and in the popular movements of the late Middle Ages students were often objects of city-dwellers' hostility along with the powerful and the privileged. That is what happened in Orléans as early as 1251, when the popular crusades known as "Pastoureaux" violently attacked students along with the bishop and his canons, and in the troubled years between 1382 and 1387, the violence was again directed against students and their privileges. The same attitude characterized the disorders in Oxford in 1355 (the Massacre of St. Scholastica's Day) and in Toulouse in 1332 and 1427. In Montpellier, during the terrible anti-tax revolt of 1379, when the duke of Anjou's officials were killed, academics stayed put or fled, but they lent hardly any support to a protest that was alien to them, since they themselves were exempt from taxes.

Once they had left the university and entered careers as clerics or officials, men of learning seem to have lost any penchant for subversion and protest. To be sure, they often participated in the factional struggles to control power at the head of the state or the Church (in the time of the Great Schism). In Oxford, from the thirteenth century on, some academics seem to have supported the king, while others, both in 1215 and in the 1250s, sympathized with the rebellious barons. Among academics in Paris in the fourteenth and fifteenth centuries, there were both loyal supporters of the monarchy and partisans of the king of Navarre, the duke of Orleans, the duke of Burgundy, and the English. These political commitments led some of them to their deaths or into exile, even though on the whole they seem to have escaped the most radical purges, often showing more skill in backing the victorious party than did the military leaders or the financiers.

Here again, however, these political commitments do not allow us to speak of a genuinely critical choice with regard to the established social and political order. What men of learning aspired to was to better serve the established order, in accord with their doctrines and without neglecting their own interests. The principal reproach they might make to the men in power was not that they had imposed an unjust or dangerous order, but rather that they did not listen to them attentively enough and had not made a sufficient place for them within the organs of power. As Robert Fossier has written, "even when they were hostile to the established order, which they reproached for not giving them enough attention, academics belonged, or gradually joined, the dominant classes; ... while they often contributed to arousing vigorous social demands, they systematically condemned any recourse to violence as a way of ensuring that these demands were met."[77] In the societies of the end of the Middle Ages, men of learning were not always men of power, as I have said, but they were at least men of authority, scorning violence and more inclined to serve and improve the existing order than to challenge it at the risk of overturning social hierarchies in which they themselves were not so badly placed, and in which they hoped to rise further.

There is no doubt that under these conditions they recognized that knowledge had an essentially incorporating and modernizing power, that they saw in it a kind of glue that ensured social and political cohesion, and that they were never so happy as when they had as their interlocutor a "wise" king who shared their convictions and was open to certain reforms, such as King Charles V of France. Was the same true of the "intermediary intellectuals" whom I mentioned earlier?

The question requires a more complex answer here. Incontestably, at the end of the Middle Ages there were individuals on this level whose incomplete knowledge, at the same time as a feeling of inferiority with respect to the true holders of power and an awareness of the socially subordinate or at least ambiguous position in which they were kept in spite of their ambitions and the efforts they had made to acquire intellectual competence, may have elicited a feeling of frustration that might itself lead to protest and dissidence in both thought and action. The history of heresies and popular uprisings at the end of the Middle Ages reveals some of these "alienated intellectuals" who are one of the classical agents of latent or overt subversion in the ordered societies of the ancien régime.[78]

It is not that these intermediate intellectuals are found everywhere at all times. Certain rebellions, and especially the briefest and most violent, such as the French "Jacquerie" of 1358, those of the English laborers in 1381, or that of the Florentine Ciompi in 1378, seem to have had hardly any leaders who did not issue from their own ranks, occasionally joined by former soldiers or a few nobles who had come down in the world.[79] However, as in many other movements, we find traces of the presence of educated or semi-educated people who contributed the outline of a theoretical foundation as well as their ability to manipulate written documents.

In actuality, the extant documents tend to obscure the link between rebellion and literacy because the documents that the rebels and heretics might have written were pitilessly destroyed, perhaps the victims of their adversaries' scorn even more than of their hatred.[80] A close examination of the events nonetheless reveals their presence, at least at an underground level.

Let us take up first the case of religious dissidence at the end of the Middle Ages. It had relatively little impact in France, except in the marginal zones (the last Cathars in the county of Foix, Dauphiné vaudois), and this certainly tended to support the image of the "very Christian" king of France. Elsewhere, on the other hand, in Italy, England, and the Empire, it sometimes took on greater proportions.

The very weak role played by the mendicant friars in this is striking. Their theological culture and their oratorical training seems to have made them much more inclined to justify the established order or to appropriate popular demands than to encourage the dissatisfaction of the crowds that came to listen to them.[81] It was only among the "Spiritual Franciscans," who were at the point of breaking with the official Church, that one could find what might at least seem to be subversive tendencies. Even then, we have to be wary; as Jean-Louis Biget has shown, there were merchants, jurists, and notaries around the Languedocian Spiritual, Bernard Délicieux, a reader in theology at the convent of Narbonne, when he tried to rouse the masses against the inquisitors at Carcassonne. May we not consider this paradoxical conjunction, which no doubt reflects the malaise of the urban élites with regard to the increasing weight of the power of the Crown and the Church in southern France, a sign of a fairly conscious appropriation in which Franciscan extremism comes to the aid of a protest that is much more regional and political in character than it is religious or social?

Constituted heresy much more often had its origin in the doctrines and teaching of secular teachers at the universities, such as John Wycliff (ca. 1330–1384) in England or Jan Hus (1369–1415) in Bohemia. Alhough they were persecuted and even, in the second case, condemned by the Church, during their lifetimes neither of these men gave rise to a genuinely popular religious movement. The latter developed after their death, referring more or less directly to their memory.

In England, there were the Lollards. We know that among these popular preachers, whose evangelism was accompanied by a vehement critique of the Church's secular wealth, were Oxford alumni such as William Taylor and Peter Payne. Without directly participating in the movement, many regents in theology at the university, including the chancellor Robert Rigg, sympathized with it, and the archbishops of Canterbury had to take the university vigorously in hand for thirty years in order to put a definitive end to the heretical ferment there. Lollardism was not strictly speaking a scholarly heresy, but because of the presence of some men of learning among its initiators and propagators, it did not cultivate the anti-intellectualism common in such movements. On the contrary, Lollard preachers accorded great importance to the production and wide distribution of manuscript pamphlets and they urged the translation of the Bible into the vernacular in order to make it accessible to all the faithful (on the condition that they knew how to read!).[82]

In Bohemia, the University of Prague remained faithful to the memory of Jan Hus; nevertheless, it belonged to the most moderate and least heterodox current—apart from the question of communion in two forms, which was emphasized by the university's theologians—in the Czech nationalist movement. This attracted vehement criticism on the part of the Taborites, who constituted the extreme, popular, and genuinely revolutionary wing of Hussism, but it allowed the University of Prague to help write, with the Council of Basel and the Emperor, the doctrinal compromise sanctioned by the *Compactata* of 1436.

Without openly breaking with the Church, other kinds of devotion and spirituality that were more or less characterized by mysticism, such as the Rhenish "Friends of God" or the Flemish Beghards and Beguines, not to mention the more traditional Franciscan third order, developed on the margins of the traditional ecclesiastical institutions and not without challenging them somewhat. This was particularly the case in the Low Countries and in the Burgundian states. These movements were also often led by cultivated men, even if they were not first-rate masters. Some of them, such as Ruysbroeck the Admirable (1293–1381), were basically self-taught, but others had gone to university, such as Gérard Grote (1340–84), the initiator of the *devotio moderna* and the holder of a Master of Arts from the University of Paris (even though he afterward harshly criticized the pride and empty knowledge of his former classmates).[83] Moreover, these pious trends gave a privileged place to personal reading and study; some, such as the Brethren and Sisters of the Common Life founded by Gérard Grote, set up a very effective and innovative school system that offered, in some respects, an alternative to shortcomings in the traditional university.

The men of learning, and especially the most modest among them, thus had their place in the various orthodox and heterodox reform movements that attempted, at the end of the Middle Ages, to respond to the crisis in the institutional Church and to satisfy the religious aspirations of the faithful, including those who sought more direct access to the very sources of Christian knowledge, that is, the Scriptures.

Men of learning also played a role in movements of political protest and revolt. Not only a few itinerant preachers, but the world of lawyers, scribes, and notaries was involved in these movements. These men often lacked university degrees and were less certain of their knowledge and their social position than were officials and prelates; they enjoyed neither the latter's privileges nor their guaranteed incomes and were thus exposed to the hazards of economic and political conditions, even though they were sometimes quite well-off. But they nonetheless had sufficient grammatical and legal knowledge to draw up a manifesto, to outline a catalogue of demands, to harangue an audience, or to open negotiations. Still close to the popular strata from which they had often come, such men easily won the confidence of these groups, which were vaguely aware of the increasing influence of knowledge in political life, and willingly relied on them to formulate their aspirations and to begin a dialogue with the superior authorities.

At the end of the Middle Ages, the archetypal though exceptional figure of these semi-educated men who had been propelled to the head of popular movements is certainly Cola di Rienzo (1313–1354).[84] The son of a Roman tavern-keeper, the young Cola learned the notary's profession from a relative; then, while practicing his profession, he acquired on his own a literary culture based on the historians and poets of antiquity, along with a little Roman law; to an extent, he was connected with the earliest Italian humanism, that of Petrarch. On the other hand, his religious convictions were rather banal and traditional. He became one of the leaders of the popular party that included merchants, artisans, notaries and the lower clergy in opposition to the baronial families which, in the absence of the pope, at that time governed Rome with a view to their own private interests alone. Cola's program was, on the contrary, to establish in Rome a regular and equitable government around which Italy as a whole could be brought together. On two occasions (1347 and 1354) Cola succeeded in seizing power, and with the ancient title of "tribune," he tried to put his policy into practice, with the aid of solemn proclamations and public ceremonies laden with allegories. But when he was rapidly abandoned by Pope Clement VI and the Emperor Charles IV, he succumbed to the nobles' attacks and was massacred by the crowd on 8 October 1354.

In the Western world of the fourteenth and fifteenth centuries, other popular leaders existed, less tragic and less colorful but comparable with Cola, so far as their social situation and their political ambitions are concerned. We will mention here only one, who has been well studied by René Fédou, the notary Jean de Condeyssie, one of the principal figures in the Lyon *Rebeyne* of 1436.[85] A notary who had come to Lyon from neighboring Dombes, lacking a university degree but a good orator, and well-off, thanks to an advantageous marriage, Jean de Condeyssie had nonetheless remained close to people in his profession, among whom he lived and on whose behalf he acted. He had long publicly expressed his attachment to the traditional communal spirit, and it was thus natural that the people of Lyon should call upon him when they rose up against both the royal officials who were trying to impose a new salt tax and against the rich whose cheating on the *taille* (the direct tax) made it necessary to increase consumption taxes. Jean de Condeyssie tried to channel popular anger to force a return to a balanced government in which the professions shared power with the oligarchy of merchants and jurists, who were too docile in their acceptance of royal orders. But this defense of communal freedoms was anachronistic; Charles VII, who could not allow the thwarting of tax measures that were necessary to win the war, had the city militarily occupied and Jean de Condeyssie was arrested along with the other leaders of the *Rebeyne*.

In any case, neither clerics who had become anti-clerical preachers nor notaries acting as improvised popular tribunes could be considered as really representative of their groups. Most of the second-rate educated people who were becoming more numerous at the end of the Middle Ages seem to have been particularly concerned about taking their place in society and rising within it. On the whole, they also zealously sought to put their competencies in the service of the Church or the state.

Parish priests, despite the fact that their preaching was often inadequate, did their best to participate in the educational work of the Church. They helped spread among the faithful a minimum of Christian culture, respect for orthodoxy and for clerics, and the elements of a worldview, generally rather disparate and traditional, that was conveyed through the lives of the saints, collections of *exempla,* and the most common encyclopedias.[86] In the prologue to his *Canterbury Tales* (ca. 1386), Chaucer sketched in the person of a country parson the most sympathetic of the thirty-two pilgrims he presents: this saintly man has not studied at the university, but he cares deeply about the education of his parishioners:

> He was also a lerned man, a clerk,
> That Cristes gospel trewely wolde preche;
> His parisshens devoutly wolde he teche.[87]

And as he exemplifies his words, he constantly advances the kingdom of God on earth.

For their part, the lay schoolteachers, in spite of the variations in their quality, inculcated a larger part of the population than was long believed with the rudiments of reading and even writing.

Finally, men of law, subordinate royal officials and notaries were effective agents of the modernization and strengthening of the state. What good would it have been, after all, for the doctors to revive Roman law had the notaries not reintroduced it into practical documents? What good would the Parlement's decisions and royal regulations have been, had there not been sergeants to proclaim and execute them? In spite of individual failures and brutalities that the people bore with difficulty, these men greatly contributed to the imposition throughout the land of the rule of law and to the omnipresence of the state's justice and sovereignty. Thanks to them, the notions of fidelity to the prince, obedience to the state, and the primacy of *bonum commune* even if it came at the expense of ancestral "freedoms" and the pretensions of local potentates, gradually became established in custom, along with a reverential fear of the monarch combined with the certainty that one could always appeal to the supreme authority.

The more modest men of learning I am talking about here played this role all the more willingly because, like the graduates of the university and the main royal officials, they found it in their and their families' interest. Some of them marked their general association with the world of the educated by showing intellectual curiosity that went far beyond the knowledge strictly necessary for their "practice" alone. We have already mentioned the extensive historical and juridical readings made by Cola di Rienzo and his humanist relationships. While many of them possessed only the few technical works necessary for their profession, others had libraries that could rival those of the graduates. The impressive list of 136 titles left by Richard de Bazoques, a modest Norman schoolteacher at the beginning of the fifteenth century, no doubt corresponds more to a sort of "ideal library" than to an inventory of the books he actually possessed or even had read,[88] but it testifies at least to his very up-to-date acquaintance with bibliography and to his appetite for knowledge. Others actually owned sizable libraries. The inventories of Sicilian books show the collection of twenty-five books owned by Niccolo da Rabuazio, a schoolteacher in Termini, as well as the decent little libraries of a few notaries: about twenty volumes on average, and as many as eighty-eight in the case of Stefano da Avillino in 1449, a notary of Messina who owned not only books on law, but also sermons and chronicles, a volume by Dante and another by Thomas Aquinas.[89]

Some of these men even rose to the level of authors. The best attorneys, and in England, the "common lawyers" educated in the Inns of Court produced practical "questions" (like those of Jean le Coq, an attorney at the Parlement of Paris from 1370 to 1400)[90] and treatises on procedure that were a useful supplement to the compendia and learned commentaries of the doctors on the faculties of law. In these works they showed both a genuine knowledge and an attention to contemporary problems, and even a sensitivity to the difficulties of humble people that corresponds well to their intermediary social situation. André Gouron has thus brought to light the modest but exemplary figure of Pierre Antiboul (?–before 1357). After studying in Montpellier, this *jurisperit* set himself up as a lawyer in Draguignan, and it was there that he wrote, in the 1340s, his *Treatise on Taxes* (*Tractatus de muneribus*). Based on both a solid knowledge of scholarly authors and experience with the concrete situations of his time, Antiboul's *Tractatus* is a vigorous plea for equality in taxation, a well-argued criticism of unjustified tax exemptions and the privileges of the aristocracy, as well as the brutalities perpetrated by officials. On the whole, it is, as André Gouron puts it, the work of a practitioner sensitive "to rural poverty and the social injustices of the time," which Antiboul attributes to the "shortcomings of the Provençal nobility and its servants . . . [as well as] certain practitioners of the time who have been accused of incompetence."[91] For all that, Pierre Antiboul was not a revolutionary or a demagogic popular leader (or at least he did not have the opportunity to become one); the more just political order to which he aspired he expected to be realized by more effective action by the prince—in this case the count of Provence. In other words, he expected it to be realized through a strengthening of the state, not by overturning social hierarchies.

At an obviously far more elevated level, but from an ultimately comparable point of view—that of a modernizing reformism favorable to the growth of the state—we may note that the greatest English jurist and publicist of the end of the Middle Ages, Sir John Fortescue (ca. 1390–ca. 1479), the author of the famous *De laudibus legum Anglie* and *The Governance of England*, had been trained at Lincoln's Inn (one of the four main Inns of Court) in London, and not at Oxford or Cambridge. Moreover, he had long practiced as a sergeant-at-law and an investigator before he took his seat on the King's Bench.[92]

This aspiration to a more and more formalized knowledge, approaching the dignity of university disciplines but retaining a more practical and more modern style (here, the texts are often in the vernacular), is particularly clear among the surgeons of the end of the Middle Ages. Schools of surgery of a kind seem to have existed at the end of the Middle Ages, at least within the orbit of the Italian faculties of medicine: their existence in Paris or in Montpellier is more doubtful. Some surgeons wrote treatises that were to have a real success, the best known being Henri de Mondeville, whose *Chirurgia* (ca. 1306) was rapidly translated into French, Provençal, English, German, and other languages.

Cultural advancement, and also social advancement. The difference in wealth among the various categories of the men of learning was not necessarily very great, for if teaching or service to God or the prince were incontestably sources of prestige, and to some extent a guarantee of stability, they were not always well remunerated. Conversely, if some men of learning vegetated in private practice, others, who had succeeded in acquiring a fine clientele, making an advantageous marriage, or supplementing their professional income with other revenues drawn from land or commerce, sometimes achieved real affluence.

Some attorneys were very rich. Jean le Coq, whom we have already mentioned, was a noble and possessed, in addition to his real estate revenues, at least five seigniories and two fiefs around Paris, plus a mansion and two or three other houses in the capital itself. Moreover, for these well-off attorneys it was not difficult to gain access to the more respected world of officials. Although not many of the attorneys who appeared before the Parlement in Paris or Toulouse seem to have become councilors on the supreme court itself, they did often serve as judges on less important tribunals.

The careers of some Florentine jurists were just as remarkable. From his *Ricordanze*, we know that around 1407 Ricciardo di Francesco del Bene (ca. 1369–1411) earned 350 florins from his practice, or if we add the salaries received for a few public offices and the income from his houses and lands, 500 to 600 florins; let us recall for the sake of comparison that at this time the net profit of the Florentine bank of the Medicis was no more than 1100 florins. Though Ricciardo was not reputed to be an exceptional jurist, belonging to an old family firmly established in the Florentine oligarchy, he had been able to build up a fine clientele.[93]

Among the notaries one can find, alongside needy scriveners, men of considerable wealth, comparable to the most well-off men of law and merchants. In Toulouse, for example, according to the 1335 *registre d'estime*, the fortune of the thirty-five notaries ranged from 30 to 934 *livres tournois*, which placed the richest of them at the level of the great merchants.[94] In Saint-Flour, in 1380, Durand Saysset, a simple notary without a university degree who had hardly left his office during a long, laborious life, led all the other men of law with 1,575 *livres* in real estate patrimony, and his fortune was exceeded by those of only two merchants.[95]

When they did not succeed in rising by themselves, through titles or through wealth, to the level of the graduates, great officials or prelates, the practitioners could at least expect to realize their ambition through their children. In the next chapter we will discuss these processes of social ascension, but we can already point out that the frequency of this kind of ascent from practitioner to official, over one or two generations, was such that we must certainly see in it a classical line of social promotion. The sons of notaries and prosecutors not only had paternal subsidies to help them along the way to studies and honors, but also had the benefit, because of their origins, of an embryonic library, some connections, and a certain familiarity with intellectual disciplines; in short, they had a minimum of "social and cultural capital" that surely gave them an advantage in relation to other newcomers.[96]

It could be said that this amounted to a kind of promotion within the group of men of learning itself. The existence and frequency of this kind of ascent show the cohesion, the dynamism, and the openness of this group. It was clearly possible to come into it at other levels. Some people went directly to the university, got diplomas, and became prelates or important officials. Conversely, others who were among the most modest of the practitioners did not succeed in making the decisive step up, or in having their children do so, with the result that they remained at the bottom of the ladder, or even moved out of the group and returned to the world of craftsmanship or commerce. But what was essential was the continuity established around a number of common cultural practices.

There may well have been occasional renegade priests, demagogic lawyers, bitter prosecutors, and notaries who had remained close to popular milieus, who were ready to put their competencies in the service of a criticism that was more or less subversive of the established order. However, in the majority of cases men of learning, at whatever level they are considered, were much more likely to feel that they could best assert themselves by accepting their integrating role. They were called upon to play an essential role in the new society that was constituting itself in place of the old feudal society. Everywhere, even in the little towns and remote countryside, they were setting up networks of supervision and obedience that allowed the princes, the cities, and the Church to impose the juridical order that was their very raison d'être. Without them, that is, without their voluntary collaboration and their daily, multiform activity, the emerging modern state would not have had the means to make itself accepted and obeyed—or even known. In the new processes of social and political regulation at the end of the Middle Ages, the men of learning sided with the élites, and it was incontestably toward the élites that most of them aspired.

But at the same time, the existence of this large stratum of "intermediary intellectuals" who ensured communication and provided the transition between the superior order of the state and ordinary subjects, kept men of learning from being merely a narrow caste of mandarins or priests, cut off from the rest of society and subject only to the caprices of the prince or of their own selfish goals. It was they, Henry of Ghent's *doctores rurales*, who established the place of the upper categories of the educated and allowed them to take their place in society by giving them a sufficiently broad and open foundation. Moreover, it was they who undertook, in an empirical manner, the diffusion, the concrete and everyday adaptation, and, on the whole, the almost consensual if not unanimous reception of theoretical knowledge, on the basis of which the new rules of the social and political game were developed.

PART III

Social Realities
and Self-Image

---•◦•---

The first part of this book offered a definition of men of learning in the Western world at the end of the Middle Ages, while the second part examined the roles their intellectual expertise allowed them to play in the societies of their time. The performance of these roles was itself part of the social and political dynamics of the general transformations of this time. These were new roles that had not existed (at least not in the same way and with the same significance) in earlier centuries. Those who occupied them created them and gave them form by occupying them.

But if the roles were new, were the men also new? Did their appearance on the social scene correspond to a general ascension and renewal? Did the cultural transformations and the emergence of previously unknown or little-developed roles permit individuals or families from the popular and middle levels of society to rise in the social hierarchy and force the old élites to accept them and even to yield positions to them? Or was there simply a functional conversion of these old élites (which had in any case never been wholly closed) and an adaptation and modernization that guaranteed the continuity of the hierarchies?

It is easy to see that in practice both solutions must have been adopted in varying percentages depending on the time and place. We will attempt to determine these in Chapter VII. But just as important as the raw data of social mechanics are the representations of oneself and of others that accompanied the phenomena of ascension and transformation (Chapter VIII). What was the image of the men of learning at the end of the Middle Ages? Did it retain the mark of their sometimes obscure origins? An indelible clerical stamp? Did it don, in order to make people forget its newness, the bright colors of the old nobility? Or were men of learning not yet able to distinguish themselves from the rest of society, to make themselves seen for what they were, a new and complex component of society with its own way of living, speaking, and thinking, its *habitus* and its values, that is, a consciousness of itself and of its historical role?

CHAPTER VII

New Men or Heirs?

The problem of the social origin of the men of learning at the end of the Middle Ages seems at first to be a simple one in which difficulties arise chiefly from a lack of adequate documentation. In reality, it also raises theoretical issues that we must immediately address.

1. Questions of Sources and Method

If the problem of the origin of men of learning comes up, it is because they clearly constitute a new group that was rapidly expanding over the last centuries of the Middle Ages, performing functions that had themselves arisen from the modernization of the state, the centralization of the Church, progress in culture, and more generally, the growing complexity of society and the economy. The men entrusted with these new functions had to come from somewhere, in other words, from the oldest social groups.

In actuality, as we have already seen, it is impossible to measure with precision the rhythm and the amplitude of the growth of the group of men of learning, which moreover must have varied considerably depending on time and place. Contemporaries were aware of this growth but they probably tended to exaggerate it. To limit ourselves to one of the cases about which we are best informed, that of royal officials in France, historical investigations seem to show that there were two phases of sustained growth in their number at the end of the Middle Ages, first between 1250 and 1314 (thus coinciding with the birth of the modern state, from St. Louis to Philip the Fair), and then during the second half of the fifteenth century, the period of "reconstruction" and the strengthening of royal power after the Hundred Years' War. However, between these two phases there seems to have been—despite the ritual denunciation, every time there was a political crisis, of the "infinite multitude" of officials—almost a stagnation, at least in absolute numbers (for this stagnation did not prevent a relatively large increase at the same time that the overall population of the kingdom diminished almost by half because of epidemics).[1]

The difficulties in determining the social origin of the men of learning (who were still largely churchmen and thus could not simply reproduce themselves as a group in a hereditary manner) are those of any kind of demographic or social research on the Middle Ages. There is no lack of documents that allow us to identify the parents of the clerics and educated laymen we are studying here. In Mediterranean countries, the multiple contracts, inventories, and wills contained in notarial sources yield abundant information concerning family links. Letters and pontifical petitions, tax rolls, judicial archives, lists of titles and pensions, etc., provide similar information. But apart from the fact that the collection of this information with a view to constituting prosopographical dictionaries, which are now computerized, is a very long-term project that has to date produced only very partial results, it may well remain difficult if not impossible to base a genuinely quantitative procedure on them, especially when it is extended over a long time.

In fact, the sources I have just mentioned, even when they are not incomplete, are rarely serial; they usually produce no more than photographic snapshots at isolated dates. In other words, they permit us to measure approximately the range of possible origins from the most popular to the most aristocratic. Diverse cases can be illustrated by more or less striking examples. But we are hardly in a position to evaluate the respective proportion of each social category and even less their respective development over time.

The incompleteness of the documentation is not the only issue here. It is likely that most of the sources, depending on their nature, privilege a given type of social origin. Overall, the powerful and the rich are obviously the most likely to appear in the documentation, or in any case, not to remain simple names but individuals who can be identified and connected with families known through their history or their economic situation. Thus men of learning of noble birth, whom we will discuss later, can usually be identified, while for other social categories both urban and rural the evidence is so aleatory that it is difficult to subject it to statistical analysis.

To this we must obviously add—and this is a general difficulty—that the "social" vocabulary used by medieval sources refers to legal status more than to professional or economic categories. For example, records in the archives of German universities in the fifteenth century divide students into "rich" (*divites*) and "poor" (*pauperes*); but in fact these terms did not refer to a social classification, which would in any case have remained very vague. It was simply a question of distinguishing students who were able to pay their tuition in the usual way from those who, because of their alleged and perhaps entirely temporary poverty, were exempt from paying tuition. There were, moreover, *semipauperes* (and *semidivites*); these were students who had obtained only a reduced tuition fee or the right to delay payment. It is clear that it would be risky to derive from such a classification any precise clues regarding the origin of the graduates of German universities.[2]

Let us also mention the ambiguity or polysemy of certain words current in medieval social vocabulary, such as *burgensis, magister,* and *clericus*.[3] And, as we will see, the very notion of nobility, which often did not distinguish between old and new nobility, hereditary status and acquired notability, is tricky to use. On the whole, then, it seems that the social history of the groups of educated medieval men remains open to many uncertainties.

We should mention here a final difficulty, one that concerns not vocabulary but method. The historian has a tendency to adopt as his starting point the individuals that he is studying, taken in themselves, and to define them socially by situating them in relation to their ancestors or their direct descendents. He hopes in this way to grasp the dynamics of social ascent or reproduction, or the progressive social decline of certain groups that are poorly adapted to their time. However, especially when highly integrated societies like those of the end of the Middle Ages are concerned, it is in fact the whole of the family structures that should be taken into account, and in particular the collateral branches—uncles, brothers, cousins—and their affiliated lineages.

The rise of the son of an artisan to join the ranks of the men of learning had differing meanings, depending on whether or not he had a relative who was a priest and was able to lend him books or recommend him to his bishop. Similarly, when the passage of a merchant's son into the world of officials and men of law marked the abandonment of the former family vocation it had a different meaning than when the new jurist was simply a youngest child who had chosen to study, whereas his brothers continued to devote themselves to commerce and business. Many additional examples of this kind could be given. We cannot fail to mention the problem that they raise, but it is clear that they make the historian's task difficult, since taking the whole of family relations into account puts a considerable burden on prosopographical research and makes even more aleatory the hope of arriving at quantifiable results.

Moreover, the family itself is doubtless an insufficient unit. In actuality, we would have to try to reinsert it into the multiple networks of neighborhoods and clienteles that structured all medieval societies. Let us return to our example of the son of an artisan whose studies allowed him to rise to an honorable position among men of learning. Today, we would be tempted to interpret this promotion as a good example of success on the basis of merit, made possible by the relatively open structures that were preserved until the end of the Middle Ages by educational institutions such as the universities. This would probably be an anachronistic view. For in reality there was every likelihood that this artisan's son—whatever his intellectual gifts and character—would have been able to pursue studies only because, as I mentioned earlier, he may have had an uncle who was a priest, and still more likely, because his family, no matter how modest, was within the sphere of influence of a powerful abbey, or because his father was a protégé and perhaps a hired hand of some important person.

For example, it is striking how many medieval colleges recruited their members, not only from the family of the founder, but also from the two or three villages specifically designated (and from which the founder came, or of which he might even be the lord). Thus places were reserved for the children of Saint-Pierre de Nazac (in the diocese of Cahors) in the college founded in Toulouse in 1341 by the archbishop of Arles, Gasbert de Laval, and places were reserved for the children of Dormans (diocese of Soissons) in the college founded in Paris in 1370 by Cardinal Jean de Dormans; neither prelate forgot the children of his less fortunate compatriots. As for the college of Pélegry (Cahors), it was largely intended to educate little grammarians born on the very lands bequeathed to this college by the founders, Hugues and Raymond de Pélegry (1365).[4] It is clear that the sons of peasants in these villages had far greater chances of going to a university than did those of equal wealth and ability in the neighboring villages.

There is no point in multiplying this kind of hypotheses, which are in no way theoretical. The preceding ones will suffice, I think, to show that many different parameters might be involved in the social mechanics of the end of the Middle Ages. The interpretation of this mechanics is thus a delicate matter, and in any case may well long defy statistical analysis. Therefore in the following pages I have for the most part limited myself to a few qualitative and descriptive notations.

2. The Path of Study

The idea that study had to be accessible to all and that through it worthy poor students ought to be able to rise to high offices in the service of God or the prince was not alien to the last centuries of the Middle Ages. Various university regulations, papal bulls, and royal commandments echo this conviction. In 1224, Emperor Frederick II promised wealth (*lucrum*), nobility (*nobilitas*) and influential connections (*amicitiarum favor*) to all those who came to study law in the *studium* in Naples.[5] In

1336, Pope Benedict XII reproached the doctors of Montpellier for discouraging poor but competent and worthy students who legitimately aspired to reach *ad altiora* by requiring them to pay excessive examination fees.[6]

Confirming this idea in their own way, certain authors of romances and chronicles who were in the service of the upper nobility expressed indignation that people "of humble extraction" (*de petite estrace*) had been able to attract royal favor and occupy places in the king's service that normally devolved upon representatives of the greatest and most ancient families of the realm. In his *Chronique métrique* (ca. 1316), the poet Geoffroy de Paris put these words in the mouths of Philip the Fair's barons:

> We have been overthrown
> By commoners and [Jewish] converts,
> Puny people who have come
> Masters at the court to become,
> . . . .
> At court our right is not respected.
> Serfs, villeins, petty lawyers,
> Have become imperial."

> *Nous sommes versez a revers*
> *Et par vilains et par convers,*
> *Chetive gent qui sont venuz,*
> *Cum a court mestre devenuz,*
> *. . . . .*
> *A la court ne nous fait on droit.*
> *Sers, vilains, avocateriaus*
> *Sont devenuz emperïaus.*[7]

The "debate between the cleric and the knight," a literary genre that goes back to the twelfth century, retained all its pertinence at the end of the Middle Ages. In the works of courtly authors, the knight, thanks to his strength, his loyalty, and his courage, generally came out the victor in this debate, as did for instance the hero of Antoine de la Sale's *Petit Jehan de Saintré* (ca. 1456), a pure product of the chivalric, courtly milieu, when confronted by the machinations of the "Seigneur Abbé." But it is evident that these literary compensations scarcely concealed many disappointments in the reality of concrete existence. And in our period, the parvenus denounced in this way were not only worldly prelates or bawdy monks, but also and especially glib students and tricky lawyers (like Maître Pathelin in the well-known farce)—in short, doctors, proud of their diplomas and their knowledge and convinced that they were henceforth indispensable to the proper functioning of the state.

Social ambition was unquestionably one of the most common motivations of those who began a course of study. The very notion of general and disinterested culture was, as we mentioned earlier, rather foreign to men of this time, as was the notion that travel to study might be not only an instrument of intellectual and professional education but also an opportunity to shape one's character and at the same time enrich one's memory with images of the places visited and the people met. Those who took the trouble to make a serious study of scholarly disciplines and fully recognized the arid character of this apprenticeship were convinced of both the prestige and social and political usefulness of this kind of studies, and they intended to derive from it the maximum advantage for themselves while also benefiting those close to them, who had often helped pay for their studies. Especially in modest families, putting a child through school must have been a difficult task to which everyone contributed as best he could.

There is no lack of examples of social ascents, some of them spectacular, by means of education and diplomas. Without mentioning all those about whose families we know nothing at all (which must indicate in many cases that they were of modest status), let us simply recall here a few classical examples. The two great English theologians and prelates of the beginning of the thirteenth century, Stephen Langton and Robert Grosseteste, were the sons of peasants, and perhaps of serfs. In France, Robert de Sorbon came from a similar origin, and a century and a half later, so did the future chancellor Jean Gerson. As for Cardinal Nicholas of Cusa (1401–1464), his father was a humble boatman on the Moselle.

We should note that these are theologians whose successful careers were essentially ecclesiastical. We could, however, find analogous examples, though perhaps less remarkable and less numerous, among jurists and physicians. Nicolas de Baye (ca. 1364–1419), a humanistic court clerk at the Parlement of Paris toward the end of the fifteenth century, was the son of a serf and had gone to the College of Dormans. His contemporary Robert Mauger, the Parlement's presiding chairman from 1413 to 1418, also studied at Dormans and was also of humble birth.[8] As for the great physician Guy de Chauliac (ca. 1300–1368), who treated three popes in Avignon, tradition maintains that in his youth he was a simple farm servant in Gévaudan. These are, in spite of all, exceptional cases. But there are more common family trajectories that are just as significant.

Let us take the example of the Pastons. This family from southeast England (the region of Norwich) left a remarkable collection of more than a thousand letters, written between 1440 and 1490, that allow us to follow its rise in society over four generations.[9] At the beginning, we find a free and well-off peasant who bears the name of his native village, Clement Paston. He had only one son, William Paston (1378–1444), and was able to send him to study law in an Inn of Court. Thanks to his competence in law, while managing the land he inherited from his father and other lands he himself bought, William had a successful career as a man of law (in the service of the duke of Norfolk and the bishop of Norwich) and a royal official. He ended up in London, at the Court of Common Pleas; he is buried in the Norwich cathedral. In the following generation, what had been only an individual success became a family vocation. William Paston's four sons followed the same course of study, first in the faculty of arts at Cambridge and then in an Inn of Court in London (clearly preferred to university law schools). Two of these jurists died young and unmarried, but the two others had careers similar to their father's; they were successively or simultaneously legal counselors to great lords and royal officials. Their social ascent continued, however, because the masters they served were increasingly high-placed and, with the help of good fortune, their landed property grew more extensive. John (1421–1466) inherited a large part of the land of his master, the famous captain Sir John Fastolf, while his brother William, Jr. (1436–1496), married the daughter of an important aristocratic family and had a seat in Parliament.

In the fourth generation, represented essentially by John's seven children, they had basically arrived, and the family destiny took diverse courses. The family had fully entered the aristocracy, since two of the sons were knighted; they attended the court and managed their manors; they were also military men who took part in battles in the War of the Roses, thereby exposing themselves to the dangers of the civil war—but without too many losses. Only one son remained a pure jurist in the tradition of his father and grandfather. Two others died young; one had been intended for the university and the Church. As for the daughters, while one of them married a simple agricultural steward, who was nevertheless very well-off, the other married the scion of a fine line of jurists very comparable to the Pastons themselves. In the sixteenth century, the Pastons gave up law and offices altogether, becoming major landholders in Norfolk; in the seventeenth century they were granted the title of counts of Yarmouth.

Obviously, several factors combined to make this exemplary success possible, and it is clear that these men (and their wives, who managed the family property when their husbands were away on business or were sitting in Parliament) lacked neither character nor intelligence. But it is no less clear that it was their competence as jurists and hence their study of law that provided the continuity of their social ascent over two and even three generations.

The history of the Pastons is remarkable in still another respect. It was not their service as royal officials alone that explains their success, even if London and the court attracted them like magnets. Although they lived at the time of the Wars of the Roses, that is, at a time of crisis for the English monarchy, it was surely not solely for that reason that they always combined service to the prince with service to one great lord or another. Their fidelity to these local potentates was moreover not always complete; but it is certain that they did not imagine that they could succeed in either the sphere of the central government or that of their native Norfolk without attaching themselves to an aristocratic clientele or clan.

Thus the history of the Paston family does not in any way contradict the results of more general investigations that have occasionally been made regarding the social origin of physicians, prelates, or officials at the end of the Middle Ages. Among both the men of law in Lyon studied by R. Fédou and the canons of Laon studied by Hélène Millet, we also see the importance of the processes of social ascent—the great majority of these men were of obscure or at least modest origin—and the decisive role played by family relationships, relationships with clienteles, and diplomas. In Laon, the decline in the number of canons coming from the old nobility (from 26 percent to 5 percent between the beginning of the fourteenth century and the beginning of the fifteenth) is exactly symmetrical with the rise of the graduates (whose proportion rises from 43 percent to 86 percent of the canons over the same period).[10]

Until the end of the fifteenth century, these diverse groups always remained open to a certain percentage of newcomers who were of relatively modest origins but held university degrees. This kind of social ascent was of little benefit, however, to isolated individuals who came, as it were, from nowhere. In order to claim to take an honorable place among men of learning, especially outside the clergy proper, it was always necessary to meet certain preconditions.

Belonging to a clientele or at least being close to an effective network of relationships was one of these preconditions. Access to a minimum of financial resources was another. When the family's resources were insufficient, and the person involved did not—or not yet—hold a college scholarship or an ecclesiastical benefice or a remunerated office, he might expect subsidies from a protector or patron. Since the thirteenth century the kings of France and England themselves had not disdained to make gifts to a few students. But traditionally it was either someone connected with the Church or an important governmental official, both of whom were usually graduates themselves, who proved most generous in assuming the burden of supporting a few young protégés.[11]

In any case, a certain basic sum of money was necessary to pay for the university studies without which access to the upper strata of the world of men of learning was almost impossible. This explains why here as elsewhere social ascent often took place in several steps. Frequently, as we pointed out in the preceding chapter, the first step was represented by becoming a notary. This was the case for at least 17 percent of the new families of men of law that appeared in Florence after 1350,[12] and without giving figures, R. Fédou estimates that jurists in Lyon at the end of the Middle Ages "came for the most part from obscure families of notaries from outside the city itself." If we can believe the genealogical trees he has reconstructed for several families, the speed of the ascent was not always the same; it took the Garbot family three generations and the Palmier family two generations to move from being notaries to being doctors of laws and judicial officials; on the other hand, the Aurillac and Bullioud families required only one generation to make the same shift. Success was not, however, always achieved, even within a single family. The example of the Bellièvres, another well-known family of officials in Lyon, is significant: of Antoine Bellièvre's two sons, Hugonin gave rise only to a long line of notaries, while Barthélemy pursued studies in law that allowed his sons and grandsons to take seats on the archbishop of Lyon's tribunal and then in the Parlement of Grenoble, of which Claude and then Jean Bellièvre became presiding chairman; finally, as a supreme success, Pomponne de Bellièvre, Barthélemy's great-grandson, became chancellor of France at the beginning of the seventeenth century.[13]

As the preceding reference to R. Fédou suggested, we cannot completely separate social mobility from geographical mobility. Men of learning, especially those who were particularly competent, were naturally concentrated in national or regional capital cities, whether on the political or administrative level or on the religious or cultural level. Conversely, apart from the most modest of them—parish priests, notaries, barbers, sergeants—they were rare if not totally absent in small villages and towns.

Traveling to study often represented the first phase of this mobility. Some remained in the town where they studied and pursued their careers there, establishing a new family line. Take, for example, Hélie Brolhet, who is well known because of a kind of private cartulary preserved in the archives of the department of Haute-Garonne (E 12005–53). He came from his native Limousin to study in Toulouse with a scholarship from the College of Périgord, earned his doctorate of laws, and in the first half of the fifteenth century became one of the city's principal attorneys. His two sons studied law in Toulouse as well. This was still a relatively common kind of migration that led talented youths from the poor lands in the southern Massif Central to go south to the large cities of Languedoc. More spectacular was certainly the adventure of the Pomeranian Jacques Rothschild, known as "Angeli" (1390–1455). He came from the distant diocese of Cammin to study medicine in Montpellier, and succeeded so well that he took up residence there, became a professor, and then, for more than twenty years, served as chancellor of the university. He married and gave rise to a distinguished line of jurists and physicians in Montpellier.[14] Any number of such examples could be given.

Others emigrated to take possession of an office. Even simple teachers in the grammar schools often came from outside, and sometimes from very far away. In Aix-en-Provence, none of the teachers we know about at the end of the Middle Ages were from the town or even the diocese.[15] We must moreover add that in certain offices, both lay and ecclesiastical, rapid rotations related to promotions or disgraces were the rule: the Avignon popes constantly shifted their bishops from one see to another and the king of France moved his bailiffs and seneschals around almost as quickly. We can thus see why many men of learning often appeared to be newcomers in cities, poorly connected and outside the traditional solidarities of the old families of notables. At the end of the fifteenth century, that was still one of the main complaints made by the merchants of Montpellier in their suit against the jurists and notaries of the town for refusing them access to the consulate.[16]

3. Shifting Social Status, Adaptation, Reproduction

While it is certain that until the end of the Middle Ages the world of men of learning, which in any case varied greatly from one country to another, was one of the most flexible and open milieus in medieval society, it nonetheless tended, like all the groups constituting the élite at this time, to close in upon itself and to become a hereditary caste. This tendency—which was, moreover, always incomplete—ended up producing in the fourteenth and *a fortiori* in the fifteenth centuries veritable dynasties of physicians and particularly of jurists, who reinforced each other by allying themselves through multiple intermarriages. We can follow these dynasties over several generations. The period of colleagues was succeeded by that of heirs, and *esprit de famille* was added to *esprit de corps*.

However, this "reproduction," which was after all rather common, is not the most interesting aspect of the social history of medieval educated men. To the extent to which these men made an increasingly important place for themselves at the end of the Middle Ages, we may ask whether this new group was not constituted at least in part by the shift in social status among the traditional élites, who were concerned to perpetuate their ancient primacy despite economic, political, and cultural changes.

Prosopographical research has brought to light at least two types of recruitment by lateral or at least oblique "slippage" rather than by ascent. The first case is that of men of learning who came from merchant families in the broad sense of the term. This classical process has often been described and is generally explained by merchants' desire, especially in the shrunken economy of the late Middle Ages, to ensure that their children would have, if not greater wealth, at least a more stable and honorable position that might even constitute a first step toward ennoblement. It would be easy to give examples; let us mention only one, that of the Le Viste family, jurists who at the beginning of the fifteenth century were the richest family in Lyon, before moving up to Paris. They descended from Barthélemy Le Viste, a draper who died around 1340.[17]

However, in addition to the fact that in the Middle Ages people may not have moved from commerce to study and to offices as often as is sometimes said, the examples mentioned suggest that certain qualifications have to be made in the description of the process. First of all, the move from commerce proper to education was often preceded by an intermediary stage, that of being entrusted with financial tasks and offices that already made it possible to approach, if not the world of knowledge, at least that of service to the prince and public power. We may cite the exemplary case of the Ysalguier family in Toulouse analyzed by Philippe Wolff.[18] Money changers and merchants at the end of the thirteenth century, the Ysalguier became councilors of the seneschal and royal tax collectors at the beginning of the fourteenth century. This allowed them to obtain titles of nobility. During the second half of the century they were able to go to the university; we find Ysalguiers taking degrees in law. They combined service to the king with service to their city as magistrates (*capitouls*). Unfortunately for them, the Ysalguiers gave up this path too soon; from the beginning of the fifteenth century on, military adventures tempted some of them to get involved in the last battles of the Hundred Years' War, while others preferred to play the role of landed gentry on fiefs that were so poorly managed that they led them into bankruptcy in the second half of the fifteenth century.

A second indispensable point is that giving up commerce for administrative or ecclesiastical careers was not general, either overall—many families remained faithful to their earlier vocation—or even among the families concerned. If the Le Viste family seems to have all at once abandoned commercial activity in order to specialize in education and offices, in other families, over several generations either in collateral family lines or among siblings, we find both lawyers and businessmen. The genealogies of some important Provençal families reconstituted by Noël Coulet show this clearly:[19] in fifteenth-century Aix-en-Provence, depending on the year, between 20 and 40 percent of the jurists married merchants' daughters and a fourth of their own children also became merchants. We therefore cannot generalize cases like that of fifteenth-century Poitiers, a city where the dominance of religious, university, and administrative functions to the detriment of economic activity allowed men of law not only to gain virtually complete control of the municipal government but also to gradually eliminate the great merchants from the urban oligarchy.[20]

The other kind of slippage, within the social élites themselves, from the earlier positions toward the new ones offered by education and intellectual competences, requires more nuanced description. The movement in question is the one that occurred within the nobility itself, and the complexity of the notion of nobility makes analysis difficult.

Things are relatively simple when one can show that a given man of learning was the heir of an ancient "feudal" lineage of unquestioned nobility and age. The famous theologian Giles of Rome (ca. 1247–1316) belonged to the most illustrious family of the Roman aristocracy, that of the Colonnas, whereas the counts of Aquino from whom St. Thomas descended were of almost equally venerable nobility in the kingdom of Sicily. But such cases are relatively rare and ultimately not very significant, for they concern only a few isolated youngest sons who were in any event expected, according to ancestral custom, to pursue an ecclesiastical career.

It is doubtless more appropriate to examine men of learning who were connected with "old families," as did Lauro Martines in his book on the Florentine men of law at the end of the Middle Ages. Martines arbitrarily chose the date 1350 as the dividing line between "old" and "new" families, the former's existence being documentable before that date, while the latter, who were themselves divided into indigenous families and families that came from the *contado*, appeared only later on.[21] This criterion allowed Martines to calculate that the proportion of Florentine jurists who were of ancient if not aristocratic origin was about 40 percent.

But this figure and Martines' method itself have only a relative value because they concentrate on a single date an evolution that was in reality gradual and continuous. In fact, among the men of learning there was always a certain proportion of "nobles." Some of them so identified themselves because the exercise of their office itself authorized them to do so, either because they had been officially ennobled, or because they were granted a sort of spontaneous social recognition attached to the dignity of their function.[22] Others were noble because their ancestors had been nobles for a relatively long time; in the Middle Ages there were many ways to gain nobility or at least to be recognized as noble. In addition to the old manor-house or chivalric nobility there were those whom the acquisition of seigniories or service to the prince had allowed, *de facto* or *de jure*, to call themselves nobles, to adopt the nobles' way of life, and to claim the corresponding privileges. In certain regions, especially in Mediterranean Europe, the urban patricians—that is, the segment of the urban population that was the most ancient, most stable, and closest in its way of life to knightly milieus—were put on the same level.

Some of these aristocratic or patrician families remained stubbornly faithful to their ancient military or landowning vocation. But in others access to the world of knowledge through study ended up happening quite rapidly, and once the habit was established it was rarely lost. Henceforth, continuity in the kind of education and culture was easily transformed into continuity in the types of careers pursued. Whether or not the earning of a university diploma and the acquisition of a judicial office were the first step, what was soon to be called the *noblesse de robe* thus constituted itself to the advantage of those who held superior intellectual competences, and who were defined by these competences far more than by the antiquity or newness of their nobility.

It would therefore be an oversimplification to speak only of the social ascension of new men or the shift in social status of old "feudal" families. In fact, there was a gradual, general adaptation of the social élites to the changes in the culture and the state through the conjunction of the ancient idea of nobility and the increased prestige of new civil and scholarly ways of serving the prince or the Church.

From then on, the great families of officials naturally tended to perpetuate themselves in their dominant position, but the self-assertion of this group in the Middle Ages was never based on its strict biological reproduction. Even if they were a little narrower, doors still remained open to new men who were late in entering the upper strata of the world of knowledge but all the more eager to join it. The blockage of careers, the constitution of the world of the men of learning in narrow hereditary castes, and the often condemned corollary, the social exclusiveness of fifteenth-century universities—all this is a historians' myth that recent research tends to refute.

The analysis we have sketched of these rather complex social phenomena is based in particular on the exemplary case of the members of the Parlement of Paris, the subject of a fine study by Françoise Autrand.[23] However, it does not seem to me to be contradicted by research on other groups of the same kind in the main European countries at the end of the Middle Ages. For example, the significant rise of the title of "gentleman" among the lay personnel of the principal administrative offices of the English Crown in the time of Henry V (1413–1422) and Henry VI (1422–1471) has been noted.[24]

However, if the processes were occasionally comparable, their chronology, as well as the respective places of the newcomers and the scions of ancient families who came from already solidly established lines of knights or doctors, varied according to the level, the period, and the country in question. In heavily urbanized zones where there were ancient scholarly networks, for example in Mediterranean countries, studies were pursued by the chivalric nobility early on, as all studies on the Italian and Provençal jurists of the twelfth and thirteenth centuries show.[25]

Conversely, in the countries of the Empire and in central Europe—where structures were more archaic and until the end of the Middle Ages the old aristocracy retained control over access to important political positions and even to scholarly culture, because the latter was still connected with lengthy and expensive travel to study—the place of new men among men of learning, who were in any case less numerous than elsewhere, long remained subject to strict quotas. Around 1400, scarcely 5 percent of the students in universities in the south of France were nobles, whereas at the same time 18 percent of the members of the "German nation" at the university of Bologna were nobles, and 25 percent of the identifiable graduates from the diocese of Liège.[26]

Yet these are still only students, that is, beginners with differing ambitions and achievements. But the world of men of learning was, as we have seen, very hierarchized. The closer one comes to the dominant positions, the more the proportion of those who call themselves nobles—whether their nobility was ancient or recent—increases. In the fifteenth century, it was almost expected in France that all the councilors in the Parlement, whatever their origin, were noble, the tensions naturally remaining high within their group depending on the relative antiquity of each councilor's nobility. Conversely, when we descend to more modest levels, nobles are rarely found, both because the sons of ancient families generally disdained these positions, which they considered insufficiently honorable, and because the holders of these offices could not derive enough prestige from them to provide a basis for their own pretensions to nobility.

We are thus once again brought back to the observation that the social position of the men of learning was less a function of their origin than of the value set upon their competence and on their political role. This was a complex play of images and representations that authorized the promotions that benefited certain people, while making changes and adaptations easier for others. Thus it is logical that we should devote the last chapter of this book to the "social image-repertory" (*imaginaire*) of the men of learning at the end of the Middle Ages.

CHAPTER VIII

Ambitions and Representations

———— •·•· ————

Despite their intellectual competencies, men of learning in medieval societies were scarcely any better prepared than their contemporaries to understand novelty, including the novelty represented by their own emergence. Thus it was naturally by way of the traditional taxonomies that they sought to legitimate their social position, and they only very gradually and sometimes awkwardly tried to bring out and make recognized what it was that constituted their collective specificity.

However, if there is one point on which they practically never had any doubts, it is the conviction that their qualifications situated them in the upper and privileged orders of society. It was thus among the latter—the clergy and the nobility—that they sought from the outset the references and models that would allow them to justify their ambitions and to define the principles of their way of life.

1. Clergy

Most men of learning retained a distinct clerical stamp until the end of the Middle Ages—and beyond. From the twelfth to the fifteenth centuries the overall tendency was certainly toward secularization. But depending on the categories of individuals and the countries concerned, this process followed quite different rhythms.

In the 1150s, the first doctors of civil law in Bologna must have seemed to their contemporaries to be laymen; they were married and had children, they lived on the income from their work (teaching and legal consultations), and the Church's suspicions regarding their discipline, which was lucrative, profane, and too favorable to imperial pretensions, could only hasten the separation between the world of the clerics and the first "lords of law" (*domini legum*) whose position within the urban élites was increasingly confirmed. At least in Mediterranean countries, physicians soon followed the jurists along this path of early secularization.

But things did not happen this way everywhere. In the countries of the northern half of Europe, many jurists, including civil lawyers, long remained clerics, which moreover often allowed them to pursue very successful ecclesiastical careers despite the theoretically profane nature of their specialty. In Paris, professors of medicine at the university obtained the right to marry only in 1452.

In any case, the proportion of churchmen among men of learning was large everywhere until the end of the Middle Ages, even in the southern societies that were secularized earlier. If jurists and physicians were dominant here, even in the universities of these regions it was nonetheless the faculties of canon law that kept the largest enrollments, including, naturally, a very large majority of clerics and religious among both students and professors. In Toulouse, Montpellier, and Avignon, at the end of the fourteenth century students in canon law still represented between 75 and 57 percent of the total enrollment; if we add to that that 16 to 29 percent of these students were canons regular or monks—and that the professors often also belonged to the regular clergy—we see that even these southern universities retained, through their faculties of canon law, a strong clerical tinge, and that they must therefore have appeared to contemporaries as populated by ecclesiastics and religious whose chief goal was to serve the Church.[27]

Service to the Church was not the only possibility, however, and we may recall that until the end of the Middle Ages and beyond, many public offices, particularly some of the highest ones (the royal council, the supreme courts, the Chambre des Comptes, the Exchequer, etc.) also continued to be entrusted to churchmen. Holding such positions was certainly not seen at the time as incompatible with their vocation and their religious status. We can therefore say that while loyally serving the prince and the state, these churchmen gave their offices a certain ecclesiastical tinge, in their own eyes as well as in those of their contemporaries.

It will perhaps be objected that in the societies of the end of the Middle Ages a cleric was not necessarily a person belonging to a major order that required celibacy (priests, deacons, and subdeacons) or a religious who had taken perpetual vows. The clergy included other categories of individuals in minor orders, and even those who were simply tonsured. These latter categories—which almost always constituted the majority of the "clergy"—enjoyed the clergy's judicial and fiscal privileges (at least in theory, since lay judges were less and less inclined to respect these privileges) but were only partially subject to the constraints imposed on it, since they were not expected to perform any pastoral or sacramental duty. They could thus easily receive ecclesiastical revenues without being in residence, and they were allowed to marry on condition that they gave up their benefices.

From our point of view, this often excessive margin of the clerical population—nearly 15 percent of the male population of a city like Reims at the beginning of the fourteenth century[28]—does not seem to have had a very marked religious character. But we must consider what the clergy represented according to the mentality and social practices of the end of the Middle Ages. In a society of hierarchized orders, clerical privileges, which had both symbolic and real value, largely defined the status of those who benefited from them. The manners a "cleric" had to adopt in order to be recognized as a cleric (solemn ways of speech, a grave attitude, tonsure, long, dark garments, a refusal to bear arms) produced an almost immediate effect of social distinction. However, the clergy was still more a cultural value. We must take care not to idealize here. To take the example from Reims already cited, Pierre Desportes noted that many of the "married clerics" in and around the city were in fact illiterate and that even if the magistrates of the archbishop's secular court—married clerics who came from good bourgeois families—could read French and knew common law, they did not know Latin, and asked the archbishop and the canons not to use Latin in proceedings in order to avoid putting them in an awkward position.

It remains that at least in theory, and even often in practice, being a member of the clergy implied what for other categories of the population was merely optional or even a mere amusement—namely mastery of writing and of Latin, knowledge of the fundamental disciplines of scholarly culture, and the possession of books. All these kinds of knowledge themselves retained a certain religious stamp and were subject to a requirement of orthodoxy of which the ecclesiastical magisterium remained the sole judge. It is true that in certain domains, such as civil law and medicine, this requirement was apparently easily satisfied by means of the ritual invocation of divine goodwill and traditional Christian virtues. More deeply, however, these kinds of knowledge continued to be inscribed within an overall framework recognized and validated by the Church; they were taught in schools and universities founded or confirmed by the ecclesiastical authority, and they therefore belonged to a cultural order that was Christian. It is significant that people continued to define "clerics" by reference to their specific intellectual practices, even men of learning who otherwise led an entirely secular life. Thus in France one spoke of both *clercs du roi* (that is, scribes and notaries in the Chancellery or the Chambre des Comptes) and *conseillers clercs* (assessors and jurists—*clers et saiges en droit*, as a document from Lyon puts it around 1450) appointed by the municipalities.[29]

2. Nobility

While most men of learning at the end of the Middle Ages claimed to belong to the clergy, "nobility" defined a horizon that was not wholly inaccessible, at least for the most talented or ambitious among them. For men of learning, the attraction of ennoblement was increased by the fact that there were many nobles in their own ranks: nobles from ancient families who had moved into teaching or offices, those who had been ennobled by the king or were simply socially recognized as noble, and the sons and grandsons of those who had been more recently ennobled, the germ of a *noblesse de robe longue* whom fidelity to study and public offices did not prevent from proudly advertising their "noble condition" and displaying titles and coats of arms.

These diverse social processes were analyzed in the preceding chapter. Here we should note that these noble men of learning never represented more than a minority within the group as a whole. They were concentrated in a narrow upper stratum, that of the prelates, royal councilors, and judges and lawyers of the supreme courts. Within this restricted élite alone they were numerous, and even, especially in the fifteenth century, clearly in the majority.

Thus neither the fascination of the aristocratic model among men of learning nor even the process of ennoblement from which some of them benefited can be explained merely by the presence among them, if not at their head, of some nobles whose nobility was unquestioned—though of varying antiquity. What was involved, I believe, was the notion of nobility itself as a paradigm of social superiority and the pressure created by the very dynamics of a group on its way up.

The aspiration to nobility shared by men of learning as a group (even if this aspiration took concrete form only for a small number of them) was expressed in two ways which were obviously complementary: reverence and precedence, on one hand, and assimilation on the other. The more the nobility of knowledge and of its bearers was affirmed, the more ostensibly respect for the nobility was expressed. This subtle, double mechanism seems more or less clearly at work in all the institutions that men of learning were taking over: religious chapters, tribunals, chancelleries, etc. Let us take the example of the universities, where it operated in a rather naïve manner as a constitutive element of the training of the intellectual élites of medieval society.[30]

University regulations of the fourteenth and fifteenth centuries show that various privileges and advantages were reserved for noble students, on the condition that they could prove their nobility either by producing a genealogy or simply by *tenant l'état noble*—"living in a noble manner" (wearing fur garments, having a sufficient number of servants, etc.). These privileges were first of all honorific, that is, they allowed noble students to sit in the first rows in lecture halls and to walk along-side the graduates, licentiates and bachelors, in university processions. They also guaranteed more substantial advantages for these noble students: the right to sit alongside graduates on university councils (as if nobles had a natural aptitude for making decisions and commands), and priority over their non-noble classmates in applying for ecclesiastical benefices reserved for university men. On the other hand, strict equality was maintained among nobles and non-nobles with regard to courses of study and the conditions that had to be met to take examinations and receive diplomas.

However, as we see, these privileges granted noble students also bene-fited non-nobles, at least those who held degrees and had thus proven their intellectual aptitudes. For nobles were not acknowledged as having precedence over others in everything. A subtle scale of equivalence was established between degrees of nobility and university degrees. The minor degrees (baccalaureate) or those earned in the least prestigious faculties (arts, medicine) was equivalent to the minor nobility, a *licence* in law to the upper nobility; while doctors of laws and theology, and the rectors, were always alone at the head in all the university's public appearances, preceding all nobles, whatever their rank. A 1389 regulation of the university of Vienna, intended to define the place of members of the university in the great Corpus Christi procession, made this system of correspondence very explicit: those holding master's degrees in medicine were to walk with the petty nobility (*minores illustres*), the regents in law with the middle nobility (*simplices illustres*), the theologians with the dukes and counts; ending the procession, the rector would walk alone, to demonstrate to all the matchless dignity of the university and of knowledge.[31]

The theme of the equivalence between knowledge and nobility— *Doctorat vaut chevalerie* ("A doctorate is equivalent to a knighthood"), as the adage would soon put it—does more than underlie the institutional practices sanctioned by the regulations. It was explicitly developed by a number of commentators. Taking the doctorate as the concrete expression of the perfection of knowledge, various authors maintained that this degree gave access to a genuine *status*, or more precisely, an *ordo*.[32] The solemnity of these rites of collation of the doctorate (presentation of the doctoral insignia, oaths, the mutual embrace of the collator and the applicant, celebrations and gifts, ceremonial lecture delivered by the new doctor, etc.) made it possible to suggest comparisons with feudal investiture or the dubbing of a knight. In the introduction to his commentary on the *Clementinae* (ca. 1370), Simon da Borsano, a doctor *in utroque jure* from Bologna who soon became archbishop of Milan and then cardinal, considers "the status of doctors" (*status doctorum*) at some length.[33] After recalling the privileges of doctors, particularly in fiscal matters, he concludes that the doctor's dignity allowed him precedence over the knight (*militem doctor precedere debet*, p. 242),and that if the doctor had taught law for twenty years or more, he should be seen as being on a par with dukes and counts. Let us note moreover that properly based on various references to Roman law, these pretensions had already appeared a century earlier, in Castille, in Alfonso the Wise's *Siete Partidas* (P. II, t. 31, § 8), and that in the fourteenth century many Italian and French jurists drew on it in adopting titles such as "lord of laws" (*dominus legum*) or "count of laws" (*comes legum*).

What justifications were given, in addition to quotations borrowed from Roman law, in support of this assimilation of knowledge to nobility? First of all there was the notion of the dignity of knowledge itself—or more precisely, of the canonical kinds of knowledge inherited from antiquity, recognized by the Church, and taught in the *studia generalia*. Law was both the vehicle of sacredness, Roman *maiestas*, and a supreme regulator of social and political life, while theology explained the meaning of Revelation and guided in a virtually infallible way—at least so it was thought until the Great Schism—the ecclesiastical magisterium. The mastery of such lofty sciences could not be possessed by unworthy or even merely ordinary men; they naturally ennobled those who had made the effort to complete long and difficult courses of study to acquire the sacred store of knowledge to preserve it and transmit it to others through writing and teaching. The nobility of the men of learning was implied by their "authority" (*auctoritas*).

It was also connected, however, and especially for the jurists, with the notion of service, which since the early Middle Ages had been a constitutive element of the concept of nobility. Bartolo da Sassoferrato (1314–57) and Baldo degli Ubaldi (1327–1400), the two great Italian jurists of the fourteenth century, emphasized the close and virtually functional link between doctor and prince. Simon da Borsano, in the text mentioned above, also stressed this aspect of the doctor's vocation, citing the *Code* to support the claim that one of the doctor's privileges was to have direct access to the prince, his court, and his tribunals.[34] This theme resonated all the more among the men of learning of the end of the Middle Ages since, without being their sole raison d'être, service to the state was in fact one of the most common outlets for university studies, as we saw in chapters four and five above. Serving the state with the weapons of the law—"The jurist is like a knight of an unarmed knighthood," said Jacques de Révigny, a professor at Orleans toward the end of the thirteenth century[35]—men of learning felt they were participating, in a way, in the prince's redoubtable majesty and in the common welfare of *res publica*. This proximity also amounted to a presumption of nobility.

Thus we can better understand what the aristocratic model signified for the men of learning. It helped both to outline the image they had of themselves and of their place in society and to assign a precise objective to the concrete ambitions of the most enterprising among them.

At first, blood and heredity were not essential considerations. It was rather a matter of nobility for one's own lifetime, connected with aptitudes and personal service. Naturally, as we have said, men of learning almost always tended to see to it that their status was preserved within their family. But if the son of a doctor was noble, it was not only because he was the son of a doctor, but also because he was himself, generally speaking, a doctor. The nobility of the men of learning was thus inseparable from their competence and their function.

That said, this nobility was also, like all nobility, synonymous with stability, privileges, and social prestige. At whatever level he was situated, the man of learning demanded the privileges, especially the fiscal privileges, that allowed him to maintain his rank. Despite their economic interest, the scope of these privileges was as much symbolic as real. The same was true of the marks of respect and deference—laudatory epithets, reverential gestures—that he expected from others—students, persons under his jurisdiction, taxpayers—and the way of life he had to maintain if he was not to lose his noble standing. Very few were those who, having moved beyond the most modest stratum, that of the sergeants and notaries, tried to combine education and offices with the practice of commerce and business, as did Hugues Jossard.[36] The son and son-in-law of farmers with large holdings in the Arbresle area near Lyon, this bachelor of laws had a successful career as an official that took him to the offices of lieutenant to the seneschal and of royal judge in Lyon. In this way he was able to get himself ennobled in 1398. But this did not prevent him from investing his fortune, in a pioneering way, in the mines at Pampailly that Jacques Coeur later took up. It is true that in contrast with commerce and craftsmanship, mining would never be considered an activity that systematically led to the loss of noble status. However, Jossard's two sons, who were also graduates, gave up both offices and mining and concerned themselves with their lands and with military activities.

But if few men of learning transformed themselves into businessmen on the scale of Hugues Jossard, we must nonetheless emphasize that most of them did not count solely on the recognition of their intellectual capacities and on services rendered to the state to get themselves admitted to the nobility, and then to maintain themselves there and to ensure the continuation of their family line. Like other categories of the population that were rising in society—rich farmers, merchants, burghers, military men—they did not disdain less specific but proven methods such as becoming part of a clientele, negotiating dowries and advantageous marriages, purchasing mansions, chateaux, and fiefs, exercising seigneurial rights, etc.

We should mention here a final trait that clearly shows the gap that still existed between the image men of learning had of their own nobility and the social realities of the time. In some families, the nobility claimed on the basis of intellectual competencies remained limited to the individual's lifetime and could thus be rapidly lost. Take for example the Montpellier family of the Rebuffi, which produced many jurists in the course of the fourteenth and fifteenth centuries. At the end of the fourteenth century, the best known of them, Jacques Rebuffi, styled himself a "count of laws" (*comte ès-lois*); but the family rose no higher; the Rebuffi of subsequent generations were second-rate jurists, no longer bore this kind of title, and seem not to have been considered nobles.[37] The far more famous family of the Bolognese commentator Odofredo (before 1200–1265) had no better luck. At the beginning of the fourteenth century, for two generations the celebrated jurist's grandsons and great grandsons managed to obtain the title of knights, but afterward this "brief parenthesis of nobility in the history of the Odofredi," as Andrea Padovani calls it, closed again and the following generations devoted themselves to dealing in spices and silks in a bourgeois manner.[38]

Conversely, in the lineages of the men of law whose success was the most brilliant, studying and holding offices seems sometimes to have lasted only a few generations. Once the situation of the family was definitively established, its members sometimes abandoned activities associated with offices and turned toward a more traditional model of nobility, one in which managing one's land and performing military service were everything. That is what happened, in the second half of the fifteenth century, with the Ysalguiers in Toulouse, the Jossards in Lyon, and the Pastons in Norfolk.[39] Only a few eminent and already well-individualized groups of men of learning and officials (in France, those associated with the Parlement, for example, families like the Marles or the Orgemonts), seem to have attained an economic and social position sufficiently elevated and a sufficiently powerful self-awareness to remain persistently faithful to their specific vocation, that of a *noblesse de robe* clearly distinct from other kinds of nobility. This awareness among members of the Parisian Parlement and other royal clerks that they formed a social group that was not only specific but stable and homogeneous, is expressed particularly in their testaments—many of which are extant for the period of Charles VI—in the proliferation of clauses intended to ensure, beyond the transmission of patrimonies, the solidity of the bonds of family relationship and alliance, as well as the perpetuity of their intellectual and political vocation.[40] Such cases of continuity are rare, but it would nevertheless be wrong to think that absorption into an undifferentiated nobility at the end of a few generations was the

only form of social ambition of which men of learning at the end of the
Middle Ages were capable.

3. A "Fourth Estate"

Montaigne saw the problem clearly when he wrote in his *Essais* (bk. 1,
chap. 23) of this "fourth estate of people that deal with trials" who
henceforth formed "a body separate from that of the nobility."[41] A century earlier, the emergence of this "fourth estate" of men of learning,
men of law and officials, was already an unquestionable reality. But how
far were contemporaries—and even these men themselves—aware that
this amounted to the birth of a "separate body" within society and not
merely an excrescence (which many regarded as unhealthy) attributable
to the recent advances of a state suddenly forgetful of the traditional and
legitimate prerogatives of the old nobility and the clergy?

We must note first that becoming aware of the specificity of the
group of men of learning does not in any way exclude the possibility that
the latter otherwise continued, as we have seen, to see themselves as clerics at the same time that they aspired to join the nobility. The early signs
of this awareness go far back in time. As early as the twelfth century,
as R. P. M.-D. Chenu has shown, the clerics in the urban schools, without giving up their ecclesiastical appurtenance, had tried to distinguish
themselves from the rest of the clergy. The terms *scolares* and *magistri*,
or more ambitiously, *philosophi*, were very early used to describe their
special status, pending the time when the universities would give it an
effective institutional framework, even though in some respects the
latter was reductive because it implied direct control by ecclesiastical authority.[42] Jurists, particularly Italian or influenced by the Italian model,
became aware almost as early of the original character not only of their
knowledge but also of their position in the society and their political
role. We can find traces of this awareness in the first Bolognese commentators.

But it is not certain that this self-awareness on the part of the men
of learning subsequently advanced in a regular and continuous manner.
If their numbers steadily grew along with their social influence, their
increasingly deep integration into ecclesiastical frameworks that were
themselves increasingly exacting and the desire to mark first of all their
appurtenance to the élites had the effect of slowing their emancipation
and obscuring the image they had of themselves. A few points emerge,
however, that are perceptible not only to the historian (who is always
tempted to abuse the privileges accorded by his retrospective viewpoint)
but no doubt also to contemporaries, and they sketch in broad strokes

what might constitute the specificity of men of learning in the societies of the last centuries of the Middle Ages. In the interest of clarity, we will classify these specific characteristics under four rubrics.

1. The first aspect may seem archaic, but it remained very marked: the fundamentally urban aspect. The man of learning, as we conceive him here, remained a man of the city more than any other. Especially if we set aside the simple practitioners, some of whom may have resided in villages or small towns, we find our men of learning essentially in the cities and even at the center of the cities. It was there that they studied; there that they exercised their functions. When they were not going to school, men of learning spent their days in public places and official residences: cathedrals and their dependencies, royal palaces and chateaux, city halls and markets. Those who did not have their own offices spent their time in the courtyards and corridors. Even practitioners who received their clients in their offices or "studies" could not go far away from the seat of the tribunals or administrations. All the studies of social topography that have been carried out on cities of any size at the end of the Middle Ages show that men of learning preferred to live there, either in the quarter where the schools were, if there was one—the Montagne Sainte-Geneviève in Paris—or in the ancient heart of the cities, in immediate proximity to the centers of power. In Lyon, for example, most of the doctors, licentiates, and notaries lived in the *quartier du Palais*, that is, just north of the cathedral of Saint-Jean, around the so-called "Roanne house" where the seneschal's tribunal was located.[43]

In addition, men of learning, as we have seen in the preceding chapters, actively participated, as much as they could, in the associative (confraternities) and political life of the cities. Everywhere where the old merchant oligarchies did not forbid them access; they invaded the urban magistracies, which also implied a constant presence in the heart of the city.

At the same time that they accorded priority to the acquisition of urban real estate, the men of learning did not disdain to buy land in the country. But in contrast to many of the nobles whose ranks they nevertheless aspired to join, they seem not to have had any inclination to live permanently in their rural residences. That would have often been incompatible with the performance of their offices and their municipal duties.

This very close link between the men of learning and the city is nowhere more striking than in certain Italian cities and in particular in Bologna. In the thirteenth and fourteenth centuries, the tombs of great professors of law were erected on public squares. Magnificent monuments in the antique manner, with marble columns and bas-reliefs, their splendor clearly demonstrated that the glory of the doctors was a constitutive element of the very history of the city and of the self-awareness of its inhabitants.[44]

2. The second trait characteristic of the world of men of learning is what I will call, briefly and not without a certain anachronism, its professionalization. The concept could perhaps also be applied to the world of craftsmen and merchants, but for the social and political élites that concern us here, it is certain that there was a great difference between men of learning and the old nobles who, even when they served the prince in particular offices, always did so as "amateurs" without special training and serving part-time. The men of learning were characterized by an entirely different relationship to their work, whether it was teaching, public office, or private practice. For them, there was an almost necessary connection between their intellectual competence, which was often guaranteed by a diploma, and the exercise of their social functions. This necessary connection explains why men of learning, unlike noble "amateurs," were not put off by the frequently austere and technical nature of their tasks, which their years of training had taught them to master. This is the reason that during the fourteenth century the number of nobles in many administrative functions declined to the advantage of new, more competent officials who willingly agreed to devote themselves full-time to the prince's service.

This development was more or less marked depending on the country. In England, many public offices continued to be entrusted to members of the local gentry. France, in contrast, was the country par excellence of royal officials who were often foreign either socially or geographically to the traditional local élites, and in any case drew their authority from their intellectual competence and their devotion to the prince's service as well as from their own esprit de corps. With the French royal officials of the fourteenth century appears the modern notion of public office. The components of this notion, taken individually, are no doubt often of ecclesiastical origin.[45] Taken together, they outline the contours of a genuine status that was to have a remarkable future. First of all, the officials could move through the stages of a veritable *cursus honorum*, depending on complex strategies determined by both the prince's will and the personal ambitions of those involved. Often on the condition that they had a certain geographical mobility, they could occupy successively increasingly important positions, whose prestige grew at the same time as their remuneration. The notion of a career, which no doubt first appeared with the holders of benefices and ecclesiastical offices, was thus extended to all those who served the prince and the state.

Similarly, whether they served the Church or the prince, men of learning participated in some way in the latter's majesty. They were therefore seen as being part of the ecclesiastical or political body itself, and hence, whenever they were acting within the framework of their functions, as simultaneously released from personal responsibility and protected by the sacred character of the institution they served. The Church defended its clerics against any attack on the part of the people or the secular powers, and the prince came to consider any attack on the person of his servants as a crime of lèse-majesté.

A final mark characterizing the service rendered by men of learning and officials was that their position was assured at most for their own lifetimes and was always revocable. Even though oaths of personal loyalty, the granting of revenues connected with lands or other real goods, or even, at the end of our period, a certain tendency, in various ways, toward a *de facto* hereditary transmission of offices were not alien to service to the prince and the Church, in the fourteenth and fifteenth centuries this service was not reducible to the traditional feudal frameworks, even when the latter were renovated in the form sometimes called "bastard feudalism." Clerics and officials were usually paid in cash and the prince could at any time dismiss an official he was not happy with (on the condition, in theory at least, that he had "heard" him, that is, had allowed him to present his defense).

3. The third trait that we note as specific to the group of the men of learning in the societies of the end of the Middle Ages is what I will call, again in a somewhat abrupt and anachronistic way, its politicization. It is not, let us repeat, that all men of learning were or even wished to be in the service of the Church or the prince. Particularly in the old Roman law countries that had long recognized a role for the private practices of knowledge in the everyday regulation of social and economic life, many men of learning pursued a personal activity without having the ambition to influence the general functioning of power. Overall, however, it remains that a majority of them no doubt ended up serving the established authorities in one way or another, and in any case, even those who exercised a private activity—such as notaries and lawyers—were more or less consciously concerned to promote through their activity the foundation of an order founded on respect for rules that had themselves issued from the canonical disciplines of scholarly culture, in other words, to lay the bases for what we should now call the rule of law. Not that the earlier order was based, whatever might have been said about it, on the rule of force alone and on arbitrary power. But the rules that had been those of feudal society had their origin in a certain number of customary or religious notions that did not in any way proceed from rational considerations. With the emergence of the men of learning, a certain political rationality also began to emerge.

The "politicization" of men of learning was manifested in their precocious interest in political literature (in the broad sense, including ecclesiology), perceptible as early as the twelfth century, and powerfully reinforced starting in the twelfth century by the triumph of Roman law and then of Aristotelianism. Even though they were neither the only ones who worked to bring about its advent nor the only ones who profited from it, men of learning almost all were unquestionably on the side of the modern state that arose in Europe in the last centuries of the Middle Ages. The "politicization" of men of learning was one of the most striking forms of their modernity.

4. But in the final analysis it is no doubt in their culture itself that we must seek the specificity of the men of learning of the end of the Middle Ages. We have already noted everything that this culture owed to traditional ecclesiastical culture, adding that it remained, in any event, under the supervision of the ecclesiastical authorities and their demands for orthodoxy. We have also noted that it did not hesitate, on occasion, to borrow a few faded ornaments from ancient aristocratic and chivalric culture. But this must not obscure its specific aspects. This specificity was not only in the content of the disciplines, philosophy and law in particular, the emancipation and rise of which the Church had accepted only reluctantly. It was also in the cultural practices themselves, in other words, in the concrete relationship between men of learning and the knowledge by means of which we have defined them.

These practices, as we have said, were characterized first of all by their laborious, technical, professional aspect. Among them, the practice of knowledge became work, with its own rules and tested methods. Its purpose was neither the poet's aesthetic enjoyment nor the pious monk's rumination, but rather the acquisition and putting into practice of socially useful knowledge that was directed toward concrete ends, usually political.

On the other hand, the cultural practices of the men of learning of the end of the Middle Ages had a dimension that was obviously individual, if not individualist.[46] Even if these practices generally imply oral and collective—familial or academic—forms of learning, in the last analysis they cannot dispense with personal labor (memorization and writing), the personal possession of books, or, very often, the acquisition of titles and diplomas obtained after the person who held them had undergone genuine trials that guaranteed, independently of any reference to person or origin, his intellectual competence.

This "individualism"—which is certainly not the only one that appeared in the increasingly complex and mobile societies of the end of the Middle Ages—also put its stamp on the religious devotion of the men of learning. Clerics or laymen, they inaugurated a kind of piety marked by the internalization of religious feeling, the relative disdain of external practices, an extreme value placed on reading, meditation, and personal prayer, and finally the gravity and restraint in behavior that long continued to be their peculiar mark in contradistinction to the arrogance of the powerful and the ostentation of the wealthy. We can easily see how *Devotio moderna* and then Erasmian evangelism rapidly found a favorable response in these milieus.

More than by the varying size of their incomes or by their fluid position in the social hierarchy, it is thus probably through their political vision and their cultural and religious practices that we can best grasp the most intimate ambitions of the men of learning of the end of the Middle Ages and the image they had—and gave—of themselves and of their role in the society of their time.

CHAPTER IX

By Way of Conclusion
From Doctors to Humanists—
Continuity and Innovations

———————•◦•———————

The old romantic idea of a radical rupture between the Middle Ages and the Renaissance has long been discredited. Without denying the mutations and considerable novelties that appeared in European civilization in the course of the fifteenth and sixteenth centuries, today's historian puts the primary accent on the continuities. That is why no one any longer takes literally Lorenzo Valla's, Erasmus's, and Rabelais's sarcastic remarks regarding Scholasticism or Rabelais's jokes about the "Sorbonagres." If the debates that these polemics refer to had an unquestionable reality within the order of the disciplines, it is nonetheless clear that the group of men of learning that appeared in the last centuries of the Middle Ages not only survived but considerably strengthened its positions at the beginning of the modern period, in an evident social, political, and cultural continuity.

A study of this new phase in the history of the men of learning would be a task for another book. Here, by way of conclusion, we will only draw attention to everything that, still completely alive in the medieval heritage at the turn of the sixteenth century, guaranteed for centuries to follow, at the cost of a few innovations and adjustments, the continuation of a historical phenomenon of very long duration.

1. Dominating and Sure of Themselves

In many European countries at the end of the fifteenth century, and in particular in the great national monarchies, demographic and economic growth and the end of wars and internal conflicts was accompanied by a resumption of the growth of the state. The latter was particularly spectacular in Spain, unified under the Catholic Monarchs and undertaking the conquest of the Kingdom of Granada and then of America, but we also see it in France under Louis XII (1498–1515) and in Tudor England. Everywhere, the development of the central organs of government was accompanied by a strengthening of local administration. In France, the proliferation of provincial Parlements in the fifteenth and early sixteenth centuries led to the rise, in the chief regional capitals, of an élite of jurists who were solidly anchored in local society and surrounded by a whole group of subordinate but ambitious court clerks, lawyers, prosecutors, and scriveners. In Senlis, for example, there were two attorneys in 1450 and sixteen in 1539.[47] Even if here and there, in Lyon and Rouen for example, economic growth made it possible to maintain or reconstitute large mercantile fortunes, men of law, proud of their offices, their diplomas and their fine libraries, established themselves more firmly than ever as the leading class par excellence, serving both the king and their own interests.

Jurists were not the only ones to benefit from this favorable conjuncture. Everywhere, educated priests and religious, physicians, secretaries accustomed to writing, and schoolmasters informed about the new ideas easily found employment in increasing numbers. This accelerated growth of the group of men of learning is clearly reflected in the growth in the number of educational institutions around 1500. While it is true that the number of new universities established dipped somewhat at the beginning of the sixteenth century (only twenty-six were founded in Europe between 1501 and 1550), enrollments in the old universities at the end of the fifteenth century, which had been through a time of stagnation (except in Germany), started to rise again after 1480. At the beginning of the sixteenth century, the University of Paris had an unprecedented enrollment of 12,000 to 13,000 students (five-sixths of them in the faculty of arts). On the other hand, new colleges were created, while others increasingly specialized in certain areas of teaching. Above all, many pre- or non-university schools and colleges, sometimes called *gymnasia* in the antique manner, were founded. In many cities, for lack of a *studium generale*, municipalities henceforth dominated by enlightened men of law favored the creation of large colleges of grammar and rhetoric, often of excellent quality, such as the College of Guyenne in Bordeaux (1533) and the Jean Sturm Gymnasium in Strasbourg (1538).

Naturally, the rapid growth of the number of men of learning allowed a fresh generation of "new men" to make their way in the world, often through education or other processes of social ascent that we have described in the preceding chapters. But the group's tendency toward stabilization, strengthened by its increasingly secure position in society, did not diminish. Soon, venality of offices and the generalized ennoblement of the upper strata of the world of men of learning, both of them encouraged by increasingly authoritarian political powers, combined to guarantee the hereditary transmission of offices and of a privileged social status. Even if their social recruitment remained fairly open—less than 10 percent of the students in Paris in the middle of the sixteenth century were noble, and less than 25 percent were sons of officials, compared with a majority of sons of merchants, craftsmen, and well-off peasants[48]—it became increasingly clear that the universities and especially the colleges served to reproduce social élites. In Spain, the six *colegios mayores* in Salamanca, Valladolid, and Alcalá, which were monopolized by the families of the great Crown officials, became an almost obligatory gateway for future members of the royal councils of government.[49]

The economic and political changes that marked Europe's entry into the modern age thus did not on the whole challenge the advantageous social position achieved by men of learning over the preceding centuries. Assured of the support of states and Churches that were more dependent than ever on their services, they appear increasingly dominating and sure of themselves in the society of their time. Only a deep challenge to the kinds of knowledge on which their competence and prestige were based could have upset this situation. But was such a challenge really possible?

2. New Ideas, New Men

To be sure, it is correct to say that if the group constituted by men of learning seems to have benefited, from the fifteenth to the sixteenth century, from an impressive continuity, in both its social structure and its political function, it is also true that the very definition of the kinds of knowledge on which its primary specificity was based was significantly transformed over a relatively short period of time.

Nevertheless, before we discuss these changes and their precise import, we must first emphasize that they must not be allowed to obscure constants whose persistence was promoted by the solidity of university institutions and the longevity of family traditions in educated milieus. The master disciplines of medieval scholarly culture (Aristotle's logic, Roman and canon law, Scholastic theology) remained basic to university curricula and thus to the training of a large part of the intellectual élites. In the same way, despite unquestionable victories on the part of the vernacular, the primacy of Latin as both a sacred and a learned language was never really challenged. The humanistic philological renewal even helped give it new life.

Intellectual innovations in the field of scholarly culture were nonetheless considerable. The movement first appeared in northern Italy and in Tuscany in the fifteenth century, or even at the end of the fourteenth century, and by 1500 it had spread over practically all of Europe with such vigor that the renewal of the *peregrinatio academica* again caused students, artists, and literary men to cross the Alps. Let us simply recall that humanism was at first essentially a literary and philological movement. Having restored to an honored place the arts of language—grammar and rhetoric—that were themselves based on assiduous study of the classics, and having rejected the ancient primacy of dialectic and the rebarbative technical character of medieval grammars, the humanists subsequently extended their curiosity to other ancient languages—Greek and Hebrew in particular, which had been practically forgotten in the West since the early Middle Ages—and more generally, all aspects of antiquity, both Hebrew and Greco-Latin. Competent hellenists and hebraists first appeared in Italy toward the middle of the fifteenth century; at the beginning of the sixteenth, they were found all over Europe. Let us mention here only a few examples: Lefèvre d'Étaples (ca. 1450–1537), the Parisian editor of Aristotle; Reuchlin (1455–1536), who restored Hebrew studies in Germany; and especially Erasmus (1469–1536), the most famous of all. The philological renewal launched by humanism benefited disciplines of the *quadrivium* only later on and to a more limited extent, while other disciplines of scholarly culture were profoundly transformed. In natural, moral, and political philosophy the rediscovery of Plato and the Stoics ended medieval Aristotelianism's near-monopoly in these fields. In law, humanistic philology led to a more critical and historical interpretation of Justinian's code. In medicine, a better understanding of Galen's texts hastened the decline of the influence of Arabic authors. Finally, in theology the rediscovery of the original Greek and Hebrew texts of the Bible put exegesis in the limelight, at the expense of dogmatic theology based on the systematic application of dialectics to the mysteries of faith. Supported by the reformatory aspirations of the time, religious humanism was, for most of the authors in this movement, a form of evangelism in which the desire to recover the purity of Christ's original message was often accompanied by a sharp (though rather traditional) critique of the established Church as too rich and too centralized.

Traditional historiography was fond of contrasting humanistic milieus, milieus of new men, of "obscure men," with traditional intellectual élites clinging to the immutable structures of the university and radically opposed to innovation. It is undeniable that the second half of the fifteenth century and the beginning of the sixteenth were everywhere in Europe a time of particularly lively intellectual debate, which was further exacerbated by the fact that writers of the time did not hesitate to go to extremes, and their works often quickly took on the character of polemical pamphlets or manifestos—in France, think of Rabelais—that has misled certain historians. It is also true that in all domains there were conservatives who contested, if not the principle itself, at least the social utility of the new ideas, and who emphasized the dangers they could pose to royal or pontifical authority. Some humanists were brutally driven out of the universities, like Lorenzo Valla in Pavia in 1433, new works were condemned, like those of Reuchlin censured by the theologians in Cologne, Louvain, and Erfurt. Often, the exponents of humanistic disciplines seem to have fled the traditional university framework to conduct their intellectual debates and pursue their publications in institutions of a new kind—*sodalitates* and circles of friends, academies, princely or episcopal courts—that proliferated, particularly in Italy, beginning in the last third of the fifteenth century. Here, humanists not only gathered together with other lovers of Latin culture and supporters of the new ideas but also experienced a form of sociability different from that current in the old universities. The latter had emphasized the most technical aspects of scholarly apprenticeship and the social utility of diplomas. *Sodalitates* and academies made it possible to forget these constraints. The cult of friendship encouraged them to reject the bitterness of dialectical argument in favor of friendly intercourse and rural *otium*. The taste for the beautiful introduced a certain gratuitous character into intellectual work, in which the literary man henceforth expected to enjoy an aesthetic pleasure produced by the masterpieces of ancient literature and art or their modern imitations. Finally, the rehabilitated feeling for nature encouraged them not to separate bodily exercise from mental exercise, and to restore concrete observation to its rightful place alongside the tireless compilation of "authorities."

Various recent studies have shown, however, that this opposition between medieval knowledge and new ideas was rather forced. Not only must we avoid being duped by the ideal picture of humanistic sociability sketched above on the basis of a few programmatic texts, for these milieus were in fact riven by personal conflicts just as ferocious as those in the medieval schools, but above all it is now clear that in the first half of the sixteenth century, the new disciplines were ultimately accepted—to a greater or lesser extent and with varying degrees of goodwill—by most European universities. The faculties of arts were usually the first to offer instruction in rhetoric and Greek and even in Hebrew; then the graduate faculties followed.[50] Colleges often played an important role in this development. Although in 1530 the University of Paris successfully opposed the incorporation of the "college of royal lecturers" founded by Francis I to teach the new disciplines (Greek, Hebrew, mathematics), a few years earlier the University of Louvain had allowed the opening of the *Collegium trilingue* (1517), and a new university that also specialized in teaching Latin, Greek, and Hebrew had existed in Alcalá de Henares since the beginning of the century. Most of the humanists attended universities and many did not hesitate to take a doctorate or to teach there. Erasmus himself, while he had bad memories of his studies at the College of Montaigu in Paris, took a doctorate in Turin, taught at Cambridge, and visited virtually all the important university towns of his time. The celebrated physician Paracelsus (1493–1541) had no less than three doctorates, not only in medicine but also in law and in theology.

Nonetheless, the academies and the courts offered those who frequented them forms of both sociability and intellectual work that differed from those practiced in the universities, though in fact the same men were often found in both kinds of institutions.[51] Their interests may have changed or broadened, and some aspects of their way of life may have evolved, but their social and political preoccupations remained the same, and jurists and officials, physicians, secretaries and notaries, canons and religious, often belonging to families devoted to education for one or more generations, continued to constitute the core of the world of men of learning.

It is not necessary to develop this point at greater length. My point is simply to show that the renewal—real, if partial—of knowledge around 1500 did not lead to profound changes in either the structure or the social and political functions of those whose raison d'être was precisely the mastery of this knowledge and the exercise of the competencies based on it.

If the group of the men of learning thus remained essentially the same from the Middle Ages to the Renaissance, while being able to adapt to new intellectual trends that had arisen elsewhere, it also began to broaden, including categories of individuals who had earlier remained rather alien to it. The early signs of this broadening are already visible in the fifteenth century, and even in the fourteenth; moreover, it was a tendency that was not to reach its full development for a long time to come.

This extension took place in two directions. First, forms of scholarly culture achieved by a still narrow élite of craftsmen (one thinks of the first German and Italian typographers and printers, some of whom had studied in the faculty of arts), artists (Leonardo da Vinci and Dürer are extreme but significant examples), technicians, engineers—military or other—and architects become sufficiently developed and abstract to allow us henceforth to call them men of learning. Printing certainly played a major role in the social and cultural promotion of this kind of activities. At the beginning of the sixteenth century their dignity was still far from equaling that of traditional religious, philosophical, literary, or juridical disciplines, but a tendency to grant scientific and technical knowledge new prestige and social recognition, previously unknown in the Western Middle Ages, was unquestionably under way.

The other extension concerns the nobility—here I refer to the old military or landed nobility that was attached to its traditional values. For a long time, this nobility had officially looked down on scholarly, Latin culture, limiting itself to a very superficial veneer—a little vernacular literature, a few social arts—displayed against the background of the old chivalric virtues: valor, honor, generosity. In the Middle Ages, the nobles of the old nobility, rather few in number, who already went to the universities were usually youngest sons who were intended for the Church or were being prepared to hold juridical offices.

With the Renaissance, things changed a bit, first of all in Italy and then north of the Alps. To be sure, many nobles felt no shame in remaining very uneducated and even illiterate, whereas others studied simply in order to try to join the clergy or the already well-filled ranks of the *robe*. But we also now see the reemergence of the figure—which the twelfth century had also known in its own way—of the cultivated *curialis* (courtier). While he retained a certain disdain for diplomas and the more technical aspects of academic practices, and had no intention of giving up the traditional pleasures of chivalric life (sporting and military exercises, worldly social arts, courtly eroticism), the *curialis* did not hesitate to attend the university, at least in an ephemeral manner, to travel to study, usually in Paris or in Italy, to collect books, and to become acquainted with the new disciplines—Latin and Greek belles-lettres, eloquence and poetry, natural curiosities, and indeed, for the most pious, the Holy Scriptures restored to their original purity. Baldassare Castiglione (1478–1529), a Mantuan gentleman who had spent most of his life in the princely courts at Mantua and Urbino, did not fail to introduce this cultural dimension into the ideal portrait he outlined in his *Book of the Courtier* (1524), which had great success throughout Renaissance Europe:

> Then the Count replied: "I blame the French [since Petrarch, Gallophobia had been a commonplace of Italian humanism] for thinking that letters are detrimental to the profession of arms, and I hold that to no one is learning more suited than to a warrior [i.e., a noble]; and I would have these two accomplishments conjoined in our Courtier, each an aid to the other . . ."[52]

This extension of education to new social categories is not explained only by fashion but also testifies to the strong social position held by men of learning, at the same time as to the great power of attraction exercised by a scholarly culture that had no doubt been modernized in certain aspects but remained in its principle fundamentally faithful to its medieval origins.

Between the time of the doctors to that of the humanists, there was therefore no sharp break—at most, modernization, adaptation, opening up, without which there is no social dynamics. The last centuries of the

Middle Ages had already marked out, for a long time to come, the place that Western societies were inclined to give abstract modes of knowledge and those who made it their profession to ensure the preservation, diffusion, and, possibly, the practical application of these modes of knowledge.

No doubt it would be possible to criticize this choice on historical grounds. No doubt medieval men of learning—and their heirs down to the end of the *ancien régime*—could be reproached for having, by their prejudice and their selfishness, slowed scientific and technical innovation, delayed economic growth, and immeasurably strengthened political and religious constraints. We will let the reader be the judge. In this book we have sought only to describe, without making any moral judgment, the emergence and self-assertion on the social scene of a group of men whose destiny illustrates, in a way, what the place and the import of culture might be in history.

Notes

⸺•◆•⸺

Introduction

1. Cf. J. Shatzmiller, "Etudiants juifs à la faculté de médecine de Montpellier, dernier quart du XIVe siècle," *Jewish History* 6 (1992): 243–255.

Part I

1. Cf. S. Lusignan, *"Parler vulgairement." Les intellectuels et la langue française aux XIIIe et XIVe siècles* (Paris and Montréal, 1986).
2. Cited in F. Autrand, "L'apparition d'un nouveau groupe social," in *Des origines au XVe siècle* (Paris, 1993), 311–443; vol. 1 of *Histoire de la fonction publique en France*, ed. M. Pinet.
3. Cited in E. Garin, *L'educazione in Europa (1400–1600): problemi e programmi* (Bari,1957).
4. Maistre Nicole Oresme, *Le Livre de Ethiques d'Aristote*, based on the text of ms. 2902, Royal Library of Belgium, ed. A. D. Menut (New York, 1940), 100–101.
5. Cf. H. Grundmann, *"Litteratus—illitteratus.* Der Wandel einer Bildungsnorm vom Altertum zum Mittelalter," Archiv für Kulturgeschichte 40 (1958): 1–65.
6. Cf. L. J. Paetow, *The Arts Course at Medieval Universities with Special Reference to Grammar and Rhetoric* (Champaign, Ill., 1910).
7. Quoted in L. Douët d'Arcq, "Acte d'accusation contre Robert le Coq," *Bibliothèque de l'École des chartes* 2 (1840–41): 380.
8. See for example Th. Renna, "Aristotle and the French Monarchy, 1260–1303," *Viator* 9 (1978): 309–324.
9. Cited in G. Beaujouan, "La science dans l'Occident médiéval chrétien," in *La science antique et médiévale* (Paris, 1966), 582–652; vol. 1 of *Histoire générale des sciences*, dir. R. Taton.
10. G. Dahan, "Les classifications du savoir aux XIIe et XIIIe siècles," *L'enseignement philosophique* 40/4 (1990): 5–27.
11. Hugh of St. Victor, *Didascalion: A Medieval Guide to the Arts*, trans. Jerome Taylor (New York, 1961).
12. For a general overview of the historical culture of the Middle Ages, see B. Guenée, *Histoire et culture historique dans l'Occident médiéval*, 2nd ed. (Paris, 1991).

13. See in particular his *Doctrine d'enfant*, French version, ed. A. Llinarès, Paris, 1969, and *The Buke of the Ordre of Knychthede*, ed. Jonathan A. Glenn (Edinburgh, 1993).

14. Cf. J. Verger, *"Ad studium augmentandum:* l'utopie éducative de Pierre Dubois dans son *De recuperacione Terre Sancte* (v. 1306)," *Mélanges de la Bibliothèque de la Sorbonne* 8 (1988): 106–122.

15. See for example his treatise *De parvulis ad Christum trahendis*, in J. Gerson, *Oeuvres complètes*, ed. P. Glorieux (Paris, 1973), 9: 669–686.

16. In editing Inghetto Contardo's *Disputatio contra Iudaeos* (Paris, 1993), G. Dahan highlighted a remarkable Genoese merchant of the thirteenth century who possessed an amazing exegetical erudition, perhaps gathered orally from mendicant preaching.

17. Ch. Bec, *Les marchands écrivains. Affaires et humanisme à Florence, 1375–1435* (Paris and The Hague, 1967).

18. M. Mollat, *Jacques Coeur ou l'esprit d'entreprise au XVe siècle* (Paris, 1988).

19. Nicolas Oresme, *Traité des monnaies, et autres écrits monétaires du XIVe siècle (Jean Buridan, Bartole de Sassoferrato)*, ed. C. Dupuy (Paris, 1989).

20. Cf. J. A. Paniagua, *El maestro Arnau de Villanova médico* (Valencia, 1969).

21. Cf. Charles M. Radding, *The Origins of Medieval Jurisprudence: Pavia and Bologna, 850–1150* (New Haven and London, 1988).

22. G. Giordanengo, "Résistances intellectuelles autour de la Décrétale *Super Speculam* (1219)," in *Mélanges offerts à Georges Duby* (Aix-en-Provence, 1992), 3: 141–155.

23. B. Guillemain, *La cour pontificale d'Avignon, 1309–1376. Etude d'une société*, 2nd ed. (Paris, 1966), 217.

24. H. Gilles, "Les auditeurs de Rote au temps de Clément VII et Benoît XIII (1378–1417)," *Mélanges d'archéologie et d'histoire* (Ecole Française de Rome) 67 (1955): 321–337.

25. In H. Kantorowicz, "The Poetical Sermon of a Mediaeval Jurist. Placentinus and his 'Sermo de Legibus,'" *Journal of the Warburg Institute* 2 (1938): 111–135.

26. *Qui docti fuerint, fulgebunt quasi splendor firmamenti, et qui ad iustitiam erudiunt multos, quasi stellas in perpetuas aeternitates* (cf. G. Le Bras, "*Velut splendor firmamenti:* le docteur dans le droit de l'Eglise médiévale," in *Mélanges offerts à Étienne Gilson* (Toronto and Paris, 1959), 373–388.

27. J. Gerson, *Oeuvres complètes*, ed. P. Glorieux (Paris, 1968), vol. 7, part 1: 1145.

28. J. Le Goff, *Les intellectuels au Moyen Age*, 2nd ed. (Paris, 1985), 187–188.

29. 32 for the period between 1200 and 1249; 48 from 1250 to 1299; 62 from 1300 to 1349; 72 from 1350 to 1399; 82 from 1400 to 1449, according to N. Orme, *English Schools in the Middle Ages* (London, 1973), 294.

30. M. T. Clanchy, *From Memory to Written Record. England, 1066–1307*, 2nd ed. (Oxford, 1993).

31. See for example, A. Rigaudière, "L'essor des conseillers juridiques des villes dans la France du bas Moyen Age," *Revue historique de droit français et étranger* 62 (1984): 361–390. Rpt. in A. Rigaudière, *Gouverner la ville au Moyen Age* (Paris, 1993), 215–251.

32. F. Autrand, "Culture et mentalité. Les librairies des gens du Parlement au temps de Charles VI," *Annales ESC* 28 (1973): 1219–1244.

33. Cf. Cl. Bémont, J. Le Goff, and J.-Cl. Schmitt, *L'exemplum* (Turnhout, 1982).

34. This last explanation is set forth in the excellent study by P. Paravy, "A propos de la genèse médiévale des chasses aux sorcières: le traité de Claude

Tholosan, juge dauphinois (vers 1436)," *Mélanges de l'Ecole française de Rome, Moyen Age, Temps modernes* 91 (1979): 333–379.

35. Cf. N. Orme, *From Childhood to Chivalry: The Education of the English Kings and Aristocracy, 1066–1530* (London and New York, 1984), 1–80.

36. *Chartularium Universitatis Parisiensis*, ed. H. Denifle and E. Châtelain, vol. 3 (Paris, 1894), #1446.

37. G. Petti Balbi, *L'insegnamento nella Liguria medievale. Scuole. maestri, libri* (Genoa, 1979), 75–76.

38. W. J. Courtenay, "The London *Studia* in the Fourteenth Century," *Mediaevalia et Humanistica: Studies in Medieval and Renaissance Culture* 13 (1985): 127–141.

39. N. Orme, *Education in the West of England, 1066–1548* (Exeter, 1976), and G. Petti Balbi, *L'insegnamento nella Liguria medievale.*

40. P. Glorieux, "La vie et les oeuvres de Gerson. Essai chronologique," *Archives d'histoire doctrinale et littéraire du Moyen Age* 18 (1950–1951): 150.

41. See, in *Enseignement et vie intellectuelle (IXᵉ–XVIᵉ siècle). Actes du 95ᵉ congrès nat. des Sociétés savantes—Philologie et histoire jusqu'à 1610*, vol. 1 (Paris, 1975), the studies by P. Desportes, "L'enseignement à Reims aux XIIIᵉ et XIVᵉ siècles," 107–122, and L. Carolus-Barré, "Les écoles capitulaires et les collèges de Soissons au Moyen Age et au XVIᵉ siècle," 123–226.

42. S. Guilbert, "Les écoles rurales en Champagne au XVᵉ siècle: enseignement et promotion sociale," in *Les entrées dans la vie. Initiations et apprentissages* (12ᵉ congrès de la Société des historiens médiévistes de l'enseignement supérieur public) (Nancy, 1982), 127–147.

43. Cf. J. Pourrière, *Les commencements de l'école de grammaire d'Aix-en-Provence, 1378–1413, d'après les documents inédits* (Aix-en-Provence, 1970).

44. J. W. Miner, "Change and Continuity in the Schools of Later Medieval Nuremberg," *The Catholic Historical Review* 72 (1987): 1–22.

45. See in particular N. Orme, *English Schools in the Middle Ages* (London, 1973), 87–115.

46. *Scientie parum cupidi, grammaticam ad necessitatem student, cetera studiorum genera parvi pendunt* (quoted in G. Petti Balbi, *L'insegnamento nella Liguria medievale*, 94).

47. G. Petti Balbi, *L'insegnamento nella Liguria medievale*, 57.

48. *Universities in the Middle* Ages, ed. H. de Ridder-Symoens; vol. 1 of *A History of the University in Europe* (Cambridge, 1992).

49. As I indicated in the preceding chapter, in Paris, starting in 1219, only teaching of canon law was authorized, by virtue of Pope Honorius III's bull *Super speculam.*

50. Cf. J. Verger, "Remarques sur l'enseignement des arts dans les universités du Midi à la fin du Moyen Age," *Annales du Midi* 91 (1979): 355–381.

51. For an overall account of the debate, see J. Verger, "A propos de la naissance de l'université de Paris: contexte social, enjeu politique, portée intellectuelle," in *Schulen und Studium im sozialen Wandel des hohen und späten Mittelalters*, ed. J. Fried (Sigmaringen, 1986), 69–96.

52. The essential book here is M.-M. Dufeil, *Guillaume de Saint-Amour et la polémique universitaire parisienne, 1250–1259* (Paris, 1972).

53. According to *A History of the University*, 1: 62–63, the active *studia generalia* were those in Bologna, Paris, Oxford, Montpellier (medicine and law), Cambridge, Salamanca, Padua, Naples, Vercelli, Toulouse, the Pontifical Curia (*studium Curiae*), Lisbon, and Lerida; in 1346, Vercelli had to be removed from this list and Avignon, Rome, (*studium urbis*), Orléans, Perugia, Treviso, Cahors, Pisa, Angers, Valladolid, and perhaps Grenoble added.

54. Cambridge was founded after 1209, as a result of the secession of a group of teachers and students from Oxford.

55. In Thomas Aquinas, *The Trinity and the Unicity of the Intellect* (St. Louis and London, 1946).

56. 10 December 1270 and 7 March 1227 in Paris, 18 March 1277 in Oxford. Cf. L. Bianchi, *Il vescovo e i filosofi. La condanna parigina del 1277 e l'evoluzione dell'Aristotelianismo scolastico* (Bergamo, 1990).

57. Cf. J. Verger, "Prosopographie et cursus universitaires," in *Medieval Lives and the Historian: Studies in Medieval Prosopography*, ed. N. Bulat and J.-Ph. Genet (Kalamazoo, 1986), 313–331.

58. Pisa, Prague, Florence, Perpignan, Huesca, Pavia, Cracow, Orange, Vienna, Pécs (according to *A History of the University in Europe*, 1: 63).

59. Erfurt, Heidelberg, Cologne, Buda, Ferrara, Wurzburg, Turin, Leipzig, Aix-en-Provence, St. Andrews (ibid., 1: 64).

60. Rostock, Dole, Louvain, Poitiers, Caen, Bordeaux, Catania, Barcelona, Glasgow, Valence, Trier, Greifswald, Freiburg-im-Breisgau, Basel, Ingolstadt, Nantes, Bourges, Pozsony (now Bratislava), Venice, Saragossa, Copenhagen, Mainz, Tübingen, Uppsala, Palma de Mallorca, Sigüenza, Aberdeen, Alcalá, Valencia (ibid., 1: 64–65).

61. *Princeps debet in suo imperio habere universitatem*. See M. Fournier, *Les statuts et privilèges des universités françaises depuis leur fondation jusqu'en 1789*, vol. 3 (Paris, 1892): 600.

62. *Valde congruum, necessarium et decens arbitrantur in patria nostra seu terra nobis subjecta, unam creare et instituere Universitatem [. . .] cum rari sint principes, in quorum territoriis universitas non sit fundata, in nostris vero nulla* (M. Fournier, *Les statuts et privilèges des universités françaises*, 3: 362.

63. J. Verger, "Les universités françaises au XVe siècle: crise et tentatives de réforme," *Cahiers d'histoire* 21 (1976): 43–66.

64. In J. Gerson, *Oeuvres complètes*, ed. P. Glorieux, vol. 7, pt.1 (Paris, 1968), 1137–1185.

65. Cf. J. Paquet, *Les matricules universitaires* (Turnhout, 1992).

66. According to J. Favier, *Paris au XVe siècle, 1380–1500* (Paris, 1974).

67. J. Verger, "Le recrutement géographique des universités françaises au début du XVe siècle d'après les suppliques de 1403," *Mélanges d'archéologie et d'histoire* (École française de Rome) 82 (1970): 855–902.

68. Cf. W. J. Courtenay, "The Effect of the Black Death on English Higher Education," *Speculum* 55 (1980): 696–714.

69. T. H. Aston, "Oxford's Medieval Alumni," *Past and Present* 74 (1977): 3–40, and T. H. Aston, G. D. Duncan, and T. A. R. Evans, "The Medieval Alumni of the University of Cambridge," *Past and Present* 86 (1980): 9–86.

70. A. I. Pini, "*Discere turba volens.* Studenti e vita studentesca a Bologna dalle origine alla metà del Trecento," in *Studenti e università dal XII al XIX secolo*, dir. G. P. Brizzi and A. I. Pini (Bologna, 1988), 45–136.

71. R. C. Schwinges, *Deutsche Universitätsbesucher im 14. und 15. Jahrhundert. Studien zur Sozialgeschichte des alten Reiches* (Stuttgart, 1986).

72. Cf. J. Verger, "La mobilité étudiante au Moyen Age," *Histoire de l'Éducation* 50 (1991): 65–90.

73. Cf. J. Verger, "Les étudiants slaves et hongrois dans les universités occidentales (XIIe–XVe), in *L'Église et le peuple chrétien dans les pays de l'Europe du Centre-Est et du Nord (XIVe–XVe siècle)* (Rome, 1990), 83–106.

74. Cf. J. Paquet, *Les matricules universitaires*, 128–136.

75. Cf. C. Carrère, "Refus d'une création universitaire et niveau de culture à Barcelone: hypothèses d'explication," *Le Moyen Age* 85 (1979): 245–273.

76. Cf. N. Gorochow, *Le Collège de Navarre de sa fondation (1305) au début du XVe siècle (1418). Histoire de l'institution, de sa vie intellectuelle et de son recrutement* (Paris, 1997).

77. Cf. in particular L. Stouff, "Une création d'Urbain V: le *studium* papal de Trets (1364–65)," *Provence historique* 16 (1966): 528–539, and L.-H. Labande, "Une fondation scolaire du pape Grégoire XI à Carpentras," *Mémoires de l'Académie de Vaucluse*, 2nd series, 15 (1915): 217–232.

78. A. L. Gabriel, *Student Life in Ave Maria College, Medieval Paris; History and Chartulary of the College.*

79. A. Grafton and L. Jardine, "Humanism and the School of Guarino: A Problem of Evaluation," *Past and Present* 92 (1982): 51–80.

80. Cf. G. Ortalli, *Scuole, maestri e istruzione di base tra Medioevo e Rinascimento. Il caso veneziano* (Venice, 1993), 24–29.

81. For a general discussion of the fifteenth-century Inns of Court and the relevant bibliography, see Orme, *From Childhood to Chivalry*, 74–79.

82. The system of *pecia*, which appeared in Bologna and Paris in the thirteenth century, consisted in providing the university librarians with officially supervised copies of the main textbooks; these copies were made of unbound fascicles (*pecia*) that could be lent to several copyists at once; the latter could thus produce simultaneously several copies of the same book Cf. *La production du livre universitaire au Moyen Age. Exemplar et pecia*, ed. L. J. Bataillon, B.G. Guyot, and R. H. Rouse (Paris, 1988), which allows the reader to follow the abundant literature on the subject back to the pioneering study by J. Destrez, *La pecia dans les manuscrits universitaires du XIIIe et du XIVe siècle* (Paris, 1935).

83. C. Bozzolo and E. Ornato, *Pour une histoire du livre manuscrit au Moyen Age. Trois essais de codicologie quantative* (Paris, 1980), 25–26.

84. Cf. for example, J. Verger, "Le livre dans les universités du Midi de la France à la fin du Moyen Age," in *Pratiques de la culture écrite en France au XVe siècle*, ed. M. Ornato and N. Pons (Louvain-la-Neuve, 1995), 403–420.

85. I take these figures from the studies by G. Hasenohr, "L'essor des bibliothèques privées aux XIVe et XVe siècles," and by M.-H. Jullien de Pommerol and J. Monfrin, "La bibliothèque pontificale à Avignon au XIVe siècle," in *Les bibliothèques médiévales du VIe siècle à 1530*, (Paris, 1989), 215–263 and 147–169, vol. 1 of *Histoire des bibliothèques françaises*, dir. A. Vernet (Paris, 1989).

86. See for example S. Stelling-Michaud, "Le transport international des manuscrits juridiques bolonais entre 1265 et 1320," in *Mélanges d'histoire économique et sociale en hommage au professeur Antony Babel* (Geneva, 1963), 1: 95–127.

87. These figures are also taken from the previously cited studies by Hasenohr and by Jullien de Pommerol and Monfrin.

88. Figures taken from M.-C. Garand, "Les anciennes bibliothèques du XIIIe au XVe siècle," in *Histoire des bibliothèques françaises*, 1: 45–63.

89. These figures and those that follow are taken from M.-H. Jullien de Pommerol, "Livres d'étudiants, bibliothèques de collèges et d'universités" in *Histoire des bibliothèques françaises*, 1: 93–111.

90. N. Ker, "Oxford College Libraries before 1500," in *Les universités à la fin du moyen Age*, ed. J. Paquet and J. Ijsewign (Louvain, 1978), 293–311.

91. Cited in H.-J. Martin, "La révolution de l'imprimé," in *Le livre conquérant. Du Moyen Age au milieu du XVIIe siècle*, vol. 1 of *Histoire de l'édition française*, dir. R. Chartier and H.-J. Martin, 2nd ed. (Paris, 1989), 165–185.

92. Cf. Jullien de Pommerol, "Livres d'étudiants, bibliothèques de collèges et d'université."

93. Cf. M. B. Parkes, "The Provision of Books," in *Late Medieval Oxford*, ed. J. I. Catto and R. Evans (Oxford, 1992), 407–483. Vol. 2 of *The History of the University of Oxford*.

94. Thus for example Juan Alfonso de Benavente, in his *Ars et doctrina studendi et docendi*, ed. B. Alonso Rodriguez (Salamanca, 1972), 90.

95. F. Autrand, "Culture et mentalité. Les librairies des gens du Parlement au temps de Charles VI," *Annales ESC* 28 (1973): 1219–1244.

96. Cf. G. Hasenohr, "Les sorts des bibliothèques privées au XIVᵉ et XVᵉ siècles," 90, n. 2.

97. At least until 1444, the date of the foundation of the University of Catania, which remained of secondary importance.

98. H. Bresc, *Livre et société en Sicile (1299–1499)* (Palermo, 1971).

99. D. Nebbiai-Dalla Guarda, *Livres, patrimoine, profession: les bibliothèques de quelques médecins en Italie (XIVᵉ–XVᵉ siècles)*. The author has permitted me to read this as yet unpublished study.

100. I draw these figures from J.-M. Dureau, "Les premiers ateliers français," in *Histoire de l'édition française*, 1: 186–202.

101. Cf. C. Bozzolo and E. Ornato, "Les bibliothèques entre le manuscrit et l'imprimé," in *Histoire des bibliothèques françaises*, 1: 333–347.

102. Cf. L. Febvre and H. J. Martin, *L'apparition du livre*, new ed. (Paris, 1971), 351–365.

103. Cf. D. Coq, "Les incunables: textes anciens, textes nouveaux," in *Histoire de l'édition française*, 1: 203–227.

104. P. Aquilon, "Petites et moyennes bibliothèques," in *Histoire des bibliothèques françaises*, 1: 285–309.

105. A German Dominican theologian (ca. 1380–1438), the author of *Fornicarius seu myrmecia bonorum*, which devotes long passages to witchcraft.

106. J. Michelet, *Oeuvres complètes* (Paris, 1978), 7: 85.

Part II

1. Cf. G. Post, K. Giocarinis, and R. Kay, "The Medieval Heritage of a Humanist Ideal. 'Scientia donum Dei, unde veni not potest,'" *Traditio*, 11 (1955): 195–234.

2. This attraction to public offices, which provided the crowning touch, often less lucrative than honorable, for careers that were first pursued privately, has been emphasized by J. R. Strayer in his prosopographical study on *Les gens de justice de Languedoc sous Philippe le Bel* (Toulouse, 1970).

3. *Henrici de Gandavo opera omnia*, V, *Quodlibet I*, ed. R. Macken (Louvain and Leiden, 1979), 195–202.

4. The records of this suit have been published in the *Chartularium Universitatis Parisiensis*, ed. H. Denifle and E. Châtelain, vol. 3 (Paris, 1894), nos. 1528–1531, 1546).

5. *Chartularium Universitas Parisiensis*, vol. 1 (Paris, 1889), no. 515.

6. Cf. J. Verger, "Les professeurs des universités françaises à la fin du Moyen Age," in *Intellectuels français, intellectuels hongrois. XIIᵉ–XXᵉ siècles*, ed. J. Le Goff and B. Köpesczi (Budapest and Paris, 1985), 23–29.

7. D. Zanetti, "A l'université de Pavie au XVᵉ siècle: les salaires des professeurs," *Annales ESC* 17 (1952): 421–433.

8. W. J. Courtenay, *Teaching Careers at the University of Paris in the Thirteenth and Fourteenth Centuries* (Texts and Studies in the History of Medieval Education, vol. 18), (Notre Dame, 1952), 29.

9. Cf. H. Grundmann, *"Litteratus—Illitteratus.* Der Wandel nach einer Bildungsnorm vom Altertum zum Mittelalter," *Archiv für Kulturgeschichte* 40 (1958): 1–65.

10. I repeat here the conclusions I drew in my study "Études et culture universitaire du personnel de la Curie avignonnaise," in *Aux origines de l'État moderne. Le fonctionnement administratif de la papauté d'Avignon,* Coll. de l'École française de Rome, 56 (Rome, 1990), 61–78.

11. Cf. J.-L. Gazzaniga, *L'Église du Midi à la fin du règne de Charles VII (1444–1461) d'après la jurisprudence du Parlement de Toulouse* (Paris, 1976).

12. In the following pages, the figures cited are drawn, unless otherwise indicated, from P. Moraw's chapter, "Careers of Graduates," in *A History of the University in Europe* Cambridge, 1992), 244–279.; vol. 1 of *Universities in the Middle Ages,* ed. H. de Ridder-Symoens.

13. J. W. Baldwin, *"Studium et regnum.* The Penetration of University Personnel into French and English Administration at the Turn of the Twelfth and Thirteenth Centuries," *Revue des Études Islamiques* 44 (1976): 199–215.

14. H. Millet, *Les chanoines du chapitre cathédral de Laon. 1272–1412.* Coll. de l'École française de Rome, 56 (Rome, 1982), 87–95.

15. J. Verger, "Les chanoines et les universités," in *Le monde des chanoines (XIe–XIVe siècle),* Cahiers de Fanjeaux, 24 (Toulouse, 1989), 285–307, esp. 302–303.

16. See, in *I canonici al servizio dello Stato in Europa, secoli XIII–XVI/Les chanoines au service de l'État en Europe du XIIIe au XVIe siècle,* ed. H. Millet (Modena and Ferrara, 1992), the studies by G. Battioni, "Il capitolo cattedrale di Parma (1450–1500)," 73–92; M. Pellegrini, "Il capitolo della cattedrale di Pavia in età sforzesca (1450–1535)," 73–92; R. Montel, "Les chanoines de la basilique Saint-Pierre de Rome (fin XIIIe siècle–fin XVIe siècle): esquisse d'une enquête prosopographique," 105–118.

17. A. Rucquoi, *Valladolid au Moyen Age (1080–1480)* (Paris, 1993), 435.

18. See the introduction by B. Guenée, "Michel Pintoin, sa vie, son oeuvre," in *Chronique du Religieux de Saint-Denys,* ed. L. Bellaguet (rpt., Paris, 1994).

19. Let us note, for example, that between the end of the thirteenth century and the beginning of the sixteenth century, the Germanic provinces of the Carmelite order (*Alemania superior* and *inferior* and *Saxonia*) alone sent no less than 3349 friars to pursue university-level *studia* in theology, 122 of which were awarded doctor's degrees. See F.-B. Lickteig, *The German Carmelites at the Medieval Universities,* Textus et studia historica Carmelitana (Rome, 1981), 416.

20. A. Vauchez, *La sainteté en Occident aux derniers siècles du Moyen Age d'après les procès de canonisation et autres documents hagiographiques,* Bibliothèque des Écoles françaises d'Athènes et de Rome, 241 (Rome, 1981), 460–472 ("Valorisation de la culture").

21. J. Verger, "L'exégèse de l'université," in *Le Moyen Age et la Bible,* ed. P. Riché and G. Lobrichon (Paris, 1984), 199–232, esp. 231.

22. H. Martin, *Le métier de prédicateur à la fin du Moyen Age. 1350–1520* (Paris, 1988), 72–75.

23. H. Millet, "Les chanoines au service de l'État: bilan d'une étude comparative," in *L'État moderne: Genèse. Bilans et perspectives,* ed. J.-Ph. Genet (Paris, 1990), pp. 137–145, esp. p. 143.

24. See R. B. Dobson, "The Canons of York Cathedral, 1400–1500" and D. N. Lepine, "The Canons of Exeter Cathedral, 1300–1445," in Millet, *I canonici,* 15–26 and 27–46.

25. See E. Lalou, "Les chanoines au service de Philippe le Bel, 1285–1314," in Millet, *I canonici,* 219–230.

26. This and subsequent paragraphs draw principally on the works of F. Autrand, *Naissance d'un grand corps de l'État. Les gens du Parlement de Paris 1345–1454* (Paris, 1981), and "L'apparition d'un nouveau groupe social," in *Des origines au XVe siècle*, ed. M. Pinet (Paris, 1993), 311–443; vol. 1 of *Histoire de la fonction politique en France*.

27. B. Guenée, *Tribunaux et gens de justice dans le bailliage de Senlis à la fin du Moyen Age (vers 1380–vers 1550)* (Strasbourg, 1963).

28. J. Bartier, *Légistes et gens de finance au XVe siècle. Les conseillers du duc de Bourgogne sous Philippe le Bon et Charles le Téméraire*, 2 vols. (Brussels, 1955–57).

29. J. R. Strayer, *Les gens de justice du Languedoc*.

30. J. Chiffoleau, *Les justices du pape. Délinquance et criminalité dans la région d'Avignon au XIVe siècle* (Paris, 1984), 285–317.

31. L. Martines, *Lawyers and Statecraft in Renaissance Florence* (Princeton, 1968).

32. Cf. A Rucquoi, *Histoire médiévale de la péninsule Ibérique* (Paris, 1993), 308–322.

33. B. Leroy, *Le royaume de Navarre. Les hommes et le pouvoir, XIIIe–XVe siècle* (Biarritz, 1995), 208–212.

34. A. L. de Carvalho Homem, *O Desembargo regio (1320–1433)*, 471–472.

35. ... *ut tandem studiosi viri moribus et scientia decorati reipublice preessent et eidem salubriter consulerent.* Quoted in M. Fournier, *Les statuts et privilèges des universités françaises depuis leur fondation jusqu'en 1789*, vol. 3 (Paris, 1892), no. 1578.

36. Cf. above, p. 32.

37. Cf. J. Verger, "Pour une histoire de la maîtrise au Moyen Age: quelques jalons," *Medievales* 13 (1987), 117–130.

38. *Magister nomen est equivocum ad plura.* See Konrad von Megenberg, *Werke. Ökonomik (Buch III)*, ed. S. Krüger (Stuttgart, 1984), 24. For Konrad, the word *magister* included three distinct elements—the university degree (*titulus*), the actual knowledge (*res*), and the social appelation (*nominacio*)—of which many *magistri* possessed only one or two.

39. Cf. E. Türk, Nugae curialum, *Le règne d'Henri II Planagenêt (1149–1189) et l'éthique politique* (Geneva, 1977).

40. F. Autrand, *Charles VI le sage* (Paris, 1994), 728.

41. Cf. *Le forme della propaganda politica nel Due e Trecento*, ed. P. Cammarosano, Coll. de l'École française de Rome, 201 (Rome, 1994).

42. See the collection of texts published under the title *Splendeurs de la cour de Bourgogne. Récits et chroniques*, ed. D. Régnier-Bohnler (Paris, 1995).

43. Cf. J. Krynen, *L'empire du roi. Idées et croyances politiques en France, XIIIe–XVe siècle* (Paris, 1993), esp. 384–414.

44. See the introduction to Pierre Dubois, *The Recovery of the Holy Land*, trans. W. I. Brandt (New York, 1956).

45. Christine de Pisan, *Le livre des fais et bonnes meurs du sage roy Charles V*, ed. S. Solente (Paris, 1940), 2: 46–47.

46. Fundamental to the superabundant literature on this subject are the works of H. Baron, and particularly his masterwork, *The Crisis of the Early Italian Renaissance. Civic Humanism and Republican Liberty in an Age of Classicism and Tyranny*, 2 vols. (Princeton, 1955).

47. S. B. Chrimes, "Richard II's Questions to the Judges," *Law Quarterly Review* 72 (1956): 365–390.

48. L.S. Domonkos, "Ecclesiastical Patrons as a Factor in the Hungarian Renaissance," *New Review of East-European History* 14 (1974): 100–116.

49. C. Beaune, *Naissance de la nation France* (Paris, 1985).
50. Cf. above, 89.
51. This is, at least, the thesis maintained in R. N. Swanson, *Universities, Academics and the Great Schism* (Cambridge, 1979).
52. J. W. Stieber, *Pope Eugenius IV, The Council of Basel and the Secular and Ecclesiastical Authorities in the Empire. The Conflict over Supreme Authority and Power in the Church* (Leiden, 1978).
53. F. Smahel, *La révolution hussite, une anomalie historique* (Paris, 1985).
54. F. J. Pegues, *The Lawyers of the Last Capetians* (Princeton, 1962), and J. Favier, "Les légistes et le gouvernement de Philippe le Bel," *Journal des Savants* (1969): 92–108.
55. F. Autrand, *Charles V le Sage*, 688–712; P.-R. Gaussin, *Louis XI, un roi entre deux mondes* (Paris, 1976), 150–152.
56. P.-R. Guassin, "Les conseillers de Charles VII (1418–1461). Essai de politologie historique," *Francia* 10 (1982): 67–130.
57. R. Cazelles, *La société politique et la crise de la royauté sous Philippe de Valois* (Paris, 1958), and *Société politique, noblesse et couronne sous Jean le Bon et Charles V* (Geneva and Paris, 1982).
58. A. Rucquoi, *Valladolid au Moyen Age (1080–1480)* (Paris, 1993), 289–291.
59. Cf. A. L. de Carvalho Homem, "O Doutor João das Regras no Desembargo e no Conselho Régio (1384–1404)—Brevas Notas," in *Estudios de História de Portugal. Homenagem a A. H. de Olivieira Marques*, vol. 1, *Sécolos X–XV* (Lisbon, 1982), 241–253.
60. G. Brucker, *The Civic World of Early Renaissance Florence* (Princeton, 1977), 269.
61. This is shown by the interminable suit before the Parlement of Toulouse from 1448 to 1470, whose essential documents are preserved in the Archives of the Commune of Montpellier (FF 75 and 76).
62. Ph. Wolff, *Commerces et marchands de Toulouse (vers 1350–vers 1450)* (Paris, 1954), 541.
63. R. Fédou, *Les hommes de loi lyonnais à la fin du Moyen Age. Etude sur les origines de la classe de robe* (Lyon, 1964), 279–292 and 375–396).
64. J. Favier, *Nouvelle Histoire de Paris. Paris au XVe siècle (1380–1500)* (Paris, 1974), 420–430.
65. P. Trio, "A Medieval Students' Confraternity at Ypres: The Notre-Dame Confraternity of Paris Students," *History of Universities* 5 (1985): 15–53.
66. F. Autrand, *Naissance d'un grand corps de l'Etat. Les gens du Parlement de Paris, 1345–1454* (Paris, 1981), 53–108.
67. The generally unsuccessful resistance of the élites, especially the ecclesiastical élites, in the south is well discussed in J.-L. Gazzaniga, *L'Église du Midi à la fin du règne de Charles VII (1444–1461), d'après la jurisprudence du Parlement de Toulouse* (Paris, 1976).
68. M. Allabert, "Les avocats devant the Parlement de Toulouse à travers les registres d'audience (1444–1483), in *École nationale des Chartes. Positions des thèses... 1989* (Paris, 1989), 7–15.
69. B. Guenée, *Tribunaux et gens de justice dans le bailliage de Senlis à la fin du Moyen Age (vers 1380–vers 1550)* (Strasbourg, 1963), 192.
70. Cf. J. Shatzmiller, "Médecins municipaux en Provence, Catalogne et autres régions de l'Europe méridionale (1350–1400)," in *Les sociétés urbaines en France méridionale et en péninsule Ibérique au Moyen Age* (Paris, 1991), 329–336.
71. D. Jacquart, *Le milieu médical en France du XIIe au XVe siècle* (Geneva, 1981), 237–257.

72. *Sicut rurales doctores et praedicatores eorum quae praedicant et docent frequenter ignorant rationes, sed tamen docent confidentur, quia sciunt ea quae docent, a magistris se accepisse.* —*Henrici de Gandavo opera omnia, V, Quolibet I,* ed. R. Macken (Louvain and Leiden, 1979), 199.

73. Cf. above, pp. 53–54.

74. Archives of the department of Haute-Garonne, Archives of the Château of Pinsaguel, 6 J 164, folio 207.

75. R. Aubenas, *Étude sur le notariat provençal au Moyen Age et sous l'Ancien Régime* (Aix-en-Provence, 1931), 72; L. Martines, *Lawyers and Statecraft in Renaissance Florence,* 15.

76. L. Stouff, *Arles à la fin du Moyen Age* (Aix-en-Provence, 1986), 1: 17 and 144; R. Fédou, *Les hommes de loi lyonnais à la fin du Moyen Age. Étude sur les origines de la classe de robe* (Lyon, 1964), 160.

77. R. Fossier, *La société médiévale* (Paris, 1991), 417.

78. The theme and expression were probably initiated by M. H. Curtis, "The Alienated Intellectuals of Early Stuart England," *Past and Present* 23 (1962): 25–43.

79. Let us note that in the list of the fifty principal leaders of the Ciompi drawn up by A. Stella in his book *La Révolte des Ciompi. Les hommes, les lieux, le travail* (Paris, 1993), 90–91, we nonetheless find a physician, a notary, and a schoolmaster; others include a tavern keeper, a baker, a locksmith, and forty-four textile workers.

80. See the studies collected in *Heresy and Literacy, 100–1530,* ed. P. Biller and A. Hudson (Cambridge, 1994).

81. See for example the analysis of the very "appropriative" themes of Florentine preaching in the time of the Compi, in Ch.-M. de La Roncière, "Pauvres et pauvreté à Florence au XIVᵉ siècle," in *Études sur l'histoire de la pauvreté (Moyen Age–XVIᵉ siècle),* ed. M. Mollat (Paris, 1984), 2: 75–93.

82. Analysis of the question in Ph. Genet, "Wyclif et les Lollards," *Historiens et Géographes* 294 (1983): 869–886.

83. G. Epiney-Burgard, *Gérard Grote (1340–1384) et les débuts de la dévotion moderne* (Wiesbaden, 1970).

84. J.-Cl. Maire Vigueur, "Cola di Rienzo," in *Dizionario biografico degli Italiani* (Rome, 1982), 26: 662–275.

85. R. Fédou, "Une révolte populaire à Lyon au XIVᵉ siècle: La Rebeyne de 1436," *Cahiers d'Histoire* 3 (1958): 129–149.

86. H. Martin, "L'Eglise éducatrice. Messages apparents, contenus sous-jacents," in *Educations médiévales. L'enfance, l'école, l'Eglise en Occiden (VIᵉ–XVᵉ siècles,* ed. J. Verger, special issue of *Histoire de l'Education* 50 (1991): 91–117.

87. *The Complete Works of Geoffrey Chaucer,* ed. W. W. Skeat (Oxford, 1894), 4:15, vv. 480–482.

88. J. Bignami-Odier and A. Vernet, "Les livres de Richard de Bazoques," *Bibliothèque de l'École des Chartes* 110 (1952): 124–153.

89. H. Bresc, *Livre et société en Sicile (1299–1499)* (Palermo, 1971), 138–140, 179–182.

90. M. Boulet, *Quaestiones Johannis Galli* (Paris, 1944).

91. A. Gouron, "Doctrine médiévale et justice fiscale. Pierre Antiboul et son *Tractatus de muneribus,*" *Analecta Cracoviensia* 7 (1975): 309–321; rpt. in A. Gouron, *La science du droit dans le Midi de la France au Moyen Age* (London, 1984), no. 10.

92. On Fortescue, see the introduction to Sir John Fortescue, *De Laudibus Legum Anglie,* ed. S. B. Chrimes (Cambridge, 1942).

93. L. Martines, *Lawyers and Statecraft in Renaissance Florence,* 103–105.

94. Cf. M.-Cl. Marandet, "Approche d'un milieu social: le notariat en Midi toulousain aux XIVᵉ et XVᵉ siècles," in *Visages du notariat dans l'histoire du Midi toulousain (XIVᵉ-XIXᵉ siècles*, ed. J.-L. Laffont (Toulouse, 1992), 81–115.

95. A. Rigaudière, "La fortune des hommes de loi sanflorains d'après le livre d'estimes de 1380," *Studia historica Gandensia* 267 (1986) [=*Structures sociales et topographie de la pauvreté et de la richesse aux XIVᵉ et XVᵉ siècles. Aspects méthodologiques et résultats de recherches récentes*], 13–49, esp. 41 (rpt. in A. Rigaudière, *Gouverner la ville au Moyen Age* (Paris, 1993), 275–318.

96. The importance of this process has been shown with particular clarity in Lyon society at the end of the Middle Ages, in R. Fédou, *Les Hommes de loi lyonnais à la fin du Moyen Age*, 153–178.

Part III

1. Cf. F. Autrand, "L'apparition d'un nouveau groupe social," in *Histoire de la fonction publique en France*, ed. M. Pinet, vol. 1, *Des origines au XIᵉ siècle* (Paris, 1993), 311–443.

2. Cf. J. Paquet, "Recherches sur l'universitaire 'pauvre' au Moyen Age," *Revue belge de philologie et d'histoire* 56 (1978): 301–353.

3. For *magister*, see above, p. 102. *Burgensis* applied to a person living in any community having its own law, and we have to remember here that at the end of the Middle Ages a country like Germany had about 4,000 towns and villages, ranging from Cologne and Frankfurt to small rural towns, all considered as urban communities. *Clericus* could designate either a cleric who had received only minor orders, or any member of the clergy, or an educated man who had attended schools (even if he was married and led an entirely secular life).

4. F. Autrand, *Charles V le Sage* (Paris, 1994), 707; M. Fournier *Les statuts et privilèges des universités françaises depuis leur fondation jusqu'en 1789*, vol. 1 (Paris, 1890), no. 595 and vol. 2 (1891), no. 1435.

5. Circular announcing the foundation of the *studium* published in *Ryccardi de Sancto Germano notarii chronica*, ed. C. A. Garufi (*Rerum Italicarum Scriptores*, VII/2) (Bologna, 1938), 113–116.

6. M. Fournier, *Les statuts et privilèges des universités françaises*, vol. 2, no. 944.

7. A. Diverrès, *La Chronique métrique attribuée à Geoffroy de Paris* (Paris, 1956), 212, vv. 6433–6442.

8. F. Autrand, *Naissance d'un grand corps de l'État. Les gens du Parlement de Paris, 1345–1454* (Paris, 1981), 75, 326.

9. *The Paston letters, 1422–1509*, ed. James Gairdner, 3 vols. (London, 1874); *The Paston letters*, ed. John Fenn and re-edited by Mrs. Archer Hind, 2 vols. (London and New York, 1938).

10. R. Fédou, *Les hommes de loi lyonnais à la fin du Moyen Age*, and H. Millet, *Les chanoines du chapitre cathédral de Laon, 1272–1412*, esp. 71–100.

11. See P. Trio, "Financing of University Students in the Middle Ages: A New Orientation," *History of Universities* 4 (1984): 1–24.

12. L. Martines, *Lawyers and Statecraft in Renaissance Florence*, 69.

13. R. Fédou, *Les hommes de loi lyonnais à la fin du Moyen Age*, 153–178, 416.

14. B. Delmas, "Le chancelier Jacques Angeli (1390–1455) restaurateur de l'université de médecine de Montpellier au début du XVᵉ siècle," *Actes du 110ᵉ Congrès national des Sociétés savantes. Section d'histoire des sciences et des techniques*. Vol. 2, *Histoire de l'École médicale de Montpellier* (Paris, 1985), 39–54.

15. J. Pourrière, *Les commencements de l'école de grammaire d'Aix-en-Provence, 1378–1413, d'après des documents inédits* (Aix-en-Provence, 1970), 28.

16. Cf. above, p. 117.

17. R. Fédou, *Les hommes de loi lyonnais à la fin du Moyen Age*, 335–350.

18. Ph. Wolff, "Une famille du XIIIe au XVIe siècle: les Ysalguier de Toulouse," *Mélanges d'histoire sociale* 1 (1942): 7–31. Rpt. in Ph. Wolff, *Regards sur le Midi médiéval* (Toulouse, 1978), 233–257.

19. N. Coulet, "Les juristes dans les villes de la Provence médiévale," in *Les sociétés urbaines en France méridionale et en péninsule Ibérique au Moyen Age* (Paris, 1991), 311–327.

20. R.Favreau,*La ville de Poitiers à la fin du Moyen Age*(Paris, 1978), 2: 487–541.

21. L. Martines, *Lawyers and Statecraft in Renaissance Florence*, 62–78 and 482–505.

22. At least in France, titles of nobility originally benefited particularly royal officials (cf. J. Rogozinski, "Ennoblement by the Crown and Social Stratification in France, 1285–1322," in W. C. Jordan, B. McNab, and T. F. Ruiz, eds., *Order and Innovation in the Middle Ages. Essays in Honor of Joseph R. Strayer* (Princeton, 1976), 273–291, 500–515). Later on, a simple *de facto* ennoblement (by social prestige, marriages, the purchase of seigneuries, etc.) increasingly sufficed for the most important men, such as councilors in Parlement; but simple notaries and royal secretaries continued to be very eager to acquire titles of nobility.

23. F. Autrand, *Naissance d'un grand corps de l'État. Les gens du Parlement de Paris*, esp.163–261.

24. R. I. Storey, "Gentleman-Bureaucrats," in C. H. Clough, ed., *Profession, Vocation and Culture in Later Medieval England. Essays Dedicated to the Memory of A. R. Myers* (Liverpool, 1982), 90–129.

25. Cf. for example A. Gouron, "Enseignement du droit, légistes et canonistes dans le Midi de la France à la fin du XIIIe et au début du XIVe siècle," *Recueil de mémoires et travaux publiés par la Société d'histoire du droit et des institutions des anciens pays de droit écrit* 5 (1966): 1–33.

26. Figures drawn from J. Paquet, *Les matricules universitaires* (Typologie des sources du Moyen Age occidental, 65) (Turnhout, 1992), 131, and Chr. Renardy, *Le monde des maîtres universitaires du diocèse de Liège, 1140–1350). Recherches sur sa composition et ses activités* (Paris, 1979), 161.

27. J. Verger, "Moines, chanoines, et collèges réguliers dans les universités du Midi au Moyen Age," in *Naissance et fonctionnement des réseaux monastiques et canoniaux* (CERCOR, Travaux et recherches, 1) (Saint-Étienne, 1991), 511–549.

28. Cf. P. Desportes, "L'enseignement à Reims aux XIIIe et XIVe siècles," in *Enseignement et vie intellectuelle (IXe–XVIe siècle)* (Paris, 1975), 1: 107–122, esp. 120–121.

29. A. Rigaudière, "L'essor des conseillers juridiques des villes dans la France du bas Moyen Age," *Revue historique de droit français et étranger* 62 (1984): 361–390; rpt. in A. Rigaudière, *Gouverner la ville au Moyen Age* (Paris, 1993), 215–251.

30. I return here to the conclusions of my study "Noblesse et savoir. Étudiants nobles aux universités d'Avignon, Cahors, Montpellier, et Toulouse (fin du XIVe siècle)," in Ph. Contamine, ed., *La Noblesse au Moyen Age. XIe–XVe siècles. Essais à la mémoire de Robert Boutruche* (Paris, 1976), 289–313. In the absence of evidence to the contrary, these conclusions seem to me applicable, *mutatis mutandis*, to all European universities of the end of the Middle Ages.

31. Regulation cited in M. H. Shank, *"Unless You Believe, You Shall Not Understand": Logic, University, and Society in Late Medieval Vienna* (Princeton, 1988), 23.

32. Cf. G. Le Bras, "*Velut splendor firmamenti*: le docteur dans le droit de l'Eglise médiévale," in *Mélanges offerts à Étienne Gilson* (Toronto and Paris, 1959), 373–388.

33. This text can be found in D. Maffei, "Dottori e studenti nel pensiero di Simone da Borsano," *Studia Gratiana* 15 (1972): 231–249.

34. *Item doctori ingredienti ad principis curiam non debet vetari ingressus sed admitti, etiam ad secreta iudicum admitti.* Quoted in D. Maffei, "Dottori e studenti," 241.

35. *Miles inermis milicie.* Quoted in M. Boulet, *Quaestiones Johannis Galli* (Paris, 1944), xcviii.

36. R. Fédou, "Une famille au XIVᵉ et XVᵉ siècles: les Jossard de Lyon," *Annales ESC* 9 (1954): 461–480.

37. J. Segondy, "Une famille de juristes montpelliérains: Les Rebuffy," in *Fédération historique du Languedoc méditerranéen et du Roussillon. XXXVIIᵉ et XXXVII Congrès (Limoux-Nimes) (1964–1965)* (Montpellier, s.d.), 143–153.

38. A. Padovani, *L'archivio di Odofredo. Le pergamene della familigia Gandolfi Odofredi. Edizione et regesto (1163–1499)* (Spoleto, 1992), 61–62.

39. See above, pp. 146–148, 151, and 161.

40. Cf. D. Courtemanche, "Les testaments parisiens sous Charles VI: des écrits sur soi au service de la mémoire collective," *Le Moyen Age* 97 (1991), 367–387.

41. Quoted by R. Favreau, *La Ville de Poitiers à la fin du Moyen Age. Une capitale régionale* (Poitiers, 1978), 2: 487.

42. See M.-D. Chenu, *La théologie au douzième siècle*, 2ⁿᵈ ed. (Paris, 1966), chap. 15, "Les *Magistri*. La 'science' théologique," 323–350.

43. Cf. R. Fédou, *Les hommes de loi lyonnais à la fin du Moyen Age*, 356–357, 363–365.

44. R. Grandi, *I monumenti dei dottori et la scultura a Bologna (1267–1348)* (Bologna, 1982).

45. J. Verger, "Le transfert de modèles d'organisation de l'Église à l'État à la fin du Moyen Age," in J.-Ph., Genet and B. Vincent, eds., *État et Église dans la genèse de l'État moderne* (Madrid, 1986), 31–39.

46. See J. Coleman, ed., *The Individual in Political Theory and Practice* (Oxford, 1996), esp. chap. 1, "The Individual and the Medieval State," by J. Coleman, and chap. 3, "The Contribution of Medieval Universities to the Birth of Individualism and Individual Thought," by J. Verger.

47. B. Guenée, *Tribunaux et gens de justice dans le bailliage de Senlis à la fin du Moyen Age (vers 1380–vers 1550)* (Strasbourg, 1963), 384, 418.

48. *Histoire des universités en France*, dir. J. Verger (Toulouse, 1986), 182.

49. Cf. A. M. Carrabias Torres, *Colegios mayores: centros de poder*, 3 vols. (Salamanca, 1986).

50. *Der Humanismus und die oberen Fakultäten*, ed. G. Keil, B. Moeller, and W. Trusen (Weinheim, 1987).

51. Cf. *Università, Accademie e Società scientifiche in Italia e in Germania dal Cinquecento et Settecento*, ed. L. Boehm and E. Raimondi (Bologna, 1981).

52. Baldassare Castiglione, *The Book of the Courtier*, trans. Charles S. Singleton (New York, 1959), 73.

Bibliography

The following bibliography is relatively brief. In the notes to this book the reader will find, in addition to a few references to medieval sources published or unpublished, the titles of many books and articles intended to support with precise examples one or another assertion made in the course of the discussion. With a few exceptions, these titles have not been repeated below.

This bibliography is essentially limited to studies that are both general enough to illuminate the chief historical problems mentioned in this book and recent enough to contain numerous bibliographical references to older research. On the other hand, only those studies have been listed that focus on the subject of this book, namely the articulation in given individuals or groups of an intellectual competency and a social practice. It would in fact have been impossible and pointless to try to present here, even in an abridged form, the whole of the bibliography relevant to either the history of scholarly culture or the history of education, not to mention, *a fortiori*, the bibliography relevant to social or political history in general.

I. Culture, Education, Books

a. Culture and Education

Garin, E. *L'educazione in Europa (1400–1600): problemi e programmi*. Bari: Laterza, 1957.
Paul, J. *Histoire intellectuelle de l'Occident médiéval*. Paris: A. Colin, 1973.
Piltz, A. *The World of Medieval Learning*. Trans. David Jones. Oxford: Blackwell, 1981.

b. Schools and Universities

Bellomo, M. *Saggio sull'università nell'età del diritto comune*. Catania: Giannotta, 1979.
Brizzi, G. P. and J. Verger. *Le università dell'Europa*. 6 vols. Cinisello Balsamo: A. Pizzi, 1990–1995. Esp. vols. 1, 4, and 5.

Catto, J. I., ed. *The Early Oxford Schools*. Vol. 1 of *The History of the University of Oxford*. Oxford: Clarendon Press, 1992.

Catto, J. I., and R. Evans. *Late Medieval Oxford*. Vol. 2 of *The History of the University of Oxford*. Oxford: Clarendon Press, 1992.

Cobban, A. B. *The Medieval Universities: Their Development and Organization*. London, 1975.

Cobban, A. B. *The Medieval English Universities. Oxford and Cambridge to c. 1500*. Berkeley and Los Angeles: University of California Press, 1988.

Fried, J., ed. *Schulen und Studium im sozialen Wandel des hohen und späten Mittelalters*. Sigmaringen: J. Thorbecke, 1986.

Grendler, P. F. *Schooling in Renaissance Italy. Literacy and Learning, 1300–1600*. Baltimore and London: Johns Hopkins University Press, 1989.

Leader, D. R. *The University to 1546*. Vol. 1 of *A History of the University of Cambridge*. Cambridge: Cambridge University Press, 1988.

Le Goff, J. *Les intellectuels au Moyen Age*. 2nd ed. Paris: Editions du Seuil, 1985.

Schwinges, R. C. *Deutsche Universitätsbesucher im 14. und 15. Jahrhundert. Studien zur Sozialgeschichte des alten Reiches*. Stuttgart: F. Steiner, 1986.

Università e società nei secoli XII–XVI. Pistoia: Centro italiano di Studi di storia e d'arte, 1982.

Verger, J. *Les universités au Moyen Age*. Paris: Presses Universitaires de France, 1973.

Verger, J., dir. *Histoire des Universités en France*. Toulouse: Privat, 1986.

Verger, J. *Les universités françaises au Moyen Age*. Leiden: Brill, 1995.

c. Books and Libraries

Glénisson, J., dir. *Le livre au Moyen Age*. Paris: Editions du CNRS, 1988.

Vernet, A., dir. *Les bibliothèques médiévales du Ve siècle à 1530*. Vol. 1 of *Histoire des bibliothèques françaises*. Paris: Promodis, 1989.

II. The Men of Learning in the Society of Their Time

a. General Studies

Classen, P. *Studium und Gesellschaft im Mittelalter*. Stuttgart: A. Hiersemann, 1983.

Genet, J.-Ph. and G. Lottes, eds. *L'État moderne et les élites, XIIIe–XVIIIe siècles. Apports et limites de la méthode prosopographique*. Paris: Publications de la Sorbonne, 1996.

Guenée, B. *L'Occident aux XIVe et XVe siècles. Les États*. 4th ed. Paris: Presses Universitaires de France, 1991.

Poirion, D., dir. *Milieux universitaires et mentalité urbaine au Moyen Age*. Paris: Presses de l'Université de Paris-Sorbonne, 1987.

Reinhard, W., ed. *Power Élites and State Building*. Oxford: Clarendon Press, 1996.

b. A Few National and Regional Monographs

Autrand, F. *Naissance d'un grands corps de l'État. Les gens du Parlement de Paris, 1345–1454.* Paris: Publications de la Sorbonne, 1981.

Brucker, G. *The Civic World of Early Renaissance Florence.* Princeton: Princeton University Press, 1977.

Bullough, V. L. *The Development of Medicine as a Profession: The Contribution of the Medieval University to Modern Medicine.* New York and Basel: S. Karger, 1966.

Clough, C. H., ed. *Vocation and Culture in Later Medieval England. Essays Dedicated to the Memory of A. R. Myers.* Liverpool: Liverpool University Press, 1982.

Fédou, R. *Les hommes de loi lyonnais à la fin du Moyen Age. Étude sur les origines de la classe de robe.* Lyon: Publications de l'Université de Lyon, 1964.

Gorochov, N. *Le collège de Navarre et sa fondation (1305) au début du XVᵉ siècle (1418). Histoire de l'institution, de sa vie intellectuelle et de son recrutement.* Paris: H. Champion, 1997.

Jacquart, D. *Le milieu médical en France du XIIᵉ au XVᵉ siècle.* Geneva: Droz, 1981.

Martines, L. *The Social World of the Florentine Humanists, 1390–1460.* Princeton: Princeton University Press, 1963.

Martines, L. *Lawyers and Statecraft in Renaissance Florence.* Princeton: Princeton University Press, 1968.

Millet, H. *Les chanoines du chapitre cathédral de Laon. 1272–1412.* Rome: École française de Rome, 1982.

Millet, H., dir. *I canonici al servizio dello Stato in Europa, secoli XIII–XVI/Les chanoines au service de l'État en Europe du XIIIᵉ au XVIᵉ siècle.* Ferrara and Modena: F. C. Panini, 1992.

Schwinges, R. C., ed. *Gelehrte im Reich. Zur Sozial- und Wirkungsgeschichte akademischer Eliten des 14. bis 16. Jahrhunderts.* Berlin: Duncker und Humboldt, 1996.

Siraisi, N. G. *Medieval and Early Renaissance Medicine: An Introduction to Knowledge and Practice.* Chicago and London: University of Chicago Press, 1990.

Index

Avignon papacy (*cont.*)
learning, 89–90, 91; and University
of Paris, 112; and Urban V, 88–89;
visitors to, 89
Avignon, University of, 29, 53, 156

baccalaureates, 85
bailiffs, 98
Balbi, Giovanna Petti, 41
Baldo degli Ubaldi, 160
Baldus, 28, 50
Balue, Jean, 115
barbers, 126–27
Bartholomaeus Anglicus, 11, 22
Bartolo da Sassoferrato, 160
Bartolus, 28, 50
Basel, Council of, 113
Basque, 10
bastard feudalism, defined, 166
Bec, Christian, 24
Beghards, 131
Beguines, 131
Bellièvre family, 149
Benedict XII, 91, 94, 144–45
benefices, 91, 95, 96
Benoîton, Roger, 69
Bernard de Chartres, 31
Bernard, Saint, 19–20
Bessarion, 111
Bible, printing of, 76
Biget, Jean-Louis, 130
bilingualism, 9, 15. *See also* Latin;
vernacular languages
bishops, 95. *See also* clerics, monks,
and ecclesiastics
Boethius, 16
Bologna, 32, 45
Bologna, University of: clerics,
monks, and ecclesiastics at, 88; law
at, 27, 46; medicine at, 26, 47;
number of students at, 53
Boniface VIII, 106, 108, 114
Book of Letters (Gasparino da
Barzizza), 78–79
Book of the Courtier (Castiglione),
175
books: access to, 66–71; Bozzolo and
Ornato on, 67–68, 69; cost of,

66–68, 77–78; on grammar, 76, 78;
importance of, 65; importing and
exporting of, 77–78; and lawyers,
69–70; and men of learning, 65–66,
69, 76; new vs. used, 67, 69; of
physicians, 70; production of,
66–67, 69, 76–79. *See also* libraries;
printing
Books of Sentences (Lombard), 25
bourgeoisie, 4. *See also specific careers*
Bozzolo, Carla, 68, 69
Bradwardine, Thomas, 112
Bragadin, Domenico, 62
Bresc, Henri, 75
Brethren of the Common Life, 61,
131
Breton, 10
Brolhet, Hélie, 149
Bullioud family, 149
burgensis, defined, 187n. 3
Burgundian states, 61, 131
Buridan, Jean, 85

Cambridge University, 53, 59, 174,
180n. 54
canon law and lawyers: as academic
discipline, 27, 156; and Catholic
Church, 27, 28, 29; commentaries
on, 27–28; and Gratian, 27;
importance of, 47, 52; and
Johannes Teutonicus, 27; and John
Andreae, 28; and libraries, 71, 76;
and Roman law, 27; at universities,
27, 28, 71, 156, 179n. 49. *See also*
law and lawyers
canons: as councilors, 96; in
Denmark, 93; in England, 96; in
France, 91–92, 96, 148; in
Germany, 93; in Italy, 92, 96–97; as
men of learning, 91–93, 96; Millet
on, 148; and nobility, 96, 148; as
notaries, 96; and public offices, 95,
96, 97; and relationship networks,
148; as royal secretaries, 96; social
ascension of, 148; in Spain, 93.
See also clerics, monks, and
ecclesiastics
Canterbury Tales (Chaucer), 133

Cardinals, College of, 111
Carmelites, 60, 94, 183n. 19. *See also* mendicant orders
Casa giocosa, 62
Casimir III (king of Poland), 110
Casimir IV (king of Poland), 55
Castiglione, Baldassare, 175
Castilian royal legislation, 33
Catania, University of, 182n. 97
Cathars, 130
cathedrals, libraries at, 70, 93–94
Catholic Church: administration of, 101; and Averroists, 16–17; and dissidence, 130–31; and education, 19–20, 36, 38–39, 42, 46, 52, 87; and Latin, 10, 11; and law and lawyers, 25, 28–29; and men of learning, 36, 101, 111–13, 122–23; Millet on, 95; and nobility, 111; and public offices, 95–96, 101; and vernacular languages, 10
Cazelles, Raymond, 116
Celtic languages, 9
Champagne, 41
chantries, defined, 42
Charles IV (Holy Roman emperor), 55, 110, 132
Charles V (king of France): Autrand on, 106; and Christine de Pisan, 108–9; and councilors, 106–7, 119; and libraries, 70, 106; and men of learning, 106, 129; and Oresme, 110–11; translations requested by, 11; and treatises, 106–7; and universities, 53
Charles VI (king of France), 93, 118
Charles VII (king of France), 107–8, 120, 133
Chartula (Anonymous), 43
Chenu, R. P. M.-D., 163
Chiffoleau, Jacques, 99
Chirurgia (Henri de Mondeville), 135
chivalric culture and literature, 107, 110
Christine de Pisan, 107, 108–9
Chronicle of the Popes and Emperors, The (Martin of Troppau), 21
chronicles, 107, 145

Chronique du Religieux de Saint-Denis (Pintoin), 93–94
Chronique métrique (Geoffroy de Paris), 145
Cicero, 11, 78–79
Ciompi, 129, 186n. 79
Cistercians, 29, 94. *See also* clerics, monks, and ecclesiastics
City of God (Saint Augustine), 11
city-states, 1–2. *See also specific countries*
civil law and lawyers: and Baldus, 28; and Bartolus, 28; and clerics, monks, and ecclesiastics, 29; commentaries on, 27–28; growth of, 52; in libraries, 76; at universities, 29, 119. *See also* law and lawyers
Clanchy, Michael T., 35
classical texts: and *contubernia*, 62; and education, 20, 44; in libraries, 76; and printing, 78. *See also* books
Clementinae (Clement V), 27
Clement VI, 89, 132
clerics, monks, and ecclesiastics: and Avignon papacy, 91; and Benedict XII, 91; and benefices, 95; as councilors, 73–74, 115, 116; in Curia, 88–89; Desportes on, 157; duties of, 25, 156–57; and education, 29, 41, 44, 88, 90, 91; in England, 90, 96; in France, 29, 91, 96, 157; and Gallican policy, 96; in Germanic countries, 91, 92; and Gersonides, 5; growth of, 170; as historiographers, 20, 21; in Hungary, 91, 92; income of, 166; as intermediary intellectuals, 126, 133; in Italy, 91; and John XXII, 91; and Latin, 12–13, 15; and law and lawyers, 28–29, 96, 156; libraries of, 68, 69, 72, 74; marriage of, 157; as men of learning, 3, 4, 87–88, 90, 91, 93–94, 122, 155–57, 163, 167–68, 183n. 19; and nobility, 92, 95, 158; prestige of, 157; and public offices, 95–96, 156; in Scandinavia, 91, 92; and

clerics, monks, and ecclesiastics (cont.)
Scholasticism, 127; in Scotland, 92;
in Slavic countries, 91, 92; and
theology, 25; types of, 25, 156
clericus, 2, 187n. 3
Cluniacs, 29, 94. See also clerics,
monks, and ecclesiastics
Coeur, Jacques, 24, 161
Coitier, Jean, 115
Cola di Rienzo, 132, 134
colleges: and Benedict XII, 94;
characteristics of, 39–40; of
Cistercians and Cluniacs, 94; in
England, 59, 94; founding of, 58;
in France, 41, 94; and Greek and
Hebrew, 173; and Gregory XI, 60;
growth of, 58, 60, 170; and Henry
VI, 61; importance of, 58; libraries
of, 70–71; purposes of, 58, 59, 60;
and sociability, 58–59; in Spain,
58–59; and Urban V, 60; and
William de Wykeham, 60–61
colleges of grammar, 61
Collegium Amplonianum, 71
Collegium trilingue, 173
commercial manuals, 24
common law, 30, 33. See also law and
lawyers
Compactata (1436), 131
competencies, 81, 84, 102. See also
men of learning
Concordia discordantium canonum
(Gratian), 27
Constance, Council of, 112
Contardo, Inghetto, 178n. 16
Contra Averroistas (Thomas
Aquinas), 48
contubernia, 62, 63
convents, libraries in, 70, 93–94
copyists: and cost of books, 66–67; in
France, 98; as intermediary
intellectuals, 126; and pecia, 67;
and printing, 77; productivity of,
66–67. See also scribes; scriveners
Corpus iuris civilis, 21, 27. See also
civil law and lawyers
Corsini, Piero, 69
Coulet, Noël, 151

Council of Basel, 113
Council of Constance, 112
Council of Pisa, 112
councils and councilors: Autrand on,
73–74, 153; canons as, 96;
characteristics of, 73, 74; and
Charles V, 119; and Charles VI,
118; and clerics, 73–74, 115, 116;
composition of, 116; conservatism
of, 74; criticism of, 118; duties of,
73; as élite, 73; in England, 116,
117; and Enguerrand de Marigny,
115; in France, 56, 113–16, 117; in
Italy, 116–17; and Joan of Arc, 114;
and lawyers, 73, 74, 116–17; and
laypersons, 115; libraries of,
68–69, 73–74; and men of learning,
97, 113–14, 115, 122; and nobility,
113–14, 116, 154, 158, 188n. 22;
and notaries, 116–17; in Portugal,
116; in Spain, 116; and Treaty of
Troyes, 114. See also public offices
and officials
Coutumes de Beauvaisis (Philippe de
Beaumanoir), 30
criados, defined, 100
culture, learned. See learned culture
Curia, 88–90, 111
curialis, defined, 175

Dauphiné, 52
Dauvet, Jean, 115
De anima (Aristotle), 16, 18
debate between cleric and knight, 145
De caelo (Aristotle), 11, 16
Decretum (Gratian), 27
Defender of the Peace (Marsilius of
Padua), 110
De laudibus legum Anglie
(Fortescue), 135
Délicieux, Bernard, 130
Denmark, 93
De regimine principium (Giles of
Rome), 106
De sphaera (Sacrobosco), 15
Desportes, Pierre, 157
Deventer, 61
devotio moderna, 61, 62, 131

De vulgari eloquentia (Dante), 14
dialectics, 15, 17, 20
dictionaries, 71
Didascalicon (Hugh of Saint-Victor), 19
diglossia, 9, 15. *See also* Latin; vernacular languages
diplomatic texts, 107
Distichs (Cato), 43
doctorates, 85, 159–60. *See also* universities
doctors. *See* law and lawyers; medicine and physicians
Doctrinale (Alexandre de Ville-Dieu), 43
Dominicans, 60, 94. *See also* mendicant orders
Dominic, Saint, 94
Donatus, 43
Dormans-Beauvais, College of, 59, 119, 144, 146
Droits de la Couronne de France, Les (Blondel), 108
Dubois, Pierre, 23, 108
du Plessis, College of, 119
Dürer, Albrecht, 174

ecclesiastics. *See* clerics, monks, and ecclesiastics
Ecloga Theoduli (Anonymous), 43
economics, 23–24
Economics (Aristotle), 11
education: and Aristotle, 15–19; Bernard on, 19–20; and canon law, 27, 28; and Catholic Church, 19–20, 36; characteristics of, 19, 33; and classical texts, 20, 44; and clerics, monks, and ecclesiastics, 41, 44; of Contardo, 178n. 16; and dialectics, 15, 20; and Dubois, 23; in England, 90; and *Ethics*, 18; in Flanders, 24; and Gerson, 23, 41; and grammar, 44; and history, 20–21; and humanism, 44; and humanities, 20; innovations in, 32–33; of knights, 23, 40; and Latin, 11–12, 13, 15; and literature, 20, 34; and Llull, 23; and logic, 15,

44; of men of learning, 38; of merchants, 24, 44; and Middle Ages, 81; and philosophy, 18; and Plato, 34; and *Politics*, 18; and *quadrivium*, 44; and Roman law, 28; and Scholasticism, 20; social utility of, 30–34, 81, 83; and specialists, 20; and theology, 44; and *Timaeus*, 16; in Tuscany, 24; and vernacular languages, 12, 20. *See also* colleges; schools; teachers and teaching; universities
Edward I (king of Portugal), 109
Elegantiae (Valla), 79
elementary schools, 39, 42. *See also* grammar schools; private schools; schools
elements and humors, 18
encyclopedias, 22, 71. *See also* books
engineers, 174
England: clerics, monks, and ecclesiastics in, 90, 96; councils in, 116, 117; education in, 35, 41, 42, 90; law in, 30, 33, 48, 96; literacy in, 35; men of learning in, 90; nobility in, 1, 96, 99, 116; peasants in, 35; printing in, 77; public offices in, 119; religious dissidence in, 130; theology in, 48; unification of, 170. *See also* specific cities
Enguerrand de Marigny, 115
epidemics, 142
Erasmus, 61, 172, 174
Essais (Montaigne), 163
ethics, 48
Ethics (Aristotle), 11, 16, 18, 110
ethics, codes of, 26
Eton College, 61
Europe, geography of, 1–2
Evrard de Trémaugon, 14
exegesis, 172
exempla, defined, 37
Exeter, 96
extraordinary professors, 87. *See also* teachers and teaching; universities
Extravagantes (John XXII), 27

France, 40, 41, 42, 44–45; growth of, 35; in Italy, 40–42, 44; Latin taught in, 43; literary culture of, 44; and men of learning, 44–45; number of, 41; Orme on, 41, 43; Pius II on, 44; purposes of, 44; in rural and urban areas, 40–41, 43; teaching methods in, 43; vernacular languages in, 43. *See also* elementary schools

Gramsci, 125

Gratian, 27

Great Schism: and Avignon papacy, 88; and Councils of Constance and Pisa, 112; effects of, 105, 114; and men of learning, 128; and universities, 50

Grecismus (Évrard de Béthune), 43

Greek, 15, 62, 172, 173

Gregory IX, 27, 105

Gregory XI, 60

Grosseteste, Robert, 146

Grote, Gérard, 131

Guarini, Guarino, 62, 63

Guenée, Bernard: on Senlis, 98

Guerre du Bien Public, 120

Guillaume de Melun, 115

Guillaume de Nogaret, 99, 115

Guillaume de Plaisians, 99

Guillaume de Rochefort, 108

Gutenberg Bible, 76

Gutenberg, Hans, 76

Guy de Chauliac, 146

Guyenne, College of, 170

gymnasia, 170

Hanseatic League, 24

Hebrew, 172, 173

Hélie de Tourette, 115

Henry V (king of England), 153

Henry VI (king of England), 61, 153

Henry VII (Holy Roman emperor), 109–10

Henry of Ghent, 84, 137

Henry the Navigator (prince of Portugal), 109

Heynlin, Jean, 77, 78

Historia pontificalis (John of Salisbury), 21

Historical Mirror (Vincent of Beauvais), 21

historiography, history, and history books, 20–22, 93

Hugues de Pélegry, 144

humanists and humanism: and Curia, 90; defined, 50; and education, 44, 50, 74, 173–74; as evangelism, 172; and Fichet, 77; in France, 97; in Germany, 71; and Greek and Hebrew, 172, 173; and Heynlin, 77; history of, 13–14; importance of, 14; in Italy, 75, 110; and libraries, 73, 76; and notaries, 74; and *païdeia,* 23; and printing, 78; and public offices, 97; and royal secretaries, 74; and *sodalitates,* 173; Valla as, 173; and Váradi, 110; and Vitez, 110

humanities, 20

humors and elements, 18

Hungary, 91, 92

Hus, John, 114, 130, 131

Hussite wars, 114

iconography, defined, 36

incunabula, 78

Innocent III, 111

Innocent IV, 28, 105, 111

Innocent VI, 88–89

Inns of Chancery, 63. *See also* law and lawyers

Inns of Court, 33, 63, 135. *See also* law and lawyers

Inquisition, 37

intellectuals, 2. *See also* men of learning

intermediary intellectuals: authors as, 134–35; barbers as, 126; characteristics of, 136, 137; and Ciompi, 129, 186n. 79; clerics, monks, and ecclesiastics as, 133; defined, 125; Gramsci on, 125; income of, 131–32; and Jacquerie, 129; lawyers as, 133–34; Lollards as, 130–31; and nobility, 129–35;

149, 151–52, 170; and Frederick II, 96, 144; golden age of, 27; growth of, 51–52, 54, 99; and Guillaume de Nogaret, 99; and Guillaume de Plaisians, 99; income of, 135–36; and Inquisition, 37; and intermediary intellectuals, 126, 133–34; and Irnerius, 27; in Italy, 46, 75, 96–97, 100, 116–17, 152, 163; and John Andreae, 50; and libraries, 72, 75; Martines on, 152; and men of learning, 24, 25, 26–27, 30, 99; and nobility, 98–100, 152, 158; and Pons d'Aumelas, 99; and popular culture, 35–36; in Portugal, 100; and printing, 78; and public offices, 98–100, 151–52, 160, 162, 170; purposes of, 160; and rationality, 28, 29; and relationship network, 148; and Rota, 29; and royal tribunals, 123–24; as scholarly discipline, 28, 29; secularization of, 96–97, 155–56; and social ascension, 146–47, 148; social utility of, 30–31, 32; in Spain, 100; Strayer on, 99. *See also* canon law and lawyers; civil law and lawyers; common law; Roman law

learned culture: characteristics of, 9–37; defined, 3; and Latin, 9–15; and Philip IV, 106; unity of, 9

Lefèvre d'Étaples, 172

légistes, 115

Le Goff, Jacques, 34

Leonardo da Vinci, 174

letrados, 2, 100, 116. *See also* men of learning

letters, republic of, 55

Le Viste family, 151

liberal arts, 15, 31, 46

Liber sextus (Boniface VII), 27

libraries: access to, 70, 71; Autrand on, 73–74; of Avillino, 134; of Benoîton, 69; of cathedrals and monasteries, 70, 93–94; characteristics of, 72–73; classical

texts in, 73, 76; of clerics, monks, and ecclesiastics, 68, 69, 71, 72, 74; of colleges and universities, 70–71, 78; contents of, 71, 72–74, 75–76; of councilors, 68–69, 73–74; in England, 71; in France, 70–71; in Germany, 71; grammar books in, 76, 78; growth of, 69; history books in, 21; and humanism, 73, 76; and law, 71, 72, 73, 74, 75, 76; location of, 70–71; manuscript collections in, 70; and medicine, 71, 76; and men of learning, 68, 71, 79; of mendicant orders, 70; minimal, 79; of Niccola da Rabuazio, 134; of nobility, 68; of notaries, 68, 134; of physicians, 72, 75, 76; of professors, 68, 69, 72; religious books in, 73, 74, 76, 78; of Richard de Bazoques, 134; of royal secretaries, 68; Scholasticism in, 76; in Sicily, 75–76; size of, 68–71, 73, 74; vernacular languages in, 73, 78. *See also* books

libri di famiglia, defined, 24

licentia docendi, defined, 85

Liguria, 41–42

literacy, 35

literary culture, 51–52

literary works, 20, 21, 34

livres de raison, defined, 24

Livro das Leis e Posturas (Edward I), 109

Livy, 11

Llull, Ramon, 23

logic, 15, 44

Lollards, 130–31

London, 41, 44–45, 63

Louis I (duke of Bavaria), 109–10

Louis IX (king of France), 106, 115

Louis XI (king of France), 52

Louvain, 59, 61, 173

Low Countries, 61, 77, 131

lucrative disciplines, 19. *See also* private service

Lyon: councils in, 117; lawyers in, 117, 148, 149; merchants in, 170; notaries in, 126

Poitiers, 151–52
Policraticus (John of Salisbury), 11,
105
political philosophy, 18
politics: and intermediary
intellectuals, 131–34; and men of
learning, 107–8, 174
Politics (Aristotle), 11, 16, 18
Pons d'Aumelas, 99
popes: and benefices, 95, 96; and
diplomatic texts, 107; libraries of,
70; and mendicant orders, 105; as
men of learning, 111. *See also*
Avignon papacy
popular culture, 34–36, 37
Portugal, 100, 116
practica della mercatura, 24
Prague, 114, 131
Presles, College of, 119
princes. *See* nobility
principalities, 1–2
printing: of Bible, 76; and classical
texts, 78; and conservatism, 76;
and copyists, 77; effects of, 79; in
England, 77; and Fichet, 77, 78–79;
in France, 77, 78; and Gering,
76–77, 78–79; in Germany, 76–77,
78; growth of, 22–23, 76–77, 78;
and Gutenberg, 76; and Heynlin,
77, 78–79; and humanism, 78; in
Italy, 76–77, 78; and law books,
78; and libraries, 79; in Low
Countries, 77; and men of
learning, 76–79; Michelet on, 79;
and scholarly culture, 174; in
Spain, 77; in Switzerland, 77.
See also books
private schools, 42. *See also*
elementary schools
private service, 123, 124, 166
profane disciplines, 19
professors. *See* teachers
propaganda: and Charles IV, 109–10;
and Henry VII, 109–10; and Louis
I, 109–10; and men of learning,
105–10; and nobility, 105–10
prosecutors, 126
Provençal families, 151

psychology, 18, 48
public offices and officials: Autrand
on, 119; and Catholic Church,
95–96, 101; characteristics of,
101–2; and clerics, monks, and
ecclesiastics, 95–96, 97, 156;
criticism of, 97, 118; duties of,
120–21; in England, 96, 119; esprit
de corps of, 120; in France, 96,
97–99, 118–21; and Gallican
policy, 96; and Gervais de Bus, 97;
growth of, 97, 118; and humanists,
97; income of, 166; in Italy, 96–97,
100; and law and lawyers, 98–100,
151–52, 160, 162, 170; and men of
learning, 83–84, 97, 101–2, 122–23,
160, 165–66, 182n. 2; prestige of,
123; private service compared to,
123; in Spain, 100; stability of, 119.
See also councils and councilors;
royal secretaries and officials

quadrivium, 15, 22, 44
Quodlibets (Henry of Ghent), 84, 125

Rabelais, François, 172
Raoul de Presle, 107
Ratingk, Amplonius, 71
Ravenna, 27
Raymond de Pélegry, 144
Rebeyne, 132–33
Rebuffi family, 162
regents in law, 52
regents of arts, 85
Reims, 41, 44–45, 157
religion. *See* Catholic Church; clerics,
monks, and ecclesiastics
religious books, 78. *See also* books
Renaissance: and Middle Ages, 4,
169–76; and nobility, 175; twelfth-
century, defined, 1
repertories, 71
republic of letters, 55
Reuchlin, Johannes, 172, 173
rhetoric, 17
Rhetoric (Fichet), 78–79
Ricciardo di Francesco del Bene, 136
Richard II (king of England), 110

Spain: councils in, 116; law and lawyers in, 100; men of learning in, 100; Muslims in, 4; nobility in, 100; notaries in, 100; printing in, 77; public offices in, 100; royal secretaries in, 100; unification of, 1, 100, 170
specialists, 20, 22–23, 25
Speyer, Johann von, 76–77
Spiritual Franciscans, 130. *See also* Franciscans
Standonck, College of, 62–63
Standonck, Jan, 62–63
Stefano de Avillino, 134
Stoics, 172
Strayer, Joseph R., 99
studia: and Catholic Church, 46; and Frederick II, 144; location of, 179n. 53; of mendicant orders, 42, 44, 60; in Naples, 144; organization of, 60; purposes of, 42; and theology, 44, 60. *See also* universities
Style de la Chambre des Enquêtes (Anonymous), 13
Summulae logicales (Peter of Spain), 16
superior faculty, defined, 46
Super speculam (Honorius III), 28–29, 179n. 49
surgeons: and Aristotle, 127; education of, 32, 63, 135; and Galen, 127; as intermediary intellectuals, 126, 135. *See also* medicine and physicians
Switzerland, 77
syllogisms, 17

Taborites, 131
taille, 132–33
taxes: Antiboul on, 134–35; and Charles VII, 133; collection of, 98; and Jean de Condeyssie, 132–33; revolt against, 128; on salt, 132–33; *taille,* 132–33
Taylor, William, 130

teachers and teaching: and *abacus,* 44, 63; and baccalaureates, 85; Buridan as, 85; as competency, 84; credentials of, 42, 43; and doctorates, 85; Dominic as, 94; in France, 150; geographic mobility of, 150; growth of, 85, 86, 170; income of, 86; as intermediary intellectuals, 126, 133; and law, 86; libraries of, 68, 69, 72; and Masters of Arts, 84–85; and medicine, 86; prestige of, 86; and theology, 86; and tonsures, 87; at universities, 86; Zanetti on, 86. *See also* education; extraordinary professors; ordinary professors
technical instruction, 22–23. *See also* education
technicians, 174
Templars, 108, 114
theology: branches of, 25; and clerics, monks, and ecclesiastics, 25; contents of, 25; and education, 44; in England, 46, 48; in France, 25, 46, 48; importance of, 25, 47; and libraries, 76; and mendicant orders, 44, 47, 51; and men of learning, 25; and popular culture, 36; social utility of, 30–31, 32; in *studia,* 44, 60; teachers of, 86; and universities, 51, 86
Thomas Aquinas, Saint, 152
Thomas de Cantimpré, 11, 22
Thomists, 50
Timaeus (Plato), 16
tonsures, 87
Topics (Aristotle), 17
Toulouse, 94, 123–24, 136
Toulouse, College of, 144
Toulouse, University of: and councilors, 56; and Curia, 89; law at, 28, 50, 117, 156; number of students at, 53
Tournai, 92
Tractatus contra rebelles suorum regum (Jean de Terrevermeille), 108

Vitez, John, 110
Vittorino da Feltre, 62

Wars of the Roses, 120
watch-making, 22–23
William of Ockham, 74
William de Wykeham, 60–61
Windesheim, canons of, 61
witches and witchcraft, 37

Wolff, Philippe, 151
Wycliff, John, 130

Yconomomica (Konrad of
  Megenberg), 102
York, 96
Ysalguier family, 151, 162

Zanetti, Dante, 86
Zwolle, 61

www.ingramcontent.com/pod-product-compliance
Ingram Content Group UK Ltd.
Pitfield, Milton Keynes, MK11 3LW, UK
UKHW041914060225
454777UK00001B/296